ig Bartholomew Strydom is a freelance writer working in ertising. His work has been featured at the London ternational Awards, the New York Festivals and *The One* ow. His writing has appeared in *Rolling Stone* and *Creative Nonfiction*, and he was a Susan Atefat Creative Nonfiction ze finalist in 2011.

tephen 'Sugar' Segerman is a music writer and co-owner the iconic record store Mabu Vinyl. He is also a former z kid. Both Strydom and Segerman live in Cape Town.

Sugar Man

The Life, Death and Resurrection of Sixto Rodriguez

Craig Bartholomew Strydom
and
Stephen 'Sugar' Segerman

CORGI BOOKS

TRANSWORLD PUBLISHERS
61–63 Uxbridge Road, London W5 5SA
www.penguin.co.uk

Transworld is part of the Penguin Random House group of companies
whose addresses can be found at global.penguinrandomhouse.com

First published in Great Britain in 2015 by Bantam Press
an imprint of Transworld Publishers
Corgi edition published 2016

A CIP catalogue record for this book
is available from the British Library.

ISBN
9780552171717

Typeset in Giovanni by Falcon Oast Graphic Art Ltd.
Printed and bound by Clays Ltd, Bungay, Suffolk.

Penguin Random House is committed to a sustainable
future for our business, our readers and our planet. This book is made from
Forest Stewardship Council® certified paper.

1 3 5 7 9 10 8 6 4 2

Contents

PART IV: THE MOVIE

For Malik

'You put together two things that have not been put together before. And the world is changed. People may not notice at the time, but that doesn't matter. The world has been changed nonetheless.'

— JULIAN BARNES, *LEVELS OF LIFE*

'You never know Rodriguez better than the first day you met him.'

— MALIK BENDJELLOUL, DIRECTOR OF *SEARCHING FOR SUGAR MAN*

'Maybe today, yeah
I'll slip away.'

— SIXTO RODRIGUEZ, 'I'LL SLIP AWAY'

Prologue

Sundance

(2012)

'What you're missing is that the path itself changes you.'

— JULIEN SMITH, *THE FLINCH*

There's a clip in the 'making of' feature on the DVD release of *Searching for Sugar Man* in which Craig Bartholomew Strydom, the so-called 'musicologist detective' featured in the documentary, arrives at a restaurant on a snowy evening in Park City, Utah. The sidewalk is slippery and he and his wife tread gingerly. Director Malik Bendjelloul, the eternally youthful former child actor, walks over, camera in hand. 'Is that video?' Strydom asks, absurdly. 'Yes, it is,' replies the director in singsong English, a tonal trait carried over from his native Swedish. Malik is intent on filming the moment because this is the first time in over twelve years that Strydom will meet up in person with Stephen 'Sugar' Segerman, his co-conspirator in the Rodriguez story. It is the opening night of the Sundance Film Festival. The date is 19 January 2012, which will turn out to be the first in a string of highly significant dates for this rogue-style documentary. What the short clip does not – and cannot – tell you about are the numerous rocky roads that have been travelled to get to this moment in the Rockies. So many trajectories have intersected in the making of this film and the story behind it, and will continue to do so. No one knows it yet, but although it feels like the end, this night is only the beginning of an extraordinary journey that will finally bring recognition to a brilliant but elusive musician, forty years after the fact.

Segerman is the next to arrive. Jet-lagged and chilled to the bone, he has just flown in from South Africa, the unlikely setting for so much of this very American story. His blood has not yet had time to thicken. Like Strydom, he is doing everything he can to keep his emotions under control. It was, after all, partially his vision that helped breathe life into the stillborn career of one of the twentieth century's most enigmatic musicians, Sixto Rodriguez. A two-album dud who, after a short brush with fame, had no choice but to go back to life as a blue-collar worker, unaware of his enormous success in South Africa, the pariah of the world, a continent away.

Strydom and Segerman shake hands in the snow. Strydom thinks back to the early eighties when his plan to find out what had happened to Rodriguez was just a crazy idea. That was before he met Segerman. The 'Red Peril' was near South Africa's borders and the masses inside the country were getting restless, so the only way to keep the white minority secure in their leafy suburbs was to send in the troops. Or so thought the near-sighted National Party government of Prime Minister P.W. Botha. There were certainly enough troops, as all white males were conscripted into the military for two years. And so it came to pass that one day in 1984, while shooting the breeze with his fellow conscripts, Strydom heard an album that would for ever change his life. It came from a small tape recorder and, refreshingly, there was nothing banal about the lyrics. Instead, the voice sang lines like 'I was born for the purpose that crucifies your mind', and 'In the factory that you call your mind, graveyard thoughts of stone'. Who was this poet, Strydom wondered. Someone answered that the singer's name was Rodriguez, and that he had killed himself on stage after reciting his own epitaph: 'Thanks for your time, and you can thank me for mine, and after that's said, forget it.' Strydom was amazed. Who would do such a thing? He made a vow to find out one day how the musician, known only as Rodriguez, had died.

The Deer Valley sun dips low and there is still no Rodriguez. By the time Segerman and Strydom make their way to the second floor of the restaurant, John Battsek is already seated at a large table, booked specially for this momentous occasion. Simon Chinn, who produced *Searching for Sugar Man* alongside Battsek, paces the floor anxiously, cellphone at the ready. Both men come across as being nervous as hell. They shouldn't be, as both have made this journey before. Battsek has midwifed several documentary features through the arduous birthing process that leads to film-festival gold. His progeny includes documentary features such as the Academy Award–winning *One Day in September*; *Restrepo*, about the Afghanistan war; and the BAFTA Award–winning *The Imposter*, about a boy impersonating a boy who is lost, not to be confused with the subject of tonight's documentary feature, the search for a man who didn't know he was lost. Rodriguez, it is announced, is running late, but Battsek is no stranger to the machinations of musicians, having also

11

produced 2010's *Stones in Exile*, a documentary about the Rolling Stones' self-imposed exile to the South of France to avoid exorbitant British taxes, a trip that led to the 1972 album *Exile on Main Street*.

The milestones on executive producer Chinn's journey are no less auspicious. His oeuvre includes director James Marsh's 2007 *Man on Wire*, a feature documentary about Frenchman Philippe Petit's audacious and illegal high-wire walk between the Twin Towers in New York City on the morning of 7 August 1974. Would *Searching for Sugar Man* follow in *Man on Wire*'s footsteps? The film of Petit's caper had opened at the Sundance Film Festival before going on to land Chinn and Marsh an Academy Award and a trove of other hardware. Chinn is also known for producing another James Marsh film, *Project Nim*, an enquiry into animal communication behaviour with respect to American Sign Language, featuring chimpanzee Nim Chimpsky. Positive reviews notwithstanding, neither man nor beast would go home with the Oscar on that occasion.

Camilla Skagerström arrives. She is in conversation with Ann-Sofie Rase, the Swedish stage actress and Malik's girlfriend. Camilla's journey to get to a place at the table in this restaurant in the Wasatch Back Mountains has also been eventful. From the day she received the call from Malik to shoot *Searching for Sugar Man*, she was under no illusion that what would be required from her would amount to more than a camera and an eye for film. Filming for Malik, his natural enthusiasm aside, would involve a level of faith that would need to grow in inverse proportion to the diminishing level of funding. Granted, faith might be a necessary ingredient of all documentaries, but faith doesn't pay the bills. Buoyed both by the recent Palme d'Or at Cannes for the short film *Micky Bader*, which she filmed, and the birth of her first child, she is delighted to be there. She sits down and smiles contentedly. It has been a long journey. The Cannes-winning documentary short in which she participated focused on the life of 100-year-old Holocaust survivor and swimming die-hard Ebba 'Micky' Heyman, who would not let the weather, her age or the seasons stand in the way of her daily swim routine in the ocean with her girlfriends. A bit like Malik's attitude to filmmaking. This is Camilla's first trip to the Sundance Film Festival, and she and Malik make nervous eye contact. Sundance, after all, was set firmly in his sights long before shooting began. She would know. She was with him almost every step of the way.

Orders are about to be taken and still Rodriguez has not arrived. Light in the Attic Records owner Matt Sullivan, seated at the far end of the table, makes a joke about having to search for Sugar Man all over again. Matt's place at the table is for reasons linked to, but different from, the other players gathered around. If Strydom was the musicologist detective in the story, Matt was the music archaeologist. And as the name of his company suggests, it is Matt's business to dig through record bins and rifle through detritus in attics, garages and storage facilities in search of that one elusive musical masterpiece that might have fallen through the cracks. Rodriguez's 1970 debut album, *Cold Fact*, was one such find.

Looking through a pile of records at a Los Angeles side-walk sale in 2006, Matt came across an album that looked interesting. The record in question was a compilation called *Come Get It I Got It* by David Holmes, with a remixed version of Rodriguez's 'Sugar Man' as the second track. Matt put the record on the turntable and could not believe his ears. Whose was this distant, mysterious-sounding voice, which sang of 'blue coins' and 'silver magic ships' and 'answers that make colours disappear'? More than anyone, Matt knows music, and for him to find an album or track that he hasn't seen or heard before is like an art curator chancing upon a previously unknown Picasso at a flea market. He spent the night poking around for more information, but other than some cyber noise from South Africa of all places, he came up largely empty-handed. The record was as good as non-existent in America. No one seemed to own the rights to it. More importantly, no one in his extended circle of music enthusiasts had even heard of the elusive musician known as Rodriguez.

He tracked down Stephen 'Sugar' Segerman through the website Sugarman.org, the only real repository of Rodriguez information at the time. Segerman put him on to *Cold Fact* and, after a lengthy quest to obtain the rights, Matt was finally able to dust off the album and reissue it on vinyl. Despite low expectations, it soon took on cult status as an underground gem on the American West Coast. But in spite of Matt's intervention, and as much exposure as he could drum up, the reissue performed no better in the US than it had on its inauguration; nothing but a fleeting blip on the niche-music listener's radar. 'Main Street' America, it seemed, the wellspring from which Rodriguez drew his inspiration, was not yet ready to hear his music.

There is a commotion downstairs. Rodriguez has finally arrived. He makes his way up to the second floor. At his side are his girlfriend Bonnie and two of his daughters, Sandra and Regan. All three daughters feature in the documentary, although Eva has not made it to Sundance. (Notably absent from the eighty-six-minute film, critics would later point

14

out, is the small bevy of ex-wives and ex-girlfriends who have accompanied Rodriguez on his life's journey.) Tonight's trip from the airport to the hotel, and from the hotel to the restaurant, has gone the way it always has: undetected. Imposing in leather and sporting a Ry Cooder hat and Roy Orbison prescription sunglasses, Rodriguez looks like a rock star one should recognise, someone whose records one should have. Unbeknown to him, he will not be going around undetected for much longer, especially not after tonight.

'Ah,' says Malik, leaping up from his chair, 'the star of the show is here.' But this statement is only partially true. The other star of the show, albeit from behind the camera, is none other than Malik himself. The waitress comes over and rushed orders are taken. They are already verging on being late for their own premiere. Strydom and Segerman take it all in. There's something surreal about the moment. Malik, an idiosyncratic eater at the best of times, is too nervous to touch his food. Instead, he walks around the room singling out each person, thanking them for the respective roles they have played in this impossible story. But there's no time for accolades. Chinn and Battsek usher everyone out.

Snow swirls into eyes and mouths as they slip-slide to the various minivans and taxis that wait to take them to their destination. A winter wonderland sweeps past. A marquee announces the film that will be opening the World Cinema Documentary Competition of the twenty-seven-year-old Sundance Festival. Three other films opened in their respect-ive categories earlier in the day, *Hello I Must Be Going* in the US Dramatic Competition, *Wish You Were Here* in the World Cinema Dramatic Competition and *The Queen of Versailles* in the US Documentary Competition. When they arrive at the theatre, each member of the *Sugar Man* team is handed a Sundance Film Festival lanyard and pass badge, giving them unhindered access to red-carpet events and other functions not available to the general public. Just to see the words *Searching for Sugar Man* and the 'official' demarcation adds to the gravitas of the moment.

A capacity audience files in slowly. The *Sugar Man* team take their seats, barely able to contain themselves. There is no reason on earth why this documentary should resonate with US audiences, and they know it. By rights it should fade like the career of the musician on which it is based. How could anyone expect otherwise? For starters, no one in America, let alone tonight's audience, is expected to know the music. And the soundtrack of a biopic, especially if it is about a musician, is half the film. And why should anyone have heard the music? In the sarcastic words of Clarence Avant, the Sussex label head and impresario responsible for signing Rodriguez to Sussex Records in 1969 who is controversially featured in the documentary, only six copies of the album ever sold: 'My wife bought one, I bought one, and maybe my daughter bought one.'

The theatre goes black. Life blinks.

PART I

THE MYSTERY

1

The other Sugar Man
(1954–1996)

'We may be through with the past . . . but the past
is not through with us.'
— Quiz Kid Donnie Smith, *Magnolia*

Like many white South Africans – including Craig Strydom
a decade later – Stephen Segerman first heard the
Rodriguez album *Cold Fact* when he was doing his compulsory stint of military service. The year was 1972; the place,
Air Force Base Swartkop in Pretoria. Two of Stephen's air
force buddies drove in to the base one day and called him
over to the car. 'Hey, man, listen to this,' they said, turning
up the volume. The car was a gold Ford Capri, bullet sleek
and 'tit', in the parlance of the day, the ultimate young man's
car in the 1970s. The first song to bleed from the speakers
was 'Sugar Man', with its haunting voice and lyrics. *'Sugar
man, won't you hurry / Cause I'm tired of these scenes / For a blue
coin won't you bring back / All those colors to my dreams.'* This was
followed closely by 'Only Good for Conversation'. *'My pocket*

don't drive me fast / My mother treats me slow / My statue's got a concrete heart / But you're the coldest bitch I know.' By the time Stephen was through listening, he was sold.

As was the modus operandi in those pre-file-sharing days, Stephen copied the album using one of those double-cassette decks that everyone seemed to own. So began the endless rotation (and endless copying) of an album that articulated the gripes of a gritty blue-collar reality an ocean away.

In spite of very little airplay on any of South Africa's state-owned radio stations (too controversial with its references to drugs; plus, it audaciously asked how many times you've had sex), *Cold Fact* took on a cult status. For twenty-five years, South Africa remained in the dark about the fate of Rodriguez, and Rodriguez remained in the dark about his fame and cult following in that remote country. How could he have known, for – bizarrely – he garnered not a cent in royalties. Unlike most albums that passed through record and later CD stores, *Cold Fact* has been on South African record racks for over forty-two years – a record in itself, surely.

But by the time Segerman heard *Cold Fact* in 1972, Rodriguez's first contribution had already faded into obscurity in the United States, along with the artist. In the words of Mike Theodore, who co-produced the album, 'America just wasn't ready.' Would it ever be? Segerman would play a crucial role in the long and winding journey of finally getting Rodriguez recognised there and around the world.

To step into Stephen Segerman's music room is to step into his mind. Thousands of posters, photographs, CDs, DVDs, albums, cassettes and tchotchkes line every inch of space.

Nothing is ever thrown away. It is all absorbed, twice. Once into his brain through the senses, the second time into his sphere as a possession. If asked a question he can go one of two routes. Rubbing his eyes as he is wont to do, he will either retrieve the answer from his mind or, failing that, he will go old school and retrieve the memory facsimile by hand, opening a drawer here, a box there, a closet elsewhere. Everything is mentally catalogued for seamless retrieval. But it took years to get this way.

Born in the liberal white Johannesburg suburb of Emmarentia in 1954, a month after Elvis went into Sun Studios, Stephen Segerman had by all accounts a normal suburban Jewish childhood, which is to say a safe, sheltered upbringing far from the realities of apartheid and the black townships that would later smoulder on the other side of town. Growing up in Emmarentia, Stephen spent most of his time riding his bicycle around a relatively small stamping ground: he attended Emmarentia Primary School, followed by a short stint at Yeshiva College in Glenhazel, and matriculated from Greenside High, with synagogues, stores, friends and sports fields all a stone's throw away.

Looking south from Bernard and Joyce Segerman's house, one might have seen the Melville Koppies, a nearby ridge and archaeological site. And in the year that Stephen was born, just over the Melville Koppies and less than a mile away, one would have stumbled upon a bustling, cosmopolitan area known as Sophiatown.

Sophiatown was an uncharacteristic (for South Africa) mixed-race suburb that had begun to encroach on the neighbouring white suburbs of Westdene and Newlands. When the National Party came to power in 1948, they put plans in motion, under the guise of the racially motivated Immorality

Amendment Act of 1950, to forcefully relocate the black residents of Sophiatown to Meadowlands, a suburb of Soweto; the coloureds (not to be confused with the blacks) to Eldorado Park; the Indians to Lenasia; and the Chinese to central Johannesburg. Anti-apartheid activists Nelson Mandela, Ruth First, Helen Joseph and Father Trevor Huddleston united with residents to thwart the forced removals, but in vain. Before Stephen's first birthday, around 2,000 armed policemen went in and forcibly removed Sophiatown's inhabitants. The newly promulgated principles of apartheid were clear: people of different races could not live together. By the time Stephen was nine, Sophiatown had been flattened to the ground, all trace of its existence erased from the map of Johannesburg. The white suburb that rose from its ashes was impudently named Triomf, the Afrikaans word for 'triumph'.

In the years to follow, with South Africa well on its way to becoming a police state, Nelson Mandela received a life sentence for high treason and Helen Joseph was repeatedly banned (her last banning order was lifted in 1985, when she was eighty). Ruth First was not so lucky. In 1982, a parcel bomb sent to her address in Mozambique by the dark forces of apartheid exploded in her hands, killing her instantly. Only Father Trevor Huddleston, who among other things had been instrumental in organising for a fourteen-year-old Hugh Masekela his first trumpet, came out unscathed, returning to Britain soon after the removals.

Because of the way South Africa operated in the fifties, sixties and early seventies, the young Stephen Segerman was oblivious to all of this. With Rosemary Clooney and Frank Sinatra gently crooning in the background, his early childhood was as happy and normal as that of any white South

African boy his age. There was never a shortage of music in the Segerman household, and no shortage of cultural ideas either. Every Friday evening – and this would become a defining factor in Stephen's life and his later obsession with music – his father, Bernard, would walk through the door with bundles of surprises under each arm. South Africa might have already started closing itself off to the world, but nothing could stop Bernard from bringing the world into his home. *Classic Comics*, *Look & Learn*, *Knowledge* magazine and assorted books entered the Segerman household and were devoured by three culture-hungry siblings, Stephen leading the charge. 'My head was just filled with that stuff,' he says today. And if the magazines and books were not enough, there were the records, plenty of them: from the soundtracks of *Mary Poppins* and *The Sound of Music* to Cliff Richard and Elvis Presley. And in spite of many South African parents' desire to 'protect' their children from 'filth' like the Beatles, Ringo, Paul, George and John were welcomed into the Segerman home.

This stuff came from American Books, a small bookshop Bernard owned with his sister. Situated in Eloff Street (right where Eloff intersects with Park Station), the shop was a treasure trove of books, magazines, records and toys, which formed the cultural nexus of an enquiring mind and further fuelled his young son's love of music.

Stephen's love of reading and knowledge led him to his first brush with fame as a 'Quiz Kid', and then much later to his role as a main player in the Rodriguez story and the subsequent documentary. It would be at the South African Broadcasting Corporation (SABC) in Commissioner Street, close to his father's next business, a jewellery factory called A. Weinberg & Co. on the corner of Kerk and Polly streets in downtown Johannesburg, that the next instalment of Stephen's story would take place.

In 1950, four years before he was born, the SABC launched South Africa's first commercial radio station. Until then there had only been the 'stiff upper-lip' English service and its dour Afrikaans equivalent. The new station was named after South Africa's national animal, the springbok. Soon Springbok Radio was the primary source of entertainment in any given white South African household, fixated on the latest twist in one of its many radio serials. This was, after all, long before the belated launch of television in 1976.

Springbok Radio's programme line-up included a show called *Quiz Kids*, based on the American equivalent. The premise of the programme involved the general public sending in questions meant to stump a panel of high-school teenagers and winning prizes, all carefully adjudicated by a charming radio host.

In the second South African run of *Quiz Kids*, Paddy O'Byrne was the quizmaster and SABC radio legend Johnny Walker was the show's producer. The panel, for the sake of photographs at least, wore black academic gowns and mortarboards.

Stephen was thirteen and in his first year of high school when the headmaster, a certain Mr Jimmy Lane, announced in general assembly one morning that Springbok Radio would be holding auditions to select a new batch of 'Quiz Kids' for the upcoming series. Panellists were typically older kids in matric, the final grade of high school. Once they finished matric, the teens would no longer be eligible to participate in the show and would be replaced on the panel. 'Any interested applicants,' concluded the headmaster, 'should meet me in my office after assembly.'

Stephen arrived at Principal Lane's office, where a handful of hopefuls were already waiting. He looked around and noticed something was wrong with the equation. There were the top students of the school, older boys and girls, intellectuals, standing around confidently with their hands in their pockets – and then there was Stephen. Photographs from the time show a fresh-faced, newly bar-mitzvahed boy of thirteen, in stark contrast to the mature seventeen- and eighteen-year-olds who would have been waiting in the headmaster's office with him that day. Finally, after several uncomfortable minutes, in walked Principal Lane, a man on a mission. 'Thanks, chaps, for coming in,' he started to say, but then, noticing the young boy standing nervously to one side, interrupted himself with, 'You – *you* I'll speak to afterwards. You go wait over there!'

'But I'm here for the quiz, sir,' implored Stephen, his voice barely audible.

'Well,' said the headmaster dismissively, 'you can't, it's only for matrics.'

With that, Stephen, and what was left of his confidence, limped back to the classroom.

Later during break in the playground, a kindly older boy, who had been in the principal's office that morning, walked over. As a youth leader, he knew Stephen well. 'Don't worry,' said the older boy, 'I'll tell you where to go for auditions.' So Stephen caught the bus, at a time when it was still safe for lone thirteen-year-olds to do so, and went through the auditioning process. He was successful, and so began the first of several years as one of South Africa's youngest ever Quiz Kids and the longest-running panellist. Shows were recorded in advance during the week, mostly at the SABC's studios. Since Bernard's factory was close by, Stephen could simply catch a ride home with his father after each taping. The show aired on Mondays and Thursdays between 6:15 and 6:30 p.m.

In many respects, Stephen's role as one of the youngest Quiz Kids was a positive one. For starters, he was able to earn some decent money and open an investment account. But he also became popular. His parents and family were extremely proud of young Stephen. Their hopes and aspirations of one day saying 'my son the doctor' or 'my son the dentist' were prematurely fulfilled with 'my son the Quiz Kid'. In Stephen's words, 'They klabbed a lot of naches from me' (which means they gained a lot of joy from him). The downsides of the experience were the things that typically happen to kids who achieve even the smallest degree of celebrity at a young age. While not quite on the scale of Quiz Kid Donnie Smith in the film *Magnolia*, Stephen nonetheless discovered the disadvantages of fame. Other children would throw out random challenges to him every day, on the playground or while walking between classes. Who wrote *this* book, they would call out. Who discovered *that* country? He took a lot of flak for it, and after a while he didn't want people to know who he was.

Stephen continued on *Quiz Kids* for several more years before making the transition back to his preferred insular life of music fan and bookworm. He didn't achieve much academically at school and had absolutely no idea what to do with his life thereafter. But his love for knowledge and natural rebelliousness made Stephen the right person to get involved in the Rodriguez story.

The year 1972 rolled around and, as a matter of course, Stephen was called up to do a year of compulsory military service in the South African Defence Force. Conscription had become mandatory for all white males in 1967, and by the time Stephen was called up it had become a serious matter, as there was trouble brewing to the north of South Africa.

The so-called Border War began in 1966, when South African security forces clashed with insurgents from the South West Africa People's Organization (SWAPO) in the north of South West Africa. Later that year the United Nations (UN) passed Resolution 2145, terminating South Africa's right to administer the protectorate, an undertaking it had inherited under a UN mandate at the end of World War II. A second resolution, 2372, followed in 1968, this one recognising SWAPO as the legitimate representative of the people of South West Africa. The same resolution also renamed the territory as Namibia, much to Pretoria's chagrin. The Republic of South Africa, then under Prime Minister B.J. Vorster, dug in its heels, holding on tight to what had effectively become its fifth province. SWAPO responded by embarking on a protracted guerrilla war to gain independence.

When Stephen was called up in 1972, the Border War was being fought mainly in the Caprivi Strip, a strange pan-handle of land to Namibia's north-east. But Stephen had nothing to do with this. After completing his basic training, he was posted to the 100 Air Force Maintenance Unit in Pretoria and performed his service as a pen-pusher, a clerk. Stephen's efforts in the military can best be described as NAAFI, a military acronym from the time meaning 'no ambition and fuckall interest'. And who could blame him? He was only seventeen years old and, like a large percentage of national servicemen during that period, reluctant to fight in a war in which he had no vested interest, let alone understanding. He got through his year without causing any ripples. He would kill time playing chess with another guy in the office, and for the rest it was 'music, music, music'.

And so it happened that Stephen heard *Cold Fact* one day in his friend's Ford Capri and became instantly hooked. It became the soundtrack of his time in the military. Truth be told, few similarities existed between the lives of the young men stationed at Air Force Base Swartkop in Pretoria and that of the man who wrote songs about inner-city USA; nevertheless, the album resonated. There was one important similarity between the two backdrops. Both countries were at war. And both wars were geographically removed from the actual lives of those fighting them: South Africa on the South West Africa/Angola border, the US in Vietnam. And, like most wars, these were politicians' wars. Yet, in the sea of anti-establishment lyrics found on the album, only two lines actually allude to war: '. . . *the government gives you your slugs*' and '*I wonder about the soldier that dies*'.

When Stephen got his hands on a copy of the LP itself, he was mesmerised by the eye-catching cover. On it a man in blue-and-white-striped trousers, a mauve leather vest, black sunglasses, sandals and a low-slung medallion sits cross-legged – Buddha-style – superimposed over (or in) what looks like a pearl or a crystal ball. Below the photograph are three graphic strips of an urban skyline laid out in a step-and-repeat fashion. Blurred but still visible in the top strip is the word 'DRUG', obviously from some indeterminate drugstore signage, but since drugstores in South Africa were known as chemist's or pharmacies, only the secondary meaning would have applied. (The three strips, black and white in the original US release, had been re-coloured on the South African version, perhaps to obscure the word DRUG and possibly, in the case of the lower strip, to conceal the repeated image of a woman in a suggestive pose. This was apartheid South Africa, after all, and the pose might have been a little too prurient for the time.)

Flipping the album over, Stephen noticed that there were no musicians credited on the album sleeve whatsoever. On the back appeared the lyrics of all twelve songs, as well as a few credits: for arrangers and producers (Mike Theodore and Dennis Coffey), the mixer (Theodore again), photography and cover design, and the New York studio where the album was remixed. The only other information was on the face of the record itself: the name Sixto Rodriguez in fine print, an A&M Records logo, a Sussex Records logo, the track listing and timings, and, in brackets, the mandatory author information. Some tracks, Stephen noticed, were credited to Jesus Rodriguez, others to Sixth Prince. Two songs were credited to Gary Harvey, Mike Theodore and Dennis Coffey. The name Sixto Rodriguez never appeared on any of the subsequent vinyl pressings, and so South Africans just naturally assumed that the artist's full name was Jesus Rodriguez. The Sixth Prince was a mystery.

The album had been pressed locally by A&M Records under the catalogue number AMLS 67000. In the days of vinyl, upon licensing the licensee would have received a master copy, which would have been used to press the record. *Cold Fact* didn't get much airplay on the radio, and while none of the songs were officially banned, certain tracks were physically scratched with a sharp object by the censors so that they could not be played on the state-owned airwaves. Other than LM Radio, the official station from Lourenço Marques that reached South Africa on AM, there were no radio stations at the time other than the SABC.

Lack of airplay notwithstanding, in due course the album became a cult classic, and was copied and recopied and played everywhere.

After his year in the military, Stephen dodged compulsory 'camps' by enrolling at the University of the Witwatersrand. It was around this time that friends increasingly began referring to him as 'Sugar', from the mispronunciation of Segerman as 'Sugarman', a much more common surname. In fact, it all began in his final year of university in 1977, when Stephen moved out of his parents' home and into a nine-person commune in a large double-storey house in the Johannesburg suburb of Parktown. Three of the new residents were called Stephen, a problem immediately spotted by the commune's head, Stephen 'Swaz' Swersky, who, without further ado, allocated them each nicknames. With that, Segerman became 'Sugar', a moniker reinforced by his obsession with the other Sugar Man and that song.

His time at university was followed by a period of articles for which Stephen could never quite stir up the requisite enthusiasm. Sadly, in this endeavour, there would be no 'naches' for the Segerman clan. And just as Rodriguez re-entered the life of blue-collar employment on the car line on the other side of the world, Stephen went to work in his father's workshop, designing jewellery and selling diamonds, and finally got married and started a family.

But his love of music never left him. Instead of incorporating music into his new family life, he incorporated his new family into his music life. He also receded further into his shell, his tortoise-like inner sanctum, a small room in the middle of his house, which he had begun to assemble and fill with every conceivable poster, book, album and sentimental item that had meant anything to him in his life. His regular Friday sorties to various record shops in Braamfontein and Hillbrow to look for new albums, books or magazines helped fill up the room. It was during one of these weekly cultural pilgrimages that he discovered *The Best of Rodriguez*, a 1982 compilation which he hadn't seen before, and which – surprisingly – featured several Rodriguez songs that he hadn't heard. How could this be? Surely there hadn't been a second album? How had he missed this? So began his quest to track down a second Rodriguez LP.

As the years passed, political change eventually came to South Africa. It withdrew its soldiers from Angola and Namibia in 1989, ending the Border War, and when F.W. de Klerk took over from P.W. Botha as state president, he began a process of reform that resulted in the release of Nelson Mandela and other political prisoners, and the first democratic election in April 1994, in which Mandela became president.

In December 1994, Sugar was sitting on Camps Bay beach with some friends, while on holiday in Cape Town. Among them was an ex-South African, Ronit Molko, who had emigrated to the United States a while before but who often returned to visit her family and friends in South Africa. Ronit asked Sugar where she could buy Rodriguez's *Cold Fact* album on CD in Cape Town. Sugar told her that she could buy it anywhere, 'even from the CNA', a nationwide newsagent with a branch across from the beach where they were sitting at the time. The answer was so obvious it seemed stupid. 'Or just buy it when you get home to America,' he said.

'I can't,' she replied, 'it is just not available in the US.'

Ronit explained that she had not been able to find it

anywhere in America. No one there had ever heard of it. This surprised Sugar, because around these parts everyone knew and owned Rodriguez's music. Rodriguez was as big as Bob Dylan and the Rolling Stones, and South Africans quite naturally assumed his music would be available everywhere. This was the first time that Sugar got an inkling that they might be dealing with a cult album. He was correct about it being in the shop across from the beach. They strolled over and bought a copy of *Cold Fact* for Ronit to take home with her.

Back in Johannesburg, Sugar's curiosity was piqued and he once again took up the search for the missing Rodriguez album that he had never seen or heard, but which he knew had to exist thanks to the *Best Of* album. He searched through all his regular Johannesburg record shops – Kohinoor Records on Commissioner Street, Hillbrow Record Centre and Look & Listen, some second-hand shops downtown, anywhere he could think of – but without any luck. Then one day, while hanging out at the house of friend Andre Bakkes in Midrand, Sugar mentioned that he was looking for the second Rodriguez album. To his astonishment, Andre casually walked over to his turntable, flipped through his record collection and pulled out a copy of the original South African release of *Coming from Reality*. Sugar was completely stunned, having never even seen a copy of this mysterious LP. Andre agreed to let him take it home.

The cover of the album featured a photograph of Rodriguez dressed in a white shirt and black trousers, sitting on a porch. Once again his eyes are hidden by black sunglasses. His hair is long, and he stares at the camera with just a hint of a smile. It is immediately clear that the porch where he is seated is part of a derelict building. Behind him is a boarded-up blue door, a broken chair back and an empty bottle. Oddly, a child's shoe, similar to his own, is placed alongside his right foot. In his hands he is holding what looks like a bag of something, or a piece of broken glass.

The album was released in South Africa in 1972, although the label lists it as 1973. It was once again from A&M/Sussex, and carried the catalogue number SXBS 7012. This time all the songs were credited simply to Rodriguez. Besides producer Steve Rowland, the only other credit read: 'Impresario: Clarence Avant'.

From the opening strains of acoustic guitar, one thing was immediately clear: a level of confidence not heard on *Cold Fact*. Rodriguez invited the listener to '*Climb up on my music, and my songs will set you free*'. Sugar sat back and listened. The lyrics were as poignant as they were on the previous album: '*Have you ever had a fever / From a bitter-sweet refrain / Have you ever kissed the sunshine / Walked between the rain.*' Sugar had the fever. Again.

What followed was the second important event in a chain of coincidences that started with Andre pulling that LP out of his collection. Shortly after Sugar found *Coming from Reality*, another of his close friends in the local music business, Andy Harrod, called to say that the record company was looking for a pristine copy of *Coming from Reality*, because they wanted to release the record on CD.

'Why don't they just press it from the master copy?' Sugar asked, another seemingly obvious question. After all, that's what record companies do.

'Um,' said Andy hesitantly, 'they don't seem to have the masters.'

How could that be? It was another spark to fuel the mystery. So Sugar, with Andre's permission, handed over the LP version of *Coming from Reality* to Andy, who passed it on to the record company. The record company was obviously thrilled to receive such a well-looked-after specimen of vinyl, and to thank and reward Andy and Sugar, they asked if they would write the liner notes for the new South African CD release of what would now be called *After the Fact – Coming from Reality*.

A week later, the friends had cobbled together the liner notes; pretty standard stuff but for two seminal lines:

There were no concrete cold facts about the artist known as Rodriguez.

It is not known if he is even alive or dead. Any music-ologist detectives out there?

2

Kimberley to the moon
(1964–1997)

'The cure for boredom is curiosity. There is no
cure for curiosity.'
— DOROTHY PARKER, AMERICAN POET AND SATIRIST

When Craig Bartholomew Strydom read those words in
the liner notes from the Rodriguez CD that he had
unpacked at the Look & Listen music store where he worked,
he couldn't believe his eyes. A couple of years earlier, Craig
had set himself the task of finding out how Rodriguez had
died. It was on a list of journalistic articles that he wanted to
write, a list that was pinned on his office wall. Now he found
that someone else was asking the same question.

Like Stephen, Craig was to play a part in the rediscovery of
Rodriguez. But when the 'musicologist detective' moniker
was perpetuated in the press release that announced the film
Searching for Sugar Man in 2012, Craig had to admit that at no
stage of his life had he been a musicologist or a detective.
Delicately, he would have to explain the genesis of this

strange title to audiences during the many film-festival Q&A sessions, including a 1,000-strong audience in New York City. Ultimately, it became easier to simply admit that he was in fact a musicologist detective, the first of his kind.

In the diamond-mining town of Kimberley where Craig was born in 1964, highfalutin dreams of being a writer or a musicologist ran up against more regional job-market realities. A large percentage of the city's population worked on the mines or for industries dependent on the mines. His father and four of his father's five brothers worked at various stages for De Beers or its subsidiaries. (Craig, too, would work for De Beers as a diamond sorter for a short period.) Had it not been for the discovery of diamonds in 1871 on the Vooruitzigt farm owned by the De Beer brothers, Kimberley would more than likely not exist on any map today.

In the decade in which Craig was born, Kimberley was no more than a sleepy mining town, a mere shadow of its former multi-ethnic self at the height of the diamond rush and the early stages of the city's inception. Fortune-seekers from all four corners of the globe had descended in droves to play Mother Nature's infectious lottery. At the height of the diamond rush, diggers from as far off as Russia, Australia, California, Britain and Brazil could be seen socialising after a day's exhausting work, making deals while watching their backs in makeshift saloons. Following closely on their heels were the tycoons, throwing money at consolidation. Mining at the time might have been a race to the bottom, hence the world's biggest manmade hole, but it soon became a race to the middle as the consolidation process brought about homogenisation and, over time, fewer but larger monopolistic corporations. Kimberley in its early days was like the

Wild West. What could a boy do but dream in a town founded on dreams?

Crouched with his father around the radio (known at the time as a wireless), less than a year before Rodriguez released *Cold Fact* an ocean away, five-year-old Craig found himself captivated by the live broadcast of the first moon landing. The next day, greeting the milkman at the front gate of their mine-allocated house on Ernest Oppenheimer Avenue, Craig excitedly told him about the moon landing, which, to his childish sense of wonder, had been nothing short of miraculous. Two men, Neil Armstrong and Buzz Aldrin, had walked on the surface of the moon! Still looking up at the sky to where the boy had been pointing, the milkman asked Craig if he, too, wanted to visit the moon. Craig could not believe his luck as the milkman graciously offered to take him to the moon on his day off. Plans were made for an early-morning departure that coming Sunday. The instructions were clear: wait in the front garden, at his mother's rockery populated with miniature cactuses, for the milkman's arrival. Sunday came. The milkman did not. An hour later, the boy's mother found him in tears, hugging his neatly packed knapsack.

Craig's parents, Bert and Gladys, were of mixed English and Afrikaans descent, but they spoke English at home. His father was a lay-preacher and both parents were unflinchingly religious. Nonetheless, his upbringing was happy. His parents were loving, nurturing, eternally youthful and involved, not an easy thing with five children and a handful of stray cousins. Craig's grandmother had been an opera singer in her youth, and he listened enraptured as she sang a Bach cantata at the City Hall one Christmas.

In contrast to the Segermans, popular culture did not beat down the door of the Strydom household, but now and then it would sneak in. Craig's earliest musical memory is 'Downtown' by Petula Clark, which he would sing in the back of the family's beige VW Variant. Once he stumbled upon a drawer in his mother's room filled to the brim with LPs – the Beatles, Rod McKuen, Françoise Hardy, Roy Orbison and Elvis. Looking back, it seems incongruent that his very religious parents would have had such music in their home. Even more inconsonant was the day his father arrived home with a copy of Barry White's 'You're the First, the Last, My Everything' as an anniversary gift for his mother. Black soul? Of course, by 1972 *Cold Fact* was already on the shelves in South Africa, albeit in a limited fashion, but there was no way Craig or his father would have heard it. It wouldn't be until 1984 that the album would cross Craig's path. Kimberley was slow on the receiving end when it came to popular culture.

When the town did get a dose, it was short and intense. Like the night he and his brother had to wait in their uncle Peter's car, both boys dressed in pyjamas and dressing gowns, when Rabbitt, Trevor Rabin's second band – and South Africa's answer to the Beatles – came to town. Disobeying orders, Craig sneaked into the lobby of City Hall where the concert was taking place and caught his first glimpse of screaming, near-fainting groupies and long-haired fans.

In 1973, Craig's father announced that they would be moving to a farm twenty-six kilometres from Kimberley. If anyone thought this would mean leaving diamonds behind, they were wrong. His father had taken the job of running an alluvial – or open-faced – diamond mine on the banks of the Vaal River. Although he now found himself even further removed from popular culture, the two-year sojourn into farm life had an important effect on Craig. Along with his brother and one of his sisters, he attended a farm school called Klipdam Holpan Primêr near the town of Windsorton. Occasionally, when the river was in flood and the bridges washed away, they were home-schooled by their mother. But far from being a daunting experience, Klipdam, which at the time had only twenty-six pupils, afforded Craig his first forays into the world of detecting. Always the dreamer, he would climb a water tower in the playground and spy on the other kids using his pocket-sized telescope. School also brought him his first fistfights, a welcome end to a cosseted life. As one of only two English boys in the predominantly Afrikaans school, it took several skirmishes to achieve a semblance of status quo. With only a few girls his age, the competition among the boys was severe. On golden summer nights, films were projected on the side of the school building and, on one such Saturday, a highly sought-after girl named Anne sat on his lap for an entire reel. This was an achievement – both in stature and early romance – and no amount of numbness and pins and needles could persuade the ten-year-old to ask Anne to get off.

Outside the farmhouse, apartheid was in full swing, and Craig's naturally philanthropic father cobbled together a makeshift church and took on the role of caregiver to the small community of black people who lived and worked there. As a way to compensate for their low wages, he would cart in large quantities of tripe, which they were able to purchase at cost price. He would also help save the township from having to hire hearses to deliver their dead for Sunday burials. Occasionally, the yellow family VW Kombi, which had replaced the Variant, could be seen transporting five children (not unlike the Waltons of TV fame), a coffin (supposedly empty: a rare white lie from Craig's father) and a twenty-five-gallon container of tripe. The ensemble, the summer heat and the olfactory consequences ensured the experience would be burnt into the boy's memory, whether he liked it or not.

In 1975 he and his family moved back to Kimberley, and in June the following year, up north in Johannesburg, the township of Soweto erupted. The black youth, objecting to being taught in Afrikaans, the language of the oppressor, began to riot. The police opened fire, and scores of dead children later a false calm settled over the townships, but not for long. The deaths had finally forced the world to sit up and take notice. A campaign of economic disinvestment intensified, as did the cultural and sports boycott. Soon it would begin to have an adverse effect on the country. For both apartheid and the National Party government – on the wrong side of history – it was the beginning of the end.

By 1983, South Africa was in the full throes of an internal revolt. Practically all the townships had become hotbeds of unrest, specifically those around Johannesburg and in the Eastern Cape. It was during this troubled time that Craig received his call-up papers to report for duty to the South African Defence Force. By now, with the escalating unrest that permeated everyday life in South Africa, and with the Border War having spread into Angola, compulsory national service had been extended to two years. Added to that were the so-called 'camps', another two years of service spread over ten years.

The army, with its early-morning inspections, guard duty, freezing route marches and politically questionable training – 'fire two shots, the first at the target, the second as a warning shot, in that order' – was a big deal for any eighteen-year-old. Training was designed to break down the conscripts and remould them into servicemen, i.e. men in service of the apartheid government and its ideologies. Unfortunately for the government, this kind of heavy-handed indoctrination had the opposite effect on many of the young men it tried to brainwash. Craig was able to wangle a transfer from 1 Parachute Battalion to 3 Military Hospital as a medic. This – a non-combat environment – went a long way towards alleviating the conscience of the budding liberal. At 3 Military Hospital, he discovered a circle of kindred spirits, such as a chef named Andy, who, as a result of his refusal to carry a weapon, was forced to walk around with a broomstick for two years, and a guy called Chris Reinders, who led the group in heated intellectual discussions.

So when the first strains of Rodriguez's *Cold Fact* impregnated the air of the sixty-four-sleeper bungalow in Bloemfontein's Tempe military base, young minds were already opening. It was a Saturday afternoon. The men – still boys, really – were relaxing, doing washing and enjoying a little R&R from the intensity of the week. They were huddled around a *trommel* – a large army-issue metal trunk – and snacking on a spread of communal snacks when someone put in a cassette that Craig had never heard before. Taken aback by the profundity of the lyrics and catchy hooks, he sat up and asked, 'Who is this?'

'Rodriguez,' said his friend David Viljoen.

'Anyone know anything about the man?' pressed Craig.

No information was forthcoming, except that the singer had apparently committed suicide on stage after reciting his own epitaph.

'How?' asked Craig.

The answers were varied, but two stood out: 'He shot himself,' said Ian Robertson, '*everyone* knows that!'

'No, he set himself alight on stage,' said someone else.

From that day on, with Rodriguez's voice emanating from the tinny sound systems belonging to the soldiers, Craig pondered this bizarre story. Importantly, over drinks one night, Craig announced to his comrades that he was going to find out how Rodriguez had died. The story was just too good to be true, and appealed to his idea of poetic mystery. He simply had to get to the bottom of it. '*Ja*, that would be kiff,' said Michael Hynek (known as Dumpy), sipping his Castle Lager. 'Go find the oke.'

It is safe to say that none of them had any idea where Craig's stated intention would lead. By the next morning, nursing a hangover, the idea was probably forgotten anyway. But then, a few weeks later, David gave him a cassette, a copy of a copy, of *The Best of Rodriguez*. It did not cross Craig's mind at the time that the album obviously had songs on it that were not on *Cold Fact*. The album was simply assimilated into the wider playlist that formed the backdrop to his army experience for the next year and a half. Finally, in July 1985, Craig's two-year stint came to an end. With their military service over, Craig, David and Ian spent a few weeks at David's house. That's when Craig saw a copy of Rodriguez's second album for the first time.

The album was called *After the Fact*, and its cover was strikingly similar to *Cold Fact*: a photograph of Rodriguez was superimposed over the same crystal ball from the *Cold Fact* cover, with the same black background and similar coloured bands at the bottom. The word 'DRUG' (from a cropped 'DRUGSTORE' sign) is visible in two places, providing a further link to the *Cold Fact* album. What Craig was looking at was in fact a retitled and rejacketed version of *Coming from Reality*, unique to South Africa. The image of Rodriguez was a cropped version of the photograph on *Coming from Reality*. All in all, the cover design was an amalgam of Rodriguez's two albums. The title, as PT Music owner Terry Fairweather recalls, came about when a sales person suggested that the album would do better if its design and its name referenced the previous record, which by that time had become quite popular.

As *Cold Fact* had done, this album blew Craig's mind. One thing was immediately clear, however: more Rodriguez music did not mean more information, just more mystery. There were no clues about who Rodriguez was or what had happened to him. Out of interest, the name Sixto Rodriguez does not appear on this version at all. While the Sussex logo is still on the record sleeve, A&M has been replaced by United Artists (SA). The back cover features the typical producer and engineer credits, plus the fact that the album was distributed in South Africa by RPM Records.

The friends went their separate ways after that, but Rodriguez's music and fate remained on the backburner of Craig's mind. During an eight-month backpacking trip around the UK in 1986, he began to ask around if anyone had heard of Rodriguez. He was shocked and surprised to find no one really had. After all, hadn't the second album been recorded there? One day, on the train to Brighton, Craig decided to actively look for information on the singer. Three or four record stores later, he returned to the village of Lenham, where he was working in a country house, with the same amount of information he had left with that morning: none. Months later, he and two of his army friends, Chris and Ian, spent the better part of the summer busking with their guitars on the Spanish Costa del Sol. Among the songs that made up their playlist were two Rodriguez classics, 'Rich Folks Hoax' and 'Hate Street Dialogue'. Craig likes to think that the Rodriguez songs brought in the most pesetas.

In 1987 Craig found himself back on South African soil and living in Pretoria. He got a job at a record store and enrolled in a three-year diploma course in 'Light Music' (in reality, jazz studies) at Pretoria Technikon (now Tshwane University of Technology). Life went on and his quest to discover what had happened to Rodriguez receded once more. Then, one day in 1988, something happened that would have a profound and complicated effect on Craig. A right-wing white extremist named Barend Strydom went on a shooting spree in the centre of Pretoria that left seven black people dead and fifteen wounded. The senseless shooting happened close to the campus where Craig was studying and near Strijdom Square, named for the uncompromising segregationist former prime minister J.G. Strijdom, a distant relation to Craig. It was unthinkable that something so extreme could happen just a few hundred metres from the technikon where Craig studied. He no longer felt comfortable using his surname, Strydom, and for the next few years he wrote under his first and middle names only, Craig Bartholomew.

After graduating at the end of 1991, Craig spent eleven months in Amsterdam on a student visa, nursing beers and slumming it in an upmarket, unfurnished apartment with some ex-students from Pretoria Technikon and a Serbian refugee named Darko. The apartment had come about as a result of a deal made by one of the student's fathers, and both the area and the apartment were way classier than any of them could afford. During this time, Craig poked around to see if there was any information on Rodriguez. A half-remembered lyric from a track called 'Can't Get Away' on the South African version of *The Best of Rodriguez* seemed to suggest that the singer had spent some time in Amsterdam. *'In a hotel room in Amsterdam / On a wild and windy August night / As a cloud passed over a cold moon / My heart was seized with terror and fright.'* He came up empty-handed. In his second month, Craig got a job as a handyman and occasional waiter at a hotel near the famed Vondelpark, very near to where John Lennon and Yoko Ono had held one of their famous 'bed-ins'. While working his way through a punch-list of odd jobs, including painting the entire exterior of the hotel, Craig would try to picture the thing that had seized Rodriguez's heart with 'terror and fright'.

Upon his return to Johannesburg in 1993, and in spite of his music diploma, Craig still had no idea what to do with his life. So he did the one thing that came naturally. He took a job at Look & Listen, a record store on Sugar Segerman's traditional Friday culture trek. (There's no doubt his and Sugar's paths would have crossed during that time.) And one thing he noticed while working there was the fact that each week, when the stock came in from the various record labels, there were two albums that were on permanent back order. The first was *Cold Fact*, and the other was *Second Contribution* by Shawn Phillips. Surprisingly, conscript soldiers had made up both musicians' core fan base. Another thing Craig noticed was the regularity with which *Cold Fact* would sell out each week. This got him thinking. So intrigued was he that he made a point of asking customers directly if they knew anything about their purchase – who this mysterious musician could be – but to everyone the question seemed absurd. Rodriguez simply 'was'.

*

By the beginning of 1995, Craig realised that he was going nowhere fast; he was a jack of all trades and master of none. He had started a relationship with a woman called Philippa and wanted to settle down. He put down his guitar and shelved any musical aspirations. The pen was going to be his tool. He just needed to find an avenue for his skill. He could not continue to work at Look & Listen indefinitely. He wanted to write great stories, to create.

That's when Craig discovered advertising. It amazed him that people actually got paid to think up all those conceptually great print and TV adverts that he was always commenting on. He suddenly felt empowered. Perhaps there was a place for misfits after all. He put together an advertising portfolio using hand drawings and Letraset transferable letters and landed a job, and so began his love–hate relationship with an industry in which today's award-winning newspaper ad is tomorrow's birdcage liner. It was not writing in its purest form, but at least it paid the bills.

As the months rolled by, even though he enjoyed his new career, Craig still yearned to write something of importance. He needed a challenge. So it was that in late 1995 Craig sat down at a coffee shop during his lunch hour and made a list of ten journalistic essays that he wanted to write. A version of the list would appear in *Searching for Sugar Man*, reconstructed by Malik Bendjelloul and Sugar Segerman during the making of the film, but the original list was different, and mostly forgotten now. It included a story about the Capuchin Catacombs of Palermo, an article about 'secondary interests' (like the art of Hitler and Churchill), an account of the platonic love affair between Salvador Dali and Amanda Lear, a piece on Shawn Phillips, and, importantly, 'Find out how Rodriguez died'. Although this was something he had been thinking about on and off since 1984, this was the first time Craig actually put the idea into writing. It was not number one on the list, which seems strange now.

Craig's girlfriend Philippa, meanwhile, was building a career as a jeweller, working at Charles Greig Jewellers in the Johannesburg suburb of Hyde Park. Interestingly, in yet another of the coincidences that characterise this story, she had business dealings at the time with a jewellery-repair expert named Bernard Segerman, Sugar's father. In mid-1996, Philippa was paired up with a new client, a woman who was larger than life, expressive and friendly, preferred to work with women and wanted discretion. It was none other than Tina Turner, who had asked to see emeralds from the Charles Greig collection. This was the start of a successful business relationship between the two women.

A few months later, in November, Roger Davies, the legendary manager of Tina Turner, Sade and Janet Jackson, among others, called the store to ask if Philippa would deliver a parcel of jewellery to Tina in Germany. Craig and Philippa took the next flight out, and a day later found themselves travelling from Dusseldorf to Dortmund to attend a Tina Turner concert. In the makeshift dressing room, filled with rails of wigs and outlandish outfits that would make any clothing boutique jealous, Philippa presented Tina with a selection of jewellery. While she made her choices, Craig stood around, taking it all in, but there was a burning question that he needed to get off his chest. He just couldn't find quite the right opening. The crowd upstairs was getting rowdy and the air had become electric.

Months earlier, Craig's army friend Dumpy had shown him an imported copy of *Coming from Reality*, which had a sticker or stamp in the right-hand corner with the words 'Impresario, Clarence Avant'. (It must have been an import, because no vinyl iteration in South Africa ever had such a stamp on the cover.) *Impresario* is a rather pretentious word for producer or manager, but its older meaning is someone who arranges and finances operas, plays or other productions. This was not the type of thing Craig had seen on records before, and it struck him as odd. It might have been prevalent in the movies of the sixties and seventies, when producers like Carlo Ponti would put their stamp on films, much to the chagrin of directors like Fellini, but not in music. Who was this Clarence Avant? This was before the days of Google searches, and although his name popped up in the music encyclopaedias Craig had consulted, it was in connection with Motown. Craig was flummoxed. Motown? The head of Motown had his name on a folk record by Rodriguez? Could it be a mistake? Perhaps there was another Clarence Avant.

Now in Dortmund, Craig thought why not ask Tina Turner about Jesus Rodriguez, as the singer was still erroneously known in South Africa. Although Tina had never been signed to Motown, it was worth a shot. She racked her brain for a minute, but she couldn't remember anyone by that name. Even with the names of the albums she still could not place the singer. Tina shook her head; it was clearly a dead end. Smiling, she changed the subject. 'When I sing "Nutbush",' she said, 'make sure you head out to the car.' She was referring to the track 'Nutbush City Limits', and since Craig and Philippa were travelling in the same car as Tina's personal assistant, masseuse and chef, they needed to be ready to escape before the crowds got out.

Back in Johannesburg, Craig continued working in

48

advertising by day and moonlighting at Look & Listen by night. Hillbrow had become dangerous and he was happy to now be working at the new Sandton Square branch of the record store. One night he opened a box of CDs for re-stocking and was amazed to find the first CD release of Rodriguez's second album, now titled *After the Fact – Coming from Reality*. This was an exciting moment. Unlike *Cold Fact*, the second album had been deleted a few years earlier and was not something one saw every day. And then it struck him. Since this was a new release, perhaps it contained the information he needed. He ripped open the plastic cover and retrieved the booklet, hungry for knowledge. It had liner notes all right, a lot of words but nothing new. Worse still, the notes reiterated the problem he'd been facing: that little was known about the singer. But two lines caught his eye:

There were no concrete cold facts about the artist known as Rodriguez.

It is not known if he is even alive or dead. Any music-ologist detectives out there?

It was the first time to Craig's knowledge that anyone other than him had even bothered to ask the question. Who was asking? The liner notes were signed off by 'Mad Andy and Sugar'. Craig went through the notes again and found a section that listed the names of those responsible for bringing the re-release to fruition. It included Mad Andy and Sugar Segerman. Perhaps because he had a surname to go on, it was Sugar Segerman he decided to contact, although he had no idea who he was. Pity he didn't know about Philippa's regular business dealings with Sugar's father, Bernard. But Craig eventually managed to secure Sugar's email

address from the record company. He fired off an email on
17 February 1997:

Dear Sugar,

I hope this is the same Sugar Segerman as credited on
Rodriguez's 'Coming from Reality' CD?

I am a writer presently doing research on the elusive life
of Jesus Rodriguez and the mystery surrounding his music.
This forms part of an extensive piece I am hoping to write
on not just him, but certain folk musicians of the seventies
who for some reason became cult figures in South Africa,
yet nowhere else in the world. (Shawn Phillips is another
such name.)

I have started to make some inroads into my research,
but have also come to some dead-ends. I sincerely hope
you are able to give me some information, as it seems
you're about the only one who knows something.

Please note that all information will be credited, and
secondly, that I will share any future information I receive
with you.

If you agree, then could I start by e-mailing you a list of
questions, or alternatively, can I meet with you face to face.
I have already had minor dealings with Chris Venter, and
others from the various record companies, and am presently also trying to glean information through back copies
of certain music publications.

I trust that you will consider my request,

Regards

Craig Strydom

So began the correspondence that would link Craig and
Sugar for many years to come.

3

Searching for the wrong man
(1997)

'Mystery is the essential element of every work
of art.'

— LUIS BUÑUEL

By now Sugar had moved his family to Cape Town. After a
stint sourcing music for a TV-commercial company, he
started working at the newly formed internet company
Intekom. The two men agreed to meet in Cape Town. Craig
checked in at a hotel on Cape Town's Greenmarket Square,
right across from Sugar's office. They met at a nearby coffee
shop and talked for about an hour. While they didn't have
much information to share, they discussed Rodriguez's lyrics
and what secrets they might contain, and agreed to join
forces to find out what had happened to the man. Sugar told
Craig that he was not entirely convinced that Rodriguez was
dead. 'I sometimes see people,' he said, 'and I wonder, could
that be Rodriguez just living out his life here in South Africa
with the earnings he has amassed? Like this guy Jimmy that

51

I know at the El Arish Café near to where I used to live. He could be Rodriguez for all we know.' The idea intrigued Craig. Why the hell not? All coffeed up and energised by the conversation, Craig found it hard to concentrate for the rest of the afternoon.

The conversation helped intensify the search on both sides, but in different ways. Back in Johannesburg, Craig began the task of deconstructing each of the twenty-six known Rodriguez songs, pasting notes on the wall. If he was not going to get clues from others, he was going to have to get clues from the man himself. He tried to find meaning in each word, but this proved to be as frustrating as it was rewarding. The poetic nature of Rodriguez's lyrics meant that, while there was an abundance of clues to go on, Craig had to separate facts from double-entendres, metaphors and pure poetic licence with a fine-tooth comb. It seemed to result in more questions than answers.

It is thanks to the non-pop nature of Rodriguez's lyrics that this type of analysis was even possible. The superficiality of most modern pop songs would have left Craig empty-handed. The word 'baby', for example, is one of the most commonly used words in pop's history, yet it occurs only once in Rodriguez's oeuvre: 'Baby I ain't joking, and it's not what I'm smoking,' he sings in 'Silver Words'.

Location seemed like a logical place to start, so Craig began by searching for places. 'The inner city birthed me / The local pusher nursed me,' Rodriguez sings in 'The Establishment Blues'. This is hardly revealing. One listen to any of his songs, with their references to crime, drugs, poverty and prostitution, leaves no doubt that Rodriguez came from the inner city. In another song, he sings of having 'tasted Hate Street's hanging tree'. With no way of verifying the true meaning of the lyrics at the time, Craig interpreted 'Hate Street' as 'Haight Street', as in 'Haight-Ashbury', the district in San Francisco famous for its hippie subculture in the sixties and seventies. As if to confirm his hunch, Craig stumbled upon another clue in 'Jane S. Piddy': *'I saw my reflection in my father's final tear . . . San Francisco disappears.'* But then what of the line from 'Inner City Blues'? *'Going down a dusty, Georgian side road / I wonder'* sounded very much like a reference to a place, too. Could it pertain to Georgia, the Southern US state? Dixie hardly fitted the picture of Rodriguez's America. The image of the inner city, with its *'acid heads, unmade beds, and Woodward world queers'* seemed far grittier than anything one would find in the American South. Craig dug deeper.

What he stumbled on next was an actual landmark. In 'Can't Get Away', Rodriguez sings: *'Born in the troubled city / In Rock and Roll, USA / In the shadow of the tallest building'.* Craig stared at the words for several minutes. Was this something tangible, something he could work with? Which city had the world's tallest building? His mind naturally defaulted to New York. The problem was that various US cities had made claims over the years to having the world's tallest building. For a period of time it had been the Sears Tower in Chicago, but after doing some research Craig discovered that building was only completed in 1974, three years after Rodriguez recorded his lyrics. Before that, the World Trade Center's Twin Towers had held the record. Craig studied the dates on the album more closely. Unless he was mistaken, the songs seemed to have been written *before* the completion of the World Trade Center, too. But what was he thinking? This had nothing to do with when the album was written, but rather the year in which Rodriguez was born. Unless Rodriguez was saying that he was born where the shadow of the world's tallest building falls today ... semantics, perhaps? In any case, the world's tallest building before the Twin Towers went up was the Empire State Building, completed in 1931, so either way it made sense to stick a pin in New York City.

Two more American place names jumped out at Craig: Lafayette ('*East Lafayette weekend sluts*') and Martha's Vineyard, the affluent island off Cape Cod ('*Lost, even, at Martha's Vineyard, again*'), both in 'A Most Disgusting Song'. He explored the Martha's Vineyard angle for some time, but of course he was never going to find Rodriguez there. The only other concrete reference to a place was to the hotel room in Amsterdam in 'Can't Get Away', but Craig had already gone down this road and it was a dead end. He had lived in Amsterdam for nearly a year in 1992, directly after his music studies, and after mixing in music circles he had met all the washed-up musicians in that city and heard all the stories about all the other washed-up musicians who had lived there. Everyone, for example, had a Chet Baker story; long yarns about how they had played with him at one stage or another. If Rodriguez had lived in Amsterdam, Craig would have known about it.

A few other places that Rodriguez sang about seemed to be figments of his imagination. From 'It Started Out So Nice' Craig pulled 'Bohemia' and 'Ixea', but they both sounded too fantastical in the song to actually exist.

Setting aside the proper nouns, Craig found several descriptions of places and situations that could form clues. But these were virtually impossible to locate in the real world. For example, in 'Hate Street Dialogue' Rodriguez sings: '*The turnkey comes, his face a grin / Locks the cell I'm in again.*' There's no doubting the meaning, but also no way of knowing which prison is being sung about. Similarly, in 'A Most Disgusting Song' he sings about the kinds of places he's performed, but without ascribing names to any of them: *'I've played every kind of gig there is to play now / I've played faggot bars, hooker bars, motorcycle funerals / In opera houses, concert halls, halfway houses.'* But then again, had he really played in these places or was it simply a case of poetic licence?

Next, Craig turned his attention to names of people, of which there are many in Rodriguez's songs. Surely some of these had meaning? From Tom the curious and James the weak – obvious references to biblical figures, but still – to playboy Ralph, disappearing sister Ruth, Linda glass maid, Molly MacDonald, Willy Thompson, Jimmy Bad Luck Butts and Mr Flood. Not to mention Heikki, Genji, Kogi and Orion – Tolkienesque names that Craig could not even begin to plot on any kind of anthropological spectrum.

As he meticulously combed through the lyrics, Craig found other clues that seemingly substantiated some of the rumours he'd heard over the years. Many South Africans had taken the line from 'The Establishment Blues', *'I opened the window to listen to the news'*, to mean that Rodriguez was blind. Then there was the abovementioned 'turnkey' reference that seemed to suggest he had written his songs in jail, another myth associated with Rodriguez. And the phrase *'Jesus at the sewer'* – was this necessarily a reference to Jesus Christ or was the artist simply referring to himself? After all, it was widely believed in South Africa that his first name was Jesus.

To further confound matters, sifting through the lyrics had an unintended narcotic-like effect on Craig. The sheer hypnotic enjoyment of the process sucked him in to the point that it became easy to forget his purpose, that of extricating information in order to find a musician. Who listens to music for clues anyway? No one.

Sugar, in the meantime, had been working on a plan of his own. After meeting with Craig in Cape Town, he went back to his office at Intekom and thought about ways to track down the musician. Soon the answer came to him. Why not build a Rodriguez website? As it was, the company had already started an e-commerce site, the Two Oceans Trading Store, which sold, among other things, the music from the TV series *Cosmos*, the only place in the world where it was available on CD, and a rare Chris de Burgh album which contained the Irish artist's tribute track to Nelson Mandela called 'Riding on a Rainbow'. This song, too, was not available anywhere else in the world.

With some very strict systems in place at Intekom to keep an eye on new projects, Sugar realised he would have to come up with a strong motivation to get the Rodriguez project approved. He spoke to a colleague in the web development division named Alec McCrindle about quickly building a Rodriguez website and putting it up before anyone found out. Once it was up, he reasoned, it would be easier to justify its presence and value. Alec agreed, but could not work on it during the day as his work was also carefully scrutinised. The 'techie' guys at Intekom liked to stay at work in the evening to play a game called Quake, which freed up Alec to spend his evening hours putting together the Rodriguez website.

With absolutely no information to go on, apart from the two albums, Sugar and Alec decided to call their website The Great Rodriguez Hunt (The word 'Great' referred to Rodriguez, not the website or the hunt.) Alec had the inspired idea to draw a milk carton with an image of Rodriguez on the side, below the words 'Have you seen this man?', as with other missing persons. Next to it was a short piece that Sugar wrote for the site:

We're after the facts . . .

I wonder how many of you know what happened to the enigmatic 60's folk singer Jesus Rodriguez?

Well, we don't, so the reason for **the great rodriguez hunt** is that we are no longer satisfied with an urban legend that is only good for conversation.

With the aid of these pages, we hope to establish a 'Rodriguez hotline', and find the whereabouts and life story of this mystical figure of <u>urban folklore</u>.

This site (the only known Rodriguez site on the internet) lets you discover his only known 'anthology', buy his album, or take part in the <u>Rodriguez forum</u>. If you see the man in a 7/11 with Elvis somewhere in downtown Johannesburg, you'll know who to contact.

The site went live in April 1997 and began attracting quite a few CD sales and some interesting emails. With traffic steadily increasing, in August Alec created a forum where fans could leave messages. It was the fourth message posted there a few weeks later that would turn out to be the most interesting.

Craig, meanwhile, had hit a wall. He could recite Rodriguez's lyrics backwards if he wanted to, but he was no closer to finding out what had happened to the singer. He talked with Sugar on the phone, but he too had stalled. Craig needed a break, so he turned his attention to another item on his ten-point list. This one simply read: 'Interview Shawn Phillips'. Shawn Phillips was the other musician who held Craig's fascination. The American folk-rocker had achieved a similar cult status in South Africa with *Second Contribution*, an album that would alternate with *Cold Fact* in the army bungalow. Aside from his interest in Phillips himself, Craig had an ulterior motive for interviewing him: to see if he could perhaps help unlock the mystery of Rodriguez. Tracking down Phillips proved relatively easy, and Craig interviewed him for ninety minutes. Phillips was surprised to hear that both he and a musician named Rodriguez had formed the soundtrack to the lives of South Africa's many white conscripts. But Craig was even more surprised to hear that neither Phillips nor his manager Arlo Hennings had ever heard of the Mexican-American singer. First Tina Turner, now Shawn Phillips: how was it possible that Rodriguez wasn't known even by American musicians who were making music at the same time as him?

Craig started hitting up the various record labels once more. PolyGram, the distributor at the time, knew nothing. RPM, an earlier distributor, knew even less. That's when it struck him. Three words. *Follow the money*. Why hadn't he thought of it before? His next step was to squeeze PolyGram until they reluctantly divulged the number of a person whom Craig believed to be the lawyer of the Rodriguez estate in the US. This was promising. He promptly typed out a letter and faxed it to the number. In 1997 the fax machine, with its slow gurgle, was still a handy space-age instrument. He waited a few days but received no response. It was time for plan B. Working out the time difference, Craig picked up the phone and dialled the number. An answering machine kicked in on the other end: 'This office is now closed. If you know your party's extension, please dial it now . . .' – had he miscalculated the time difference? Los Angeles was nine hours behind, right? Or was it nine hours ahead? – '. . . please leave a message after the tone.' In his naivety, Craig left a long and detailed message outlining the reason for his call, and then went to bed. He tried the number again the next day: 'The number you have dialled has changed. Please consult your local directory for the new number.' How bizarre. Could it be that whomever he was trying to contact was not in the mood to be contacted? Or was it just coincidence?

Craig went back to PolyGram and bugged them again, but the one LA number was all they had. A few weekends later he headed down to visit his brother Adrian in Wilderness. Adrian, a computer technician, had moved to this sleepy seaside town on the Garden Route to escape the hustle and bustle of Johannesburg. His computer and internet setup was faster than anything Craig could lay his hands on back home, and Craig was able to use it throughout the night while his brother went out partying.

But despite the great hardware, the internet at that stage was still in its infancy, accompanied by the gurgling sound of the dial-up modem. This was a time before Google, when the go-to search engines were Netscape Navigator, AltaVista, Lycos and Ask Jeeves, which are now primitive in comparison. But Craig was happy to have the opportunity to trawl the net for information on Rodriguez.

He began with births and deaths, but unlike South Africa, there seemed to be no national database for the United States. Instead, each state functioned as its own entity, so it was a little like dealing with fifty countries. To make matters worse, births and deaths were also sometimes ordered according to county or parish, a foreign concept to a South African. The name was another problem. Rodriguez is the second most common Hispanic surname in the US, surpassed only by Garcia, and the ninth most common surname overall. And then there was the little issue of first name. Christians had already co-opted the internet as their own, so the name Jesus produced a glut of results but no glory. And to make matters worse, Jesus, pronounced *hey-soos* in Spanish, is one of the top 100 most popular Spanish first names. Looking for Jesus was like looking for a needle in a haystack.

Of course, unbeknown to Craig, he wasn't even looking for Jesus Rodriguez. Who would have thought to look for Sixto Rodriguez? Granted, the name Sixto (pronounced *seez-to*) Rodriguez does appear on the label of the early vinyl versions of *Cold Fact*, but the songs themselves are credited to Jesus Rodriguez and Sixth Prince. The name Sixto fell away on later versions, and it never appeared on any of his album covers. It didn't matter though: in South Africa everyone knew without a doubt that the person who wrote and sang the songs was Jesus Rodriguez.

Craig managed to hook up with a few fellow cyber travellers who offered to help him with his search. One sent over the URL for a database that contained many hundreds of Rodriguezes. 'Pour yourself a stiff drink,' read the subject line. Craig prepared for a long night of looking at births and deaths, which unfortunately by the next morning had produced nothing. He went for a walk on the beach. There had been a severe storm the night before. Thick, arm-like stems of kelp had washed ashore. One piece looked so much like an arm that for a second he thought he might be hallucinating. It was the lack of sleep. Determined to achieve a breakthrough, he went back to the house to resume his search. As usual, he hit play on the sound system. *Cold Fact* in shuffle mode kicked in for the umpteenth time. It was the slow, lazy tune of 'Inner City Blues' that poured from the speakers: *'Going down a dirty inner city side road, I plotted . . .'*

Still delirious from exhaustion, Craig now decided to list every name that he could find on either of the two albums. The list was quite long. Each would need to be researched in its own right. But that's when it hit him. Right in the middle of his sleep-deprived search, a line filled the air that he had heard a hundred times before, but for some reason had never taken full cognisance of: *'Met a girl from Dearborn / Early six o'clock this morn / A cold fact.'* How had he missed it? What was Dearborn? It had to be a place. A town, a neighbourhood? Excited by the prospect, Craig typed the word into the computer. He found numerous Dearborns in America. Montana, Massachusetts, Missouri, Michigan, New Hampshire and Indiana all hosted either a Dearborn or a Fort Dearborn, named for the fifth US secretary of war, Henry Dearborn. Craig sat back. What now? He glimpsed an old school atlas on his brother's bookshelf. That might be the way to go. He retrieved it, blew off the dust and went straight to the index. There were several Dearborns listed, but one seemed to stand out to him more than the others: Dearborn, Michigan, a city within the Detroit metro. None of the other states or towns felt right in terms of Rodriguez's inner-city descriptions. Craig paged to Dearborn, Michigan. This had to be it. Over the years he had heard much of the blue-collar woes and industrial pain and grit of Motor City. Detroit had to be the place. With this in mind, every search, every lyric and every clue from that moment on became fil-tered through the prism of Detroit. Had Craig not read that Clarence Avant, the so-called 'Impresario', had been the head of Motown at some stage? Didn't Motown derive from 'motor town'? For the longest time Craig had thought the answers lay in New York, but now he was almost certain they were in Detroit. He walked outside to get some fresh air, and looked up as the sky began to cry. It was time, at nine o'clock in the morning, to call it a night.

Back in Johannesburg, Craig took the list of names he had drawn up using the albums and began several mini-searches. Not surprisingly, each time a name came up, so did Detroit in some way, shape or form. Except for one that appeared to be UK-based: Roger Armstrong from Ace Records, the cata-logue distributor for two other names that appeared on the albums, co-producers Dennis Coffey and Mike Theodore. The pieces were falling into place now. Craig hoped Armstrong would have contact information for either Coffey or Theodore. He trawled the internet until he finally managed to track down a UK telephone number. At last, there would be a voice at the end of the line that knew something. Unfortunately, and this was becoming a pattern, he would have to wait until the next morning.

As early as the two-hour time difference would allow, Craig got on the phone to London. The English receptionist was friendly and put him straight through to Roger Armstrong. Craig couldn't believe how easy it was. Armstrong came on the line and he, too, sounded genial.

'Can't help you with Rodriguez,' he said, 'but I'd be happy to help you with Mike Theodore.'

'What? Say that again?' asked Craig.

'Mike Theodore,' said Armstrong pointedly, 'the record producer. I can give you his number, if you like.'

Yes. *Yes!* Craig air-punched with his fist. He reached over for his pen and notepad. The thrill of writing down Theodore's number was immeasurable, so much so that he forgot to ask Armstrong any further questions. Craig immediately dialled the US number, forgetting the time difference. An answering machine kicked in and a nasal American voice invited him to leave a message, which he promptly did. Craig could barely sleep that night. He was so close to finding the truth, just one degree, one remove, from finding out what had happened to Rodriguez.

The next morning, his phone rang. When he answered, he heard the same voice from the answering machine. The blood drained from his legs. It was Mike Theodore, co-producer of the masterpiece *Cold Fact*. Craig introduced himself and reached for his pen and notepad once more. Mike was curt at first, unsure what this call from South Africa was all about.

'What can I do for you?' he asked.

Craig explained the situation. He told Mike how, for the past however many years, the music of Jesus Rodriguez had sold and sold and sold in South Africa. How no one knew anything about the musician, not even the record companies that had distributed his albums over the years. How nearly every white person on the streets of South Africa could recite any one of a number of Rodriguez songs if asked to do so, in their sleep. How Rodriguez was a household name, perhaps one of the most famous musical artists. And finally, how no one knew how he had died.

When he had finished, there was a pause at the other end of the line. Mike seemed genuinely surprised by what he was hearing. And then came the moment that Craig will never forget.

'Jesus is alive,' said Mike, dropping the bombshell, 'but he ain't the man you're looking for. Jesus is only the brother. The one you're looking for is Sixto – the principal solo artist known as Rodriguez.'

Craig was dumbstruck. All those years of wondering and over nine months of focused research had come down to this one moment. 'Wait . . . wait a minute,' he stammered, 'you mean the one whose voice we hear on *Cold Fact*, the one you call Sixto . . . *he's* still alive?' He just had to ask the question in a different way to be sure he was hearing correctly.

Mike, calm and professional, answered in the affirmative. 'Alive and kicking.'

'*Alive?*' Craig's jaw dropped. He could feel his heart pounding.

Mike went on to say that he had absolutely no idea about the things Craig was telling him, no idea that the albums had sold in South Africa, let alone the cult status they had achieved. It was all news to him, and would be news to Rodriguez, too. Mike and Motown session guitarist Dennis Coffey, both from Detroit, had recorded *Cold Fact* in 1969 on Sussex Records, a label then owned by one Clarence Avant, 'a great believer' in Rodriguez and the current head of Motown. *Bingo!* thought Craig. His instinct about Detroit had been spot on. It was all coming together now. Except for one thing.

'But then,' asked Craig, 'how come most of the songs are credited to Jesus and not Sixto?'

There was a pause before Mike said, 'Well, that was a political move.'

Craig was frantically taking notes. He was hoping for an explanation that would shed light on the drug, jail and fire theories that circulated in South Africa, but none was forthcoming. So he asked Mike what he meant by 'political'.

'Well, there's political . . . and there's political.'

The producer was being somewhat vague on that issue, so Craig decided on a different tactic. 'Will Jesus . . . er . . . Sixto speak to me?'

'If Sixto wants to speak to you, then he will.'

'Did you actually tell him I called?' asked Craig, referring to the detailed message he'd left the day before.

'Yeah, it's personal, you know. We're trying to ascertain the status of each album. In fact, we're in touch with Clarence Avant as we speak.'

Craig wanted to probe a little deeper. 'Does Rodriguez own the rights to his songs?'

'Yes.'

'Did he play Woodstock?'

'No, but he did tour Australia. Lots of money of his was being held there at one time.'

Craig scratched his head. The plot thickened. Australia? 'So what's he doing today?'

'Same as before, playing music.'

'But will he talk to me?' Craig repeated.

'Well, let me just say this,' said Mike, 'he has his own concept of the universe . . .'

When the call ended, Craig sat in front of his computer. This was usually the best way to start writing, whether words were readily available or not. It felt strange. Sitting there, he suddenly realised that he had information in his head that no one else in South Africa could even imagine. Forget about confirming rumours of Rodriguez's suicide – the man was alive! Craig wanted to run down the street and shout the news to anyone who would listen, but instead he turned to his computer and broke the news to Sugar via email. Later on the phone, he told his fellow searcher about his call with Mike Theodore in greater detail. He asked Sugar to keep the story under wraps until he was able to get an article published. 'Although we were a thousand kilometres apart,' Sugar would later write in his blog post 'Sugar and the Sugar Man', 'Craig and I shared a telephone hug and dance when he told me the great news. What a day it had been.'

A few days later, Craig opened a new document on his computer and typed the words 'What happened to Rodriguez?' And so began the first draft of the article that would break the story. The title would change to 'Climb up on my music' and 'Looking for Jesus' before becoming 'Looking for Rodriguez'. As the words of the article fell onto the page, Craig had no idea where this strange story would take him.

After finishing the first draft, Craig started looking for a place to get the story published. His first port of call was the *Mail & Guardian*, a respected liberal newspaper, one of only two surviving papers of its kind from the apartheid era (the other being Max du Preez's Afrikaans *Vrye Weekblad*). He could have approached magazines, but Craig felt the gravitas of the story deserved a serious newspaper.

The *Mail & Guardian* said they were quite happy to publish the piece, but the conversation stalled over money. Craig thought he had a story that was worth something. The person on the other end of the line thought otherwise. When he asked for a better rate, he was summarily shut down. 'What do you think this is, a bargain basement?'

Lesson learnt, Craig faxed off the story to several other newspapers, but with no takers he changed tack and pitched it to a popular magazine new to the South African market. *Directions* had its requisite share of semi-clad girls on every page, but it also saw itself as a magazine with a brain and enough smart content to satisfy the intelligentsia. Brendan Cooper was the editor and was keen to publish the story. The Rodriguez lyric '*I wonder how many times you've had sex*' could easily have been a *Directions* headline. Craig initially wanted to hide the fact that Rodriguez had been found and publish the story over two issues, with the first instalment being more of a teaser. Brendan originally acquiesced, but then changed his mind. He rightly felt that since several newspapers had already seen the story from Craig's pitch, they might be scooped. The article went into editorial and Craig was ecstatic.

The timing could not have been better; he and Philippa were about to get married. Due to years of animosity between Philippa's divorced parents, the couple had decided to elope to Italy. After a wedding in Orvieto, they took a four-week honeymoon traversing the four corners of the boot, during which time they stopped off at Positano on the Amalfi Coast. Shawn Phillips had dropped out of the US music scene and taken up residence in Positano in the seventies. One of his most popular songs, 'Landscape', portrays his life on the Amalfi Coast during that period. With the long-distance interview with Phillips still on his desk, and with the Rodriguez article now in editorial, while in Italy Craig decided to research what was hopefully going to be his next feature, and perhaps even score a double whammy. He spent many hours with Phillips's old landlord, an eccentric artist named Federico Apuzzo, and built a story around what he heard. The article was never published.

Mr and Mrs Strydom flew back home just in time for the

October issue of *Directions* magazine. Craig rushed out to purchase a copy. Carmen Electra graced the cover with her grainy cleavage on full display and the headline 'Beware, High Voltage'. The Rodriguez story did not make it onto the cover; nonetheless, tucked near the back on page 154 was 'Looking for Rodriguez: Has anybody seen the Sugarman?' (The magazine had insisted that the title 'Looking for Jesus' be changed to 'Looking for Rodriguez'.) It may not have been Craig's finest piece of journalism, but it was his most important. He had sent an earlier draft to Mike Theodore, who had sent it to a certain Eva Koller in Junction City, Kansas. Eva ran an internet search on Sixto Rodriguez's name and South Africa. She had been shocked and surprised on reading the article to discover that the Sugar Man, who she knew as a failed musician-cum-handyman-cum-social activist, was actually a 'somebody', albeit on the other side of the world. And if Craig Bartholomew Strydom was to be believed, he had been a 'somebody' for some time, give or take twenty-five years. And unless she was mistaken, the hard-working 'singer' had not – to her knowledge – received as much as a dime from South Africa. During her internet search she stumbled upon the Great Rodriguez Hunt website. She couldn't believe it. Navigating to the forum, she typed a message. Hers was the fourth message posted:

> Rodriguez is my father! I'm serious. He recently received an article from a journalist there who told him of the following. I went on line to try to find out more info and was shocked to see he has his own site. Truly amazing. Do you really want to know about my father? Sometimes the fantasy is better left alive. It is as unbelievable to me as it is to you.

She wrote that her email system was down, but gave a phone number and address in Junction City where she could be contacted, and signed off as Eva Alicia Rodriguez Koller. The date was Friday 12 September 1997.

When Sugar went back to work, Alec called him over to show him something truly incredible. Sugar could not believe what he was reading. A message from Rodriguez's daughter! Thrilled, he picked up the phone to call her, but then remembered the time difference. He'd have to wait until that evening. When he eventually dialled and got through, it was an exciting conversation. Sugar told Eva the whole surreal story about her father's fame at the southern-most tip of Africa, and she in turn told Sugar about Rodriguez, how he was something of a recluse and was reluctant to give out his number. Sugar respected that, but said that if Rodriguez ever felt like it, he was welcome to call. It was midnight by the time he put down the phone and, although he had work the next day, he struggled to sleep. Instead, he sat and mulled over the conversation.

At around 1 a.m., just as he finally fell asleep, the phone rang. It was a strange hour for phone calls. His wife, Ronit, answered the phone, which was on her side of the bed. She looked at Sugar with an expression of awe as she mouthed the words, 'It's him!'

Sugar picked up the phone and said, 'Hello?' The voice at the other end of the line was unmistakable, with its soft 'R's and American accent. In an unassuming tone, the voice said, 'Is that Sugar? This is me, Rodriguez.'

Sugar almost dropped the phone from sheer excitement. Miraculously, the line was clear, allowing them to have a calm and quiet conversation. Sugar told Rodriguez about his cult status in South Africa and that all his albums, including the *Best Of* compilation, were available on CD and cassette. Rodriguez in turn told Sugar that he would love to tour South Africa, as he had completed a very successful tour of Australia over fifteen years earlier. In a manner which Sugar would later learn was typically Rodriguez, the singer mentioned that he did not own a CD player but did have a reel-to-reel copy of *Cold Fact*. Only someone like Rodriguez would not even have CDs of his own work. Before saying goodbye, Sugar promised to send him all the CDs via Eva. And that was how, for a brief moment, two continents collided and the frayed ends of a mystery were finally reconnected. It's tempting at this point to throw out the hackneyed phrase, 'And the rest is history.' But this was really just the beginning.

4

Dead men don't tour
(1998)

'Thank you for keeping me alive.'
— RODRIGUEZ DURING HIS FIRST TOUR TO SOUTH AFRICA

Among the people Malik Bendjelloul was indebted to for the success of his 2012 documentary *Searching for Sugar Man*, one who played an unknown but crucial role was Tonia Selley – or Karla Krimpalien, as she was known during her days as part of the eighties alternative Afrikaans music scene. When it became clear that Rodriguez was coming to South Africa, there was a lot of fanfare and excitement. But at the height of it all, no one thought to bring a camera. Except for Tonia, the percussionist in the backing band for the 1998 tour. She alone anticipated the magnitude of the event and decided to do something to record it for posterity.

In early 1998, South Africans woke up to the news that a man most thought had died in some fantastical way was in fact now planning to tour South Africa. The immediate feeling by many was that this was perhaps a tribute band. Many such bands had passed through the country over the years. In the seventies and eighties, South African kids had listened to *Springbok Hit Parade* LPs, with scantily clad women on the sleeves and featuring cover versions of the latest hits. It was something they were used to. Also, for the better part of both Craig's and Sugar's lives, the only way to see a live act was to travel to Sun City in the ostensibly independent homeland of Bophuthatswana. It was a form of sleight of hand; everyone knew on some level that playing in the homeland was just a roundabout way of flouting the 'cultural boycott' on South Africa. Many acts, including Elton John, Rod Stewart and Queen played Sun City at a time of growing mass resistance to apartheid. It wasn't until Steve Van Zandt's protest song 'Sun City' was released by Artists United Against Apartheid in 1985 that people couldn't pretend any more that they didn't know what was going on.

The job of arranging Rodriguez's first tour to South Africa went to an old business associate of his, tour promoter Zev Eizik, and a Swede by the name of Magnus Erickson. There were other tour promoters on the sidelines who might have done a better job, or who were better equipped to understand the unique complexities of touring South Africa, but because they had worked together before, Eizik was the only one Rodriguez trusted.

The proposed tour was to be a quick one, with just six performances between 6 and 13 March 1998. The first two concerts would take place in Cape Town, followed by two in Johannesburg, one in Pretoria and one in Durban. The biggest fear among those who knew Rodriguez, his family included, was whether he would still be able to perform live gigs and cope with the rigours of touring a foreign country at age fifty-seven. Some musicians' careers are finished by twenty-seven, let alone fifty-seven. And Rodriguez had not played live for nearly twenty years! Did he even own a professional guitar, for that matter? It turned out he didn't, so, according to Magnus Erickson, tour management 'had to in fact buy Rodriguez a guitar before the tour started'.

On 16 February, the *Cape Times* confirmed the rumours of a Rodriguez tour in an article titled 'Rodriguez? He's playing here in fact'. The newspaper also added another highly imaginative 'cause of death' to the already long list of ways in which Rodriguez had supposedly kicked the bucket: 'His death was blamed on an unfortunate accident with an electric guitar and a faulty wall-socket.'

While the tour was being planned, Craig approached Rodriguez for an interview. After talking on the phone to Eva, who was facilitating the process, Craig realised that the best way to get the singer to open up would be to formulate a list of questions, which he sent through to Rodriguez via Eva. The idea was to reformulate the subsequent back-and-forth emails into a conversation.

Craig was surprised and delighted by Rodriguez's responses, which playfully included his own line of questioning. 'So tell me about yourself,' Rodriguez began by saying. Craig answered that he was from Kimberley, to which Rodriguez shot back: 'Next question . . . How do they celebrate a diamond festival?'

'Hey! Who's doing this interview?' Craig replied. Rodriguez was trying to turn the interview on its head, and it was clear that he was doing his research, most likely during trips to the Detroit Public Library, where he was a frequent visitor. Craig had to bring the conversation back.

'I've had a hard time in South Africa convincing people that you are in fact alive and kicking,' he wrote. 'Why do you think this impression exists?'

'Imaginations working overtime,' Rodriguez suggested. 'Your personal intervention, though, has energised my tour to South Africa.'

Craig chose an unusual approach in the interview. Instead of asking straightforward questions, he made a list of personal statements that most of the time, but not always, led to a question. He felt that if he could capture Rodriguez's imagination by offering up some information about himself, he would be able to get the singer to open up. It was a trade-off of sorts, and it worked.

Craig told Rodriguez that he had lived in Amsterdam, and that he'd been so homesick that whenever he bought Cape apples he would stick the blue 'Cape' sticker on his bicycle handlebars, resulting in a blue handlebar.

Rodriguez's response gives a sense of his gentleness and poetic turn of phrase: 'I only went through Amsterdam. I enjoy your scenarios . . . your expression about longing for familiar places; your riff about missing home is deliciously portrayed.'

In answer to further questions, Rodriguez revealed that his parents came from Mexico in the 1920s, that he had started playing the guitar at sixteen, that he was involved in organising a Native American 'pow-wow' ceremony at Wayne State University campus in 1974, and that he had played at the Tanelorn Festival in Australia in 1981, appearing on the same bill as Midnight Oil, a band that he admired.

After Craig disclosed that he had once been arrested in Spain for possession of dagga (the South African word for marijuana), Rodriguez replied that 'Arrest is a traumatic scene', and then frankly expressed his views on cannabis:

Clearly alcohol is a much more destructive substance. Weed is a natural substance. Less harmful and helpful in some cases, i.e. the ageing of senior citizens . . . good issue! The way I see it is when the law catches up with reality, change will come. There's a group in Michigan called N.O.R.M.A.L. trying to 'decriminalise' dagga and a guy on the west coast running for governor of California who produces the substance for medical purposes.

Asked about the significance of the little grey shoe on the *Coming from Reality* album cover, Rodriguez replied:

The shoe had no real meaning. The photographer, Hal Wilson, came in from New York. We walked around Detroit and saw the house. Debris was lying around and the shoe nearby. I took it and placed it beside mine. We only took seven shots for the album cover. Milton Sincoff designed the cover with Buddah Records and we said at the time, 'If the album doesn't make it, the cover will.'

As for characters in his songs like Jane S. Piddy, Molly MacDonald and Willie Thompson, he explained, 'The people are fictional. I tapped on the writer's poetic licence, giving them names and shape. Almost as a caricature works for the visual artist.'

One thing that stands out in the interview is the sharp, creative and unorthodox mind of the man who wrote *Cold Fact*. At one point Rodriguez muses that 'art is in all of us. We all have a talent. It is up to us to listen and draw within ourselves and pull out the words, the form or some creative action.' He highlights the importance of music: 'In my opinion, the guitar is central in popular music. Guitars have evolved, changed shape, become electrified. It is one of the most unifying language tools in the world. I'd be lost without one.' And: 'I feel we live in the age of sound. Like the Bronze Age or Stone Age. Today, we are given so many clues about life through sound.'

At one point Craig put the question to him: 'Why was your masterpiece, *Cold Fact*, largely ignored in America?'

Rodriguez's response epitomises his humility and philosophical outlook: '"Masterpiece", you're too kind. It was the first product released on the Sussex label, owned by Clarence Avant. I think it's all right that it happened this way.'

The interview appeared in the *Mail & Guardian* on 20 February 1998 under the title 'Fact: Rodriguez lives'. This time there was no haggling over money. It was the first interview with Rodriguez of *any* kind to appear in South Africa. These were early days in the resurgence of the musician's career, and the fact that publicity-shy Rodriguez was open to being interviewed at all did not seem as strange then as it would today. Perhaps he acquiesced because he was not yet as jaded by celebrity.

Compared to all the interviews Rodriguez has given since then, it is in this one that he seems to be his most accommodating, in which his guard is most down. Even the piece that would later air on CBS's *60 Minutes* after the success of *Searching for Sugar Man*, when transcribed and analysed, seems to have many words but very little information. It is especially devoid of Rodriguez's insight and personality. The *Mail & Guardian* only printed a truncated version of the original interview, but the full text is available on Sugarman.org.

In spite of some initial scepticism, fans flocked to buy tickets to see the artist who had added colour to their dreams. Many of them had not even been born when Rodriguez recorded his first album. It was no exaggeration to say that a large percentage of white South Africans knew every lyric, every hook, every chorus by heart, so the interest in his concerts came as no surprise.

The next challenge on the tour promoters' list was to find Rodriguez a suitable band, and one that actually believed he was alive. Guitarist Willem Möller was one of the first musicians recruited. Möller, no stranger to South African audiences, was one of the leading musicians in the Voëlvry movement, a group of alternative Afrikaans musicians such as Johannes Kerkorrel (Ralph Rabie), Koos Kombuis (André du Toit), Bernoldus Niemand (James Phillips) and Karla Krimpalien (Tonia Selley) who performed concerts in university campuses and town halls across South Africa to oppose apartheid and Afrikaner nationalism in the eighties. It was the first time young Afrikaners stood up to the South African government en masse.

In 1998 Möller was the guitarist in the band Big Sky, with his old friend Steve Louw. In an interview with *YOU* magazine, Möller recalls getting a phone call from Steve. 'Willem,' said Steve. 'You remember Rodriguez?'

'The guy who sang "I Wonder" and "Sugar Man"?' said Willem. 'Of course I remember him. Why?'

'He's coming to tour and they want Big Sky to open for him. You in?'

'Sure,' said Willem. 'But isn't he dead?'

'Apparently not. Can you get the musicians together?'

Willem made a few calls, and the reaction he got was the same. 'Opening for Rodriguez? You sure he's not dead? Okay, we're in.' The line-up was Steve Louw on vocals, Willem on electric guitar, Russel Taylor on keyboards, Reuben Samuels on drums, Willem's wife Tonia Selley on percussion and backing vocals, and Graeme Currie on bass. (Coincidentally, Currie had been Craig's college bass teacher.)

A few days later Steve phoned again. 'It seems Rodriguez doesn't have a band,' he said. 'Do you think you guys could also be his backing band?'

'Not a problem,' Willem recalls. 'As it turned out, not only were we all Rodriguez fans, we'd all played his songs in cover bands. It was on – rehearsals in Cape Town, then six shows around the country. Just one question remained: was Rodriguez really alive?'

The band started rehearsing without Rodriguez. They knew the songs and, as seasoned session musicians, it took no time to perfect them.

During this time Craig went into the studio with former Slam Factory drummer and producer Barry Dean, Philippa Berrington-Blew and rapper Tazz to record and co-produce a hip-hop version of the song 'I Wonder', adding to a long list of cover versions. David Gresham, a South African music-industry stalwart, liked what he heard and signed the band for the one song. It appeared on a compilation album called *Dance Connection 17* under the name 'Generation EXT'. It soon became the hit pick-of-the-week on Radio Metro, but earned the musicians very little apart from a small amount of recognition. It would, however, have been the first time Rodriguez received any royalties from South Africa, assuming that the payments made by the David Gresham record company made their way to him.

A world away in Detroit, the fifty-seven-year-old singer put away his work gear. Leaving the cold behind, Rodriguez, his wife Konny and his daughters took a taxi to the airport for the twenty-plus-hour flight to sunny South Africa. It is not known what Rodriguez told his colleagues, if he told them anything at all, but one thing's for sure: it probably wasn't 'I'm off to play six sold-out shows in South Africa.' That would have seemed certifiably insane coming from a man who didn't even own a professional guitar. For someone who sang about escape, it must have been like going down his own private rabbit hole.

The Rodriguezes landed in Cape Town and were put up in an ultra-luxurious guesthouse in the scenic suburb of Camps Bay. So taken was Rodriguez by the level of extravagance that he invited the band to come and see the bidet, which was not something he had seen before. In the meantime, Craig was assigned to cover the first concert for the *Sunday Independent*. Excitedly, he called Sugar to tell him the news and took the next flight to Cape Town, where he met up with his friend David Viljoen, who had introduced him to Rodriguez's music in the first place, and Brian Currin. Brian was a home-audio sales representative and music fanatic who had posted a message on the forum of the Great Rodriguez Hunt on 23 October 1997, and who had just built a Rodriguez memorial website. Little did he know that Rodriguez had just been found alive and that, a few postings earlier, Rodriguez's daughter had made herself known to his fans on the website. Brian immediately converted the memorial site to a new site of Rodriguez facts and trivia. He called the site Climb Up On My Music and for the longest time it would be the go-to site for all things Rodriguez. At the same time, Sugar renamed his own site the Great Rodriguez Site, as the 'Hunt' was now over. The two sites would later merge as Sugarman.org.

The backing band, now pretty tight with the solid rhythm section of Currie on bass and Samuels on drums, was rehearsing to the CD of *Cold Fact* at Milestone Studios on Bloem Street in Cape Town when Rodriguez walked in. Indicating for them to continue, he went over to the CD player, turned it off and picked up the microphone. Then he began to sing along with them. 'I could not believe my ears,' Tonia recalls, 'his voice was exactly as it had been when I first heard it in the seventies.' That was the band's introduction to the singer. They established an instant rapport. With the big day swiftly approaching, there was barely time for more than three or four rehearsals.

In the midst of these rehearsals, on Wednesday 4 March 1998, Rodriguez flew up to Johannesburg. His first stop was an appearance the following morning on *The Breakfast Club* TV show for SABC 2, where, for the first time, South Africans got to see that he was actually the real deal and not an imposter. Later that evening, Rodriguez was interviewed on a show called *Front Row*, hosted by Khanyi Mkhize (now Dhlomo). After the interview, Rodriguez played an un-plugged version of 'I Wonder'. His playing was solid and his voice seemed to be on top form.

The next day Craig met up with daughters Eva and Regan, accompanied by their bodyguard and driver Juan, at Greenmarket Square in the centre of Cape Town. It was good to finally meet Eva, with whom he had been liaising. She struck Craig as being deeply serious and as sharp-minded as her father. Craig was surprised to learn that she was one of the first female helicopter pilots in US military history. Regan, at nineteen, was good-humoured and clearly excited to be touring with her musician father. With an assignment at the back of his mind, Craig was happy to be invited to travel with the girls and Juan to Cape Town International Airport to meet Rodriguez's flight from Johannesburg.

Seeing the singer at arrivals, walking towards them with his guitar, Craig began to formulate his latest article in his head. *Gandhi with a guitar.* It was unforgettable seeing Rodriguez for the first time, especially after all the hours he had spent poring over the man's lyrics and their meaning. Just to see his eyes! No one in South Africa had ever seen the singer's eyes. In the handful of photographs on the three albums that South Africans had seen over the years, he was never without his trademark sunglasses. In fact, the rumour of his blindness still persisted. Also noticeable was how young and fit he appeared in spite of being in his late fifties. It was clear that manual labour had had a positive effect on his physical well-being.

Craig rode with Rodriguez, Eva, Regan and Juan back to the city, where they met up with David Viljoen, Sugar and Brian Currin for lunch. It was the first time Craig and Brian would meet in person.

On the afternoon of the first show, the complete entourage arrived at the concert venue. The band was already doing a sound check when it was discovered that Rodriguez couldn't remember the words to 'A Most Disgusting Song'. And who could blame him? It had been seventeen years, after all. And, more than that, Rodriguez was in a state of nervous exhaustion after rehearsing throughout the night in the guesthouse, the constant tapping of his shoe keeping all in attendance awake in what was otherwise a well-sound-proofed building. Viljoen and Brian scrambled to make photocopies of the lyrics.

As the sun started to set, fans descended on the Bellville Velodrome. There was very little difference in the levels of enthusiasm between those older fans who remembered Rodriguez from the seventies and the younger ones who had only recently discovered him. Big Sky, with Steve Louw at the helm, came on first and played a charged set. Russel Taylor's keyboards were tight, Tonia Selley's percussion was crisp, and Willem Möller's guitar was shred-ready. Craig, Sugar and their friends and family were seated near the front. Many of the fans in the audience still believed that when Rodriguez came on stage they would discover someone else, a lookalike perhaps.

Finally the moment arrived. The crowd began to chant, 'Rodriguez . . . Rodriguez . . . Rodriguez . . .' The tall bassist Graeme Currie began the bassline that each and every person in the audience knew by heart. It was the bottom of 'I Wonder', a motif that the bass player describes as a secondary hook. The crowd, already coiled to breaking point, sprang loose as one when they recognised the beguiling line. The band recycled the groove. And there it was again. A wave of energy rippled through the audience. Magnus Erickson and Zev Eizik stood in the wings, worried sick. It was their investment after all. The bassline snaked across the floor once more. Where was Rodriguez? What was taking him so long? And then finally, with the repetitive bassline now on permanent loop and smoke filling the air, the ghost-like form of Rodriguez appeared, dressed in a black waistcoat and hat. He started to make his way up onto the stage, one step at a time. Erickson and Eizik had by now bitten their nails to the quick. By the time he reached the top step, every last person was on their feet. They were all watching him now. Five thousand sets of eyes drilled into him. He couldn't screw up now. This was the moment of truth. For Rodriguez and all involved, it was like a perilous dream; they just had to wake up. But this was not a dream. In a state of severe stage fright, Rodriguez was half-cowering behind the drums. Tour management was now in full panic mode. Rodriguez's wife Konny had her head in her hands. 'Get him to play,' someone in the audience shouted. Ever the level-headed individual, Graeme Currie walked over to Rodriguez and escorted him to the microphone. He had to find a way to snap the singer out of his stage fright. 'They've all come to see you,' he said, gesturing to the mass of people that was fast becoming hysterical. Then he leant over and whispered something into Rodriguez's ear. The singer burst out laughing. The spell was broken. The bassline kicked in once more, Rodriguez walked up to the microphone, strummed his first official chords in a concert on South African soil and began to sing . . . 'I wonder, how many times you've been had?' At that moment, the entire audience – in full *fortissimo* – joined in. This wasn't going to be a concert after all; it was going to be a mass karaoke. And the words whispered by Currie into the sage's ear? 'Leaning over I smelled that he had washed his hair and I simply said, "Your shampoo smells good."'

Tonia recalls being nearly too overwhelmed to play. She spent most of the evening trying to see through her tears. At some point during the show it struck her that apart from Konny's small, non-professional video camera, the show was not being recorded. How could this be, a historically significant event such as this, after years of being in the dark about Rodriguez's fate? With great urgency she called Georgina Parkin, the producer from the production company where she worked when not touring. 'We have to do something about this,' she said. 'It's a travesty.' Georgina agreed and leapt into action. By the time Rodriguez and the band were setting up for the sound check for the second show, Georgina had presented a hastily drawn-up contract to Zev Eizik, who in turn presented it to the Rodriguez family, and an agreement to film the remaining concerts was in place, without which Malik Bendjelloul would not have had the climax to his film.

At around the same time that Georgina was typing up a contract to film the shows, Craig was adding the finishing touches to his article. 'In search of Rodriguez: From hooker bars to opera houses', which told the story of the quest to find the singer, appeared in the 8 March 1998 edition of the *Sunday Independent*.

Rodriguez played six sold-out shows in South Africa. Graeme Currie recalls how playing with Rodriguez was a magical experience, how the band gelled, and how it was as thrilling for Rodriguez as it was for the band. There was a heightened sense of camaraderie as they conquered one show after the other. And the audiences? In spite of seeing their childhood idol with their own eyes, many still felt suspended in disbelief. They were not alone. From the Rodriguez family and the tour managers to Craig and Sugar and even the press, it was like a dream. Journalist Rian Malan said of the phenomenon:

That sort of thing does not happen in the rational universe. It does not happen. It's against the laws of God and nature. This guy who has come to tour here must be an imposter. It's a clever public relations scam. Actually, not even a clever public relations scam, it's a stupid public relations scam, because it so obviously can't be true. Only idiots would believe it . . . but I was wrong.

It is not often the straight-shooting Rian Malan admits to being wrong.

The video footage bears testimony to that incredible

moment. Interviewed on camera for Tonia Selley's documentary, *Dead Men Don't Tour*, Rodriguez and his people describe the range of emotions they felt at the time.

REGAN: We didn't believe it right away. We thought South Africa . . . what's in South Africa? We didn't believe it until we were on the plane, you know, honestly. We thought it was ten people . . . we had no idea the magnitude, you know.

RODRIGUEZ: I was expecting 800-seaters.

REGAN: We cross the equator and everything flips upside down . . . honestly, it's not like this at home.

SANDRA: It's been shocking . . . shocking, shocking, shocking, shocking.

REGAN: I am like all these fans, seeing him for the first time in like eighteen years, you know, [it's] crazy.

EIZIK: I've seen kids eighteen, twenty, twenty-two, twenty-four years old. I anticipated a crowd of thirty-six, forty-six, fifty-six, seventy-six, like me, but no, the youth, for them, he's a new artist.

RODRIGUEZ: How sweet they are to even notice me . . . because there's so much music out there . . . and that they made me happen . . . I owe them so much, man.

KONNY: He didn't want to play any more. He had played enough in Detroit [. . .] a lot of people took advantage of the fact that [. . .] anytime he would just pull his guitar out and play, so they could hear him for free. He wasn't making money off it or anything so he just said . . . he quit. That was it.

RODRIGUEZ: It was an incredible time. Now that this has happened in 1998, you know, it's incredible. What I wrote then, applies to today.

KONNY: He has absolutely no use for money. He will give it away; if he sees somebody on the street, he will give him a hundred-dollar bill, whatever he has in his pocket. It doesn't matter if he comes home and he doesn't have anything. He doesn't buy things. He is not at all materialistic. He is very generous to people he knows.

RODRIGUEZ: What I do as a performer, I let the guitar win them over. I accept my craft, and I give it back to them, and they recognise it.

Rodriguez played several encores for each and every performance. Audiences left the respective venues in various states of delirium. Craig and Sugar couldn't believe what they'd inadvertently made happen by seeking out a dead musician. They had quite unintentionally energised the next chapter of a man's life. Rodriguez embraced South Africa as if it was his own and, even today, a huge affinity exists between him and his fans on the southernmost tip of Africa. 'Acceptance is like home,' says Craig in *Searching for Sugar Man*. The Rodriguezes were genuinely sorry to leave the shores of what was fast becoming their alternate reality, a world where Rodriguez could not walk down the street without being recognised, to return home to a city where he was just a regular guy. Detroit was the complete opposite for Rodriguez: it represented an insular, hard-working life. Would he ever get the recognition he deserved in his home country, or would this be it? Rick Emmerson, a jobsite colleague of Rodriguez's, said it best in *Searching for Sugar Man*:

> What is demonstrated very clearly is that you have a choice. He took all that torment, all that agony, all that confusion and pain and he transformed it into something beautiful. He's like the silkworm, you know, you know you take this raw material and you transform it, and you come out with something that wasn't there before, something beautiful, something perhaps transcendent, something perhaps eternal, insofar as he does that I think he is representative of the human spirit of what's possible, that you have a choice, this has been my choice, to give you 'Sugar Man', now have you done that . . . ask yourself?

PART II

THE MAN

5

Seamy seesaw kids
(1942–1966)

'I'd rather see Hitler and Hirohito win than work
next to a nigger.'
— UNKNOWN PROTESTER, DETROIT RACE RIOTS, 1943

The recurring image of Rodriguez – dressed in black,
guitar slung over his back – walking through Detroit, as
seen through the expert lens of Camilla Skagerström in
Searching for Sugar Man, is not imagery for imagery's sake.
This is how those who knew him during his most fertile
period musically – 1966 to 1972 – describe their memories
of him. But just to picture the artist half-stumbling through
the snow is to know nothing about him. Likewise, the images
Rodriguez paints with his lyrics offer only small glimpses
into his largely private universe. What at times seems obvious
to the listener often turns out to be a poetic sleight of hand.
And double, even triple, meanings abound, such as this from
'Sandrevan Lullaby': *'She asks me up to her place, but I won't be
down anymore.'* When we see him in public, he shies away

from the limelight, just as he turned his back to the audience during his early performances. And when he speaks, his words trail off, almost as if he is at pains not to be a bother to the interviewer. Granted, when he finally gets the answer out, his ideas are considered and insightful, like this response to a reporter's (now forgotten) question: 'When you repeatedly darn a sock, at what point is it no longer the same sock?' His extreme humility doesn't make understanding Rodriguez any easier. In 2012 on the CBS show *60 Minutes*, he summed up South Africa's wholesale acceptance of his music – decades of persistent record sales – with this euphemistic comment: 'South Africans had obviously picked up on my music.'

All of this means that it is nearly impossible to reconstruct Rodriguez's early life, harder still to find anyone close to him prepared to dish out even the tiniest morsel of information. Even his foes bottle up the past. The best one can do to understand the man behind the legend is to identify the moments where he surfaces in society – in a travel guide or newspaper, on an election ballot, or from others' recollections – however rarely, and to connect the dots.

Sixto Diaz Rodriguez came into the world on 10 July 1942 in Detroit, the Motor City. It was a Friday, during the hottest part of summer. He was the youngest of six children, and his parents, Ramon and Maria, named him for that reason – *sixto* means 'sixth'. 'I was born on Michigan Avenue, five blocks from the centre of Detroit,' he said in an interview in 1998. So when he sang that he was born '*in the shadow of the tallest building*' in 'Can't Get Away', he wasn't referring to the tallest building in the world, as Craig would later suppose, but probably to the tallest building in Detroit – meaning that he was born in the inner city.

The year 1942 was not a good time to be born. The world was in the throes of the deadliest military conflict it had ever seen, in which over sixty million men, women and children would die. America had only recently been drawn into the war that it had for so long tried to avoid. A day after the surprise bombing of Pearl Harbor on 7 December 1941, and seven months before Rodriguez was born, the United States declared war on Japan.

Detroit was not a particularly good place to be born either. Just beyond the window of the Rodriguez home, another conflict was brewing, this one racial. The new factories that popped up all over Detroit to service the war effort offered blacks and whites from mostly the Southern states employment opportunities and higher wages than they were used to down South. This led to mass migration, especially by black people, to the area. To their surprise, the migrants found a level of bigotry no different from that in the conservative South. Access to public housing was denied, except in the Brewster-Douglass Projects, named partially for African-American abolitionist Frederick Douglass. Many lived without indoor plumbing and were charged rents up to triple the amount paid by families in white areas. Most faced large-scale discrimination from the general public and unfair treatment by the Detroit Police Department, a cause later taken up by a young activism-minded musician named Sixto Rodriguez.

When it became impossible to house the number of job seekers arriving daily in the city, the Detroit housing commission approved two sites for housing projects, one for whites and one for blacks, but, for a host of reasons, the US government stepped in and chose a site for blacks in a predominantly white neighbourhood. The completed housing development, named Sojourner Truth after the black aboli-tionist and women's rights advocate, became a thorn in the side of Detroit's white population, which, to a man, opposed the project.

Tension escalated, and in early 1942, a few months before Rodriguez was born, a small group of armed whites burnt a cross in a field near the site and declared their intention to keep black tenants out of the neighbourhood. By the next day the group had grown to over 1,200. A number of blacks, many of whom had already signed leases and paid advance rent, attempted to cross the picket line, resulting in clashes between blacks and whites. Despite the opposition, many black tenants were able to move in, but ultimately it would take over 1,000 city and state police officers plus 1,600 Michigan National Guard troops to secure the area.

The situation remained combustible, and the spark came in the month before Rodriguez turned one, when the Packard Motor Car Company shocked many by promoting three black workers to work alongside whites in the assembly line. In reaction, it is said that 25,000 whites walked off the job, negatively impacting the war effort. It was during this pro-test that a Southern-accented white man could be heard shouting through a loudhailer: 'I'd rather see Hitler and Hirohito win than work next to a nigger.' A cartoon in a newspaper at the time shows Hitler giving a medal to Jim Crow to thank the draconian separatists for the adverse effect their race-based influence was having on the American war industry in Detroit and other parts of the country. 'For Aid and Comfort to the Enemy,' reads the caption. By the time Rodriguez celebrated his first birthday, 34 people would be dead and 433 injured. Of course, no one had any idea of the effect baby Sixto would one day have on the soldiers whose job it was to uphold apartheid in a stubborn southern African country an ocean away.

According to several sources, Rodriguez's mother Maria died when he was three. What effect this had on the boy is unknown. It is also not known if his father Ramon remarried, or if the lyric in 'Hate Street Dialogue' about being nursed by a local pusher was in any way a reference to his own life or merely a figment of his imagination. Either way, Rodriguez would go on to tell a Detroit city guide for young people in the late sixties that 'his education and childhood on the streets of the Mexican near Westside was not fit for children'. It was Rodriguez's older sister who stepped into the shoes vacated by their mother, taking on the role of primary caregiver to the young Sixto. Their father, a proud man, would have been too busy in his job at Great Lake Steel 'working the foundries and later making foreman', as Rodriguez remembers.

Ramon and Maria had immigrated to the state of Michigan from Mexico in their twenties in search of a better life. In a 2013 interview, Rodriguez confirmed that his parents came from Santa Maria del Rio in the Mexican state of San Luis Potosi. His Americanised pronunciation of the Spanish place names in the interview, however, bears testimony to the fact that the young Sixto embraced the American way, culture and language he was born into, gently setting aside his Hispanic roots. As he always says when asked about his origins, 'I didn't come here on no ship!'

Santa Maria del Rio is one of fifty-eight municipalities that make up San Luis Potosi. The municipality is located in the southern part of the state and has a land area of 1,655 square kilometres. While the municipality has just over 37,000 inhabitants, the town of Santa Maria del Rio has a population of around 12,000. The area is known for its *rebozos*, the colourful hand-woven Mexican shawls made famous in the West by the artist Frida Kahlo. According to *A Singer with Mexican Blood*, a 2014 documentary short on Rodriguez's Mexican origins, the actual mountain community from which his mother and father hailed is known as Labor de Bagres (loosely translated it means 'plantation of catfish'). In 2015, Labor de Bagres had seventy-four inhabitants and an adult-literacy rate hovering around 11 per cent.

At sixteen, Rodriguez dropped out of school and tried to join the US army. Why a future pacifist would want to enlist is anyone's guess, but the urge to join the military is not unusual for a teenager who has not yet grown into his full beliefs and is looking for escape. In addition, it was only in 1959, the year in which he tried to sign up, that the first Americans died in Vietnam, when a number of US military advisers were killed. Most Americans supported the war at first, believing it necessary in order to contain communism and to help the Vietnamese people. As time passed and the tide began to turn, however, this support waned. Increasingly, the press portrayed the war as something the US had no business with, which would go a long way towards changing opinions. By the time of the My Lai Massacre in 1968, public opinion had almost completely turned against US involvement in the war. It is doubtful that Rodriguez would still have been eager to join the military in light of these events, and it is fair to say that many of his astute views of the world captured in his lyrics would have grown out of atrocities such as these. As it turned out, for unknown reasons, the army rejected him.

It was around 1958/59 that Rodriguez began to play music. 'I started playing the guitar at sixteen and it changed my life,' he told the *Mail & Guardian* in 1998. His earliest cited influences were the songs sung by his father in Spanish. In an interview for the new *Cold Fact* album liner notes, he recalls that he grew up listening to artists like Henry Mancini and Jimmy Reed, and various doo-wop groups. His daughter Eva has 'fond memories of my father and his brothers sitting on his father's porch jamming and singing Mexican music, James Taylor, Billy Joel, Hank Williams and others'. It is not surprising that Rodriguez absorbed Hank Williams into his early repertoire. Just as *Cold Fact* was the soundtrack to the lives of many young white South Africans, Hank Williams accompanied many young Americans growing up in the post-war period before rock 'n' roll. According to *Billboard* magazine, Williams's 'Lovesick Blues', 'Cold, Cold Heart' and 'Kaw-Liga' were the top country singles of 1949, 1951 and 1953 respectively. Interestingly, the top country singles in the rest of the early fifties were filled by an assortment of 'Hanks' – Hank Snow in 1950 and 1954, and Hank Thompson in 1952 – proving that in the five-year stretch from 1949 to 1954, it didn't hurt to be called Hank if you wanted to be crowned country crooner of the year.

Rodriguez began to play small gigs in the southwest part of Detroit. While not much is known about his movements at this stage, the new *Cold Fact* liner notes tell us that establishments like the Decanter on Palmer and Cass and Morey Baker's on Livernois Avenue were important meeting places for him during that period. At Morey's he would watch guitarist Dennis Coffey play with the Lyman Woodard Trio without any intimation as to the influential role Coffey would play in his life a few years later. It was around this time that he married a Detroit native and part-Cherokee named Rayma Barrett, who was forced to drop out of school when she fell pregnant. With Rodriguez no more than twenty years old, and Rayma still in her teens, the couple started a family. Eva Alicia Rodriguez was born on 4 February 1963, followed by Sandra in 1964.

For an aspiring musician with two small kids, life was hard. To make ends meet, Rodriguez took up employment at one of Detroit's many auto factories. Never afraid of hard work, he would have had no qualms about putting his shoulder to the wheel. In answer to numerous questions over the years about his Zen-like acceptance of backbreaking labour, both in the auto industry and in demolition work, his response has always been modest: 'It keeps the blood circulating.' But the wheels of industry take their toll on the men and women who dutifully go in to work each day. On a bridge in another blue-collar town, Trenton, on the border of New Jersey, there's a sign that reads: 'Trenton makes, the world takes.' This sentiment could easily have applied to Detroit.

One day in the early sixties, with music constantly on his mind, Rodriguez's attention must have wandered. The details of what happened are scant, mostly because of the man's intense privacy. What we do know is that when he came home that day, he had only four fingers on his left hand. An accident on the factory floor had taken a finger. For a right-handed guitarist like Rodriguez, the left hand is used to play chords. For any lesser musician, the mishap would have meant the end of whatever musical aspirations he might have had. For Rodriguez, with less than $900 in compensation, it meant having to learn to play the guitar all over again, having to find new fingerings for chords. It also meant strengthening his resolve to never look back. Complaining was a luxury reserved for those in other neighbourhoods. In a recent interview, a long-time friend said: 'Once Rodriguez makes up his mind, he doesn't usually change it [. . .] He is very generous, but he never looks back. It's all forward to him. He has no desire to go over his past. His future as a musician and "bread winner" is his only focus.'

One night in the mid-sixties Rodriguez met legendary organist T.J. Fowler, then already in his mid-fifties. In a varied and fruitful career, Fowler and his group had for the longest time served as the backing band for one Aaron Thibeaux Walker, aka T-Bone Walker, and Fowler himself had been instrumental in helping Berry Gordy establish Motown. At the time he and Rodriguez met, Fowler was gigging in and around the Motor City and south-eastern Michigan. Through Fowler, Rodriguez met Harry Balk, without question one of the seminal meetings of the young musician's life.

It was Harry Balk who gave Rodriguez his first crack at the music business. The head of Impact Records at the time and a producer in his own right, Balk had produced Del Shannon's 1961 Billboard Hot 100 number-one hit 'Runaway' and would later persuade Berry Gordy to release Marvin Gaye's 1971 'What's Going On', a song that the near-sighted Gordy at the time said was 'the worst thing I have ever heard in my life'. No doubt he changed his mind when it later became a number-one hit. Interestingly, 'What's Going On' was born out of witnessing police brutality, a cause close to Rodriguez's heart.

In 1966, soon after their first meeting, Balk offered to listen to some of Rodriguez's compositions. Rodriguez had by that stage found new fingerings for old chords. Balk was impressed by what he heard and thought the young

Mexican-American with the broad, disarming smile had potential. He offered him an 'exclusive writer agreement' for a period of five years with Gomba music. The date was 25 July 1966. Rodriguez, at twenty-four, a father of two and not yet in his trademark black getup, now found himself in the enviable position of having a record deal. He must have felt some pride as he walked home that day, ever observant of the city around him as the lyrics crystallised in his head.

Going down a dusty, Georgian side road
I wonder
The wind splashed in my face
Can smell a trace
Of thunder.

6

And I'll forget about the girl that said no

(1967)

'In the music business, all roads lead to Motown.'
— Unknown

In a story filled with ironies, coincidences and bizarre book-ends, it comes as no surprise that the song 'I'll Slip Away' would be both the first and last studio track Rodriguez recorded. (It's uncertain whether it was also the first song he ever wrote. On his live album, he claims to have written 'Half Way Up the Stairs' first.) The days leading up to his first 'real' recording at a 'real' studio must have been filled with nervous anticipation. For one thing, the world was changing. On the streets of Detroit there was an undercurrent of racial tension. Further afield, unusual events were occurring that would set a new tone globally, a counterculture and revolution in social norms that would later reflect in Rodriguez's music. Just days earlier, world heavyweight boxing champion Muhammad Ali had been banned in every American

101

state and stripped of his passport for refusing to be inducted into the armed forces. Of course, it didn't help that he had embraced Islam. 'No Vietcong ever called me nigger,' he said at the time. Over in London, Jimi Hendrix had just shockingly burnt his first guitar on stage, and the cover image of the Beatles' *Sgt. Pepper's Lonely Hearts Club Band* album was photographed, featuring at least three Eastern gurus, the father of communism, Karl Marx, and a long list of other polarising figures; it was an 'instant touchstone for psychedelic culture', in the words of journalist Bryan Wawzenek. The world faced an unprecedented openness toward drug experimentation, an attitude that resulted in colourful fashions, new art movements and an outpouring of musical talents.

Harry Balk, proving his belief in the young Rodriguez's abilities, put together some seasoned musicians to take his songs, which until that point were nothing more than guitar and vocals, to a higher level. Rodriguez had arrived and session guitarist Dennis Coffey was already plugged in and tuning up in the old Studio One of Tera Shirma Studios on Livernois Street when arranger Mike Theodore walked in on 20 April 1967. Theodore and Coffey knew each other well, but Theodore had not yet met Rodriguez in person. He was aware of him, having seen him gig at the Sewer by the Sea with his back to the audience, but this was their first proper meeting. Neither Theodore nor Coffey were strangers to studio work; the paths that led them to Tera Shirma on that day in April were already well beaten.

Theodore, a Detroit native, had started on drums, sax and trumpet at an early age. He got his first record contract with the Starlighters when he was still in high school. Sadly, the band was not able to take advantage of the record deal, as one of the members was still a minor and the boy's parents refused to agree. The band would later sign with Anna Records, the label founded by Berry Gordy's older sister Anna Gordy. Theodore tried unsuccessfully to make it with different groups, but, in his own words, 'couldn't break through the payola game'. (Payola, a contraction of the words 'pay' and 'Victrola', is the act of paying cash or gifts in return for airplay.) He eventually defaulted to a college course in biology instead. Tera Shirma's Ralph Terrana recalls that the first time he ever met Theodore, 'Mike had a stack of biology books under his arm.' Finally, with the band Shades of Blue, Theodore had his first hit. 'Oh How Happy' finished 1966 at number eighty-five on the Billboard Year End Top 100. It had been a good year.

Dennis Coffey, the other half of what would become Theo-Coff Productions, was no slouch either. A child prodigy, he started on guitar at age thirteen. By fifteen he had played his first gig as a session guitarist, backing Vic Gallon. In the early sixties he enjoyed a fruitful association with the Royaltones, playing sessions with Del Shannon, which – just as all roads led to Motown – led to Harry Balk. In 1967, Coffey became part of the Funk Brothers, historically one of the most important studio bands in the chronicle of soul music, contributing to scores of Motown hits.

Tera Shirma Studios was named for its owner Ralph Terrana and his silent partner, Al Sherman. The studio in which Rodriguez made his first recordings was, in the words of Terrana, 'a room within a room ... a very tight studio, with great acoustics'. The control room was no bigger than twelve-by-twelve feet and in the beginning had a Scully four-track recorder with an archaic spring-driven echo unit, hardly the setup on which to make magic. To get to the control room, one had to go up five or six steps. Milan Bogdan was the engineer, and the studio rates had only recently gone up from $25 to $40 an hour.

For any musician walking in off the street, there was one constant: the diminutive, attractive Neica Lee Rompollo, the glue holding things together. As Tera Shirma Studios secretary, Neica had seen it all. Like the day a hippie band recorded their almost-hit 'Freakout Freddie's Psychedelic Used Car Lot Blues'. Or the time she single-handedly, in spite of her size, tried to fend off an intruder who had broken a window to gain entry. And then there was the time Eartha Kitt came in for overdubs, and the other time when Clive Davis, a young hotshot at Columbia Records, called in person (Columbia would occasionally send spill-over jobs to Tera Shirma). 'Upbeat and very friendly, she all but ran the studio,' says Theodore of Neica. 'She was the in-house consulting shrink and adviser.' Not surprisingly, the endless stream of musicians who passed through the doors to follow their dreams loved her. These were the late sixties, after all, and there was a lot of bonhomie to go around. But it was Harry Balk who left the greatest impression on Ralph Terrana. In the early days, when the studio was struggling financially, Balk came in to make some dubs, but the studio had run out of quarter-inch tape. So Balk pulled out $100, a large sum in those days, and sent Terrana off to buy more.

Little is known of the process that was used for Rodriguez's first recordings. It was just another day in the studio. But generally it is believed that five or six tracks were put down. The official list of Impact-era recordings, which were all made on that day, reads as follows: 'I'll Slip Away', 'You'd Like To Admit It', 'Forget It' and 'To Whom It May Concern', and there was also an instrumental version of 'To Whom It May Concern'. Historian and music writer Tim Forster adds one more track to the mix, 'That Discotheque', which is a surprising title for a Rodriguez song, especially since the word, originally used to describe a record library in France, had not yet made its way into common parlance as a seventies disco-era dance hall. The track was not released, and in fact, no proof has been found of its existence, despite the rumours that persist. When pressed for information, Theodore said, 'Urban legend as far as I know . . . The word discotheque wasn't even around at the time.' Either way, by the time Rodriguez's old auto factory was shutting shop for the night, the band was putting the finishing touches on the day's sessions.

The process of birthing his musical offspring must have been a happy one for Rodriguez, but his happiness was to be short-lived. On the night of Saturday 23 July, barely three months after recording the songs, the Motor City came off the tracks. The catalyst was a police raid of an unlicensed after-hours bar, the kind of illegal establishment then known as a 'blind pig' or speakeasy, on the corner of 12th and Clairmount streets. Police confrontations with patrons and observers on the street turned into one of the deadliest and most destructive race riots in America's history. The 12th Street Riot, as it came to be known, lasted five days and was far worse than the Detroit race riots of the early forties. It would take the National Guard and the army, sent in by Governor George Romney and President Lyndon B. Johnson respectively, to bring order to the city, by which time forty-three people had died and nearly 2,000 were injured. Over 7,000 arrests were made after untold numbers of businesses were looted and hundreds of buildings were razed to the ground. It was left up to Mike Theodore to rescue the recently recorded music from Tera Shirma. 'I can remember running out the door with tapes under my arm,' he says. 'They were firebombing outside.'

Amazingly, the Tera Shirma building didn't suffer any loss or damage. Terrana recalls:

> During the riots of '67, the neighbourhood really took a hit. A couple of days after the riots settled down I had to go down there to see what was left of the studio. When I got there, I was surrounded by total devastation. Broken windows, burnt-out buildings, etc. but there stood Tera Shirma without a scratch. Not even a cracked window. I often wonder if the black rioters knew that a lot of brothers made a living out of these premises.

A month later, in August 1967, the tracks 'I'll Slip Away' and 'You'd Like to Admit It' were released as a single by Impact Records. Interestingly, the seven-inch record did not come out under the name Sixto Rodriguez, but under the pseudonym Rod Riguez. In *Searching for Sugar Man*, Malik Bendjelloul suggests that this was done because the singer's real name was too 'Hispanic' for popular tastes. But this might not be true. José Feliciano – whose last name, Garcia, heads the list of most common Hispanic surnames – sold extensively in America despite his Hispanic-sounding professional name 'Feliciano'. His 1968 version of the Doors' 'Light My Fire' reached number three on the US pop charts, with over one million copies sold in the US alone. And besides, America was at the beginning of a cultural crossroads that saw more racial integration in music than ever before. (Interestingly, on the 1997 *Best of Impact Records* CD produced by Jerry Schollenberger, 'I'll Slip Away' is credited to Sixto D. Rodriguez. This is the only time his name appears in this way on an album or single.)

Only one review of the single exists. In the September 1967 issue of *Cash Box*, a popular weekly music trade magazine, the following appeared: 'Rod Riguez could make a name for himself with this bluesy, mid-tempo rock ballad. Keep it in sight. Flip: "You'd Like to Admit It".'

Schollenberger claims that the 45-rpm single was not sold commercially to the public:

> The record is near-impossible to find due to the fact that few copies were pressed, and Impact Records went out of business shortly after the record was released. In my many years of collecting records, I have only seen ONE copy of that record for sale, and it was much too expensive for me to buy. It was about 175 US dollars.

This information, however, was refuted by a record collector who posted on Sugarman.org in 2003:

> I can confirm that a regular (NOT a promo) release of Impact #1031 does exist. A speculation to the contrary exists [. . .]
> – Steve Jones, Canada, August 2003

The two songs, both of which at first listen come across as being slightly prosaic, offer themes that thread through Rodriguez's oeuvre. The first that comes to the surface in 'You'd Like to Admit It' is his manner of handling rejection, especially when it comes to matters of the heart. The rejected lover, his guitar as weapon, gets the last word with a well-aimed song in an early form of sniping, perhaps as a means of self-defence.

At first he lays out the situation – the snub – that he can't forget:

> You were the girl who laughed when I tried
> You were the one who smiled when I sighed
> You didn't like my style or my songs
> Now tables turned and you find you were wrong.

Then, with the power of the song, he takes the upper hand:

> Now there's a hint of regret in your eyes,
> But you won't tell me, and your smile's your disguise
> So when I see you again I'll just grin,
> 'Cos I'm happy I'm here and that you're way the heck over there!

I'll get the last laugh, he seems to be saying, because I don't care. A little like Bob Dylan's 'Don't Think Twice, It's All Right'.

The second theme is 'escape', a motif that recurs in his songs more than any other. In 'I'll Slip Away', he sings:

> And you can keep your symbols of success
> Then I'll pursue my own happiness
> And you can keep your clocks and routines
> Then I'll go mend all my shattered dreams
> Maybe today, yeah
> I'll slip away.

But for now, in the early part of September 1967, the gentle poet from the modest side of town – who would later comment on those *'who mislay their dreams and later claim that they were robbed'* – had momentarily found his dream, in spite of nearly being robbed by the sharp-toothed cogs of blue-collar commerce.

7

Giving substance to shadows
(1968–1969)

'Madness passed me by, she smiled hi, I nodded.'
— RODRIGUEZ, 'INNER CITY BLUES'

When Rodriguez insisted on playing with his back to the audience, Harry Balk, the promoter and owner of Impact Records, the man who had only recently given Rodriguez his first break, turned his back on the musician. Ralph Terrana recalls:

The only thing I remember [Balk] telling me about Rodriguez is that he decided to quit recording him, and bounce him after Rodriguez told him he could only sing with his back to the audience during any future performances.

The poor sales figures of the single might also have had something to do with it. It's hard to say. The fact that, according to Balk, Rodriguez was not really willing to get involved in promotions, and sometimes inadvertently sabotaged them when he did, might have been a contributing factor. Either way, Rodriguez soon found himself with a lapsed record deal. On the plus side, he now had a calling card that he could carry around with him in the form of a catchy seven-single. But then Impact Records folded in 1968.

Balk, now out of work, sought and found employment with Berry Gordy at Motown. Dennis Coffey and Mike Theodore went on to work as in-house producers for the newly formed Sussex Records. And that's where Clarence Avant – to some, 'the Godfather of Black Music' – entered the scene.

Born in North Carolina, Avant came from humble beginnings. He began as a manager in the music business in the fifties. Later he did a mentorship under Joe Glaser, Louis Armstrong's manager from the mid-thirties until Armstrong's death in 1969. One of the artists Avant managed was Little Willie John, the very same Little Willie John who Harry Balk had once produced. After a short stint with Venture Records, Avant launched Sussex, an amalgam of 'success' and 'sex'. In order to start a label, however, one needed an artist. So one night, in their new roles as A&R (artists and repertoire) people, Theodore and Coffey went to see Rodriguez (at the time still musically known as Rod Riguez) at the infamous Sewer by the Sea. Located down an alley off Jefferson Avenue, the Sewer was, as the name suggests, definitely a little seedy, and, contrary to the name, *not* by the sea, unless one counts the river as the sea. Then again, perhaps one should. The Detroit River is big enough to serve ocean and lake freighters. Its water comes from the Great Lakes and is dark blue with a twelve-knot current.

Rodriguez was performing solo that evening, and the duo

from Theo-Coff hatched a plan to take the man and his music to Clarence Avant. But first they needed a demo tape. So they took Rodriguez back to Tera Shirma and recorded a quick in-and-out session of some new and original material. They presented the tape to Avant, who took an instant liking to Rodriguez and decided to sign him up as the newly formed Sussex label's first artist. 'That's my boy,' Avant would go on to say years later with tears in his eyes, after being shown a photograph of a young Rodriguez in the film *Searching for Sugar Man*.

During this period two significant things happened in Rodriguez's life. First, his marriage to Rayma ended. Second – at some stage between the Balk sessions and the Avant recordings – he enlisted the help of a music manager. Whether this was an organic process or something quite deliberate is not known. 'I reality-test everything,' Rodriguez likes to say, so perhaps it was well thought out. Either way, by the time they reconvened at Tera Shirma Studios in the summer of 1969 for the recording of *Cold Fact*, Margaret Moore, in the function of business manager, was at his side. 'Rainy', as everybody knew her, would play an important role in his life from around 1968 until sometime after the recording of his second album in 1971. 'In fact,' Theodore says, 'Rainy was involved from the beginning. She invited us to see Rodriguez at the Sewer. It might be safe to say that without her, he may never have reached out. She handled all his scheduling, etc.'

Rainy was a complex but creative personality and had been an on-and-off talent scout for Avant. For a period she played a stabilising role in Rodriguez's life. Her association with Detroit's music world ran deep, but before meeting Rodriguez it had also become increasingly challenging. The trouble began when she started an affair with one-time Temptations lead singer Dennis Edwards. The scandal that her relationship with a black man caused in her conservative white family and community was so severe that she was soon being threatened in all kinds of ways. The tension deepened when she came home one day to announce that she was pregnant. Kelly Moore, Rainy's only son, describes the situation:

She went through hell; my grandparents did what they could to stop the relationship. Her parents told my mother that if the baby came out black, there would be consequences. And then, when I came out black, they had her committed. This continued while she was with Rodriguez.

For several years, Rainy had to endure sessions of electroshock therapy and visits to mental institutions, which only intensified her anguish. Of course, Kelly knew nothing about his true father at the time. 'I knew Dennis as Mom's friend, not my father,' he recalls. 'Mom dropped the bombshell when I turned eighteen.' By all accounts, the open-minded Rodriguez was completely accepting of her situation.

According to Kelly, Rainy started seeing Sixto when he was four or five, after she had separated from Dennis Edwards. 'By the time I was five or six, I was living with Rodriguez downtown,' he says. 'I can remember Sandra and Eva. We played together as kids . . . Until eight or nine, I remember growing up knowing Sixto as my mom's boyfriend.' Looking back, Kelly has only fond memories of the singer. He remembers hearing Rodriguez play the guitar and attending his shows.

Rainy was at Rodriguez's side for the recording of *Cold Fact*, which began in August 1969. Rodriguez arrived at the session with ten songs, some new, some old, and all ready for a fresh treatment. 'Forget It', a song that had been recorded at the Balk sessions two years earlier, was one of the old songs. Theodore and Coffey, with numerous sessions under their belts, including some highly avant-garde contributions, arrived in an experimental mood. This was 1969, after all, and there was a touch of 'psychedelia' in the air. They had just completed work on a largely experimental Paul Parrish album called *The Forest of My Mind*, also through Avant.

Besides Theodore and Coffey, filling up the roster on the day were a host of seasoned session musicians, specially selected to create a different sound. On bass was the larger-than-life Bob Babbitt (born Robert Kreinar), who would later play on many rock, soul and disco albums, including Coffey's million-selling *Scorpio* and others from the likes of Marvin Gaye, Stevie Wonder, the Temptations and Jimi Hendrix. On drums, the very capable Andrew 'Fingers' Smith, who would go on to record with Marvin Gaye and the Plastic Ono Band, among others. On percussion was the seasoned Bob Pangborn, who would later serve as the principal percussionist for the Detroit Symphony Orchestra. All guitar leads, with an assortment of guitar pedals, went to Coffey. Keyboards were the domain of Theodore. The duo from Theo-Coff were responsible for running the session, with Rainy, as Rodriguez's manager, in the control room. Last but not least, there were seven violins and a piccolo under the leadership of Gordon Staples from the Detroit Symphony Orchestra, and a horn section made up of three trombones and a baritone sax led by trombonist Carl Raetz (who would also end up recording with Gaye). Why Theodore and Coffey went for the unorthodox line-up of three trombones and a baritone sax, omitting the more traditional trumpet, is anyone's guess, but it worked. Evident on the album are several modern-sounding, dense, lower-register horn arrangements reminiscent of Charlie Haden's *Liberation Music Orchestra*, also recorded in 1969.

The late-summer recording lasted for about thirty days. Typically, Theodore recalls, Rodriguez's vocals and guitar parts were recorded first, with congas as accompaniment to set the rhythm. Then the process of recording the other instruments, layer upon layer, followed. 'This was done on four-track, and later, if necessary, bumped up to eight-track,' Theodore says. The musical experimentation is clear from the first song. Bookending side one are the tracks 'Sugar Man' (originally called 'Sugar Man on Prentis', referring to a dealer known as Volkswagen Frank on Detroit's Prentis Street) and 'Forget It'. Both songs share the same synthesiser-like effects (to highlight the drug-related nature of the lyrics, perhaps) created by Theodore. Except, they were not made on a synthesiser. Theodore explains:

I see reviews of 'Sugar Man' and they always refer to the synthesiser making the eerie effect in the background of the song. The fact is the synth had not been invented yet. The background was created with a string track and a piccolo run through a tape delay on a quarter-inch machine. I would slow the tape by hand to create the swirling pitch bends.

The differentiating aspects of the arrangements of subsequent tracks are immediately apparent. Lest we forget, the genesis of each track was simply vocals and guitar.

All the way through, the voice is treated with a fair amount of echo and reverb, making the end result completely unique, and haunting. It is widely believed that this is one of the factors that helped the album resonate in South Africa. It also helped seed the mystery of Rodriguez. Like the dark shades that blocked our view of his eyes in the cover artwork, a layer of reverb did the same with his voice, keeping him at arm's length, a bit like what the Harmon mute did for the sound of Miles Davis – place it just outside the door.

The experimentation continues. On certain tracks, drums and guitar parts that might begin in the right ear (microphone right) pan left before the song is through. Bob Pangborn, in his role as percussionist, adds to the tenor of the album with accents placed throughout. Occasionally it's a rattlesnake-like vibraslap (on 'Sugar Man'). At other times it's a vibraphone or cowbell. There is even a loud thud of a tympani drum at the end of 'Inner City Blues', an instrument normally reserved for classical orchestras.

Carefully arranged strings, recorded and then time-manipulated, swirl through the album. At times, we find a call-and-answer motif between the strings and the horn section ('Inner City Blues'). Unlike Motown, Theodore's horn line-up gives much of the album a dark, dense feel, almost in denial of the lower interval limits observed by music arrangers. In fact, it is the deep, dense and dark guide-tone harmonies found in 'Crucify Your Mind' that give that song (and other parts of the album) an almost otherworldly undertone.

There is minimalistic use of drums. It's sometimes what's been left out that makes the album so brilliant. Andrew Smith's crisp, tight snare-work nudges certain songs along. Occasionally it's just the bass drum that drives the composition. Cymbals are used sparingly. And when they are, it's usually nothing more than a tightly closed hi-hat, mostly in unison with the muted downward strum of Rodriguez's acoustic guitar.

'I Wonder' – generally considered the most popular track on the album aside from 'Sugar Man' – is also musically the least interesting track on the album. But the enduringly catchy bassline (written and played by Coffey and not Bob Babbitt in this case), plus the lyrics with their reference to 'sex', make it instantly memorable.

Only two of the tracks were not written by Rodriguez. But despite that – and because of the cohesive nature of the album – they feel as if they could have been. These are 'Gommorah' (misspelt on the cover) and 'Hate Street Dialogue', which, in Craig's initial research he assumed was a veiled reference to the Haight-Ashbury area in San Francisco, the epicentre of the famous Summer of Love, and the first Human Be-Ins. Years later, in a radio interview, Rodriguez vindicated Craig's interpretation (suggesting that this might be a misspelling too). In answer to a listener's question, 'Rodriguez said that although the lyrics of that particular song were not written by himself they did refer to the Haight and not the opposite of love.'

The two non-Rodriguez tracks came about when it was felt that twelve songs, not ten, were needed to complete the album. To make up the shortfall, lyricist Gary Harvey was brought in, and Theodore and Coffey worked on the arrangements. Stylistically, both songs fit neatly into the métier of the album, in spite of the dreamlike children's choir used as a chorus in 'Gommorah' (voices courtesy of the friends and family of Joyce Vincent and Telma Hopkins of Dawn fame). Yet even here the experimentation continues when the words and melody at the end of the second chorus – in a fitting counterpoint – morph into strains of 'America the Beautiful'. All in all, both tracks fit in so well that for years in South Africa, where no one was the wiser, people naturally assumed the songs were Rodriguez's work. Remarkably, at the time there was a fair amount of resentment from both Rodriguez and Rainy about having to include the two tracks on the album, and even today the musician never plays them live.

Overall, what makes the album a gem is the restraint shown by Theodore and Coffey in terms of the arrangements – the sparing use of drums and the sparse instrumentation – which makes each song perfect and accentuates the meaning of the words wherever possible. Surprisingly, there are no backing vocals whatsoever, and the order of the songs seems just right.

Everyone involved held out high hopes for the album. Theodore remembers:

> After the completion of the album Dennis and I felt that we had just finished a Grammy winner. I thought this was the big ticket and Rodriguez would be as big as any of the current songsmiths. Everyone we were involved with felt the same as we did. It never entered my mind that this project would fail.

Bob Flath of Ransier-Anderson Photography took the iconic image of Rodriguez seated cross-legged and superimposed over a crystal ball. The crystal ball was Mike Theodore's idea, because he thought the songs 'predicted the future'. The new album, Cold Fact, was mixed in New York City and then released to little or no fanfare on the Sussex label in March 1970. It was distributed by Buddah Records.

By now, Rodriguez had ditched the Rod Riguez moniker. But for legal reasons he had ceded the writer's credits on his songs to various other newly formed publishing entities. When questioned about this in 1998, daughter Eva responded:

The name Jesus Rodriguez was used as a 'political move' to avoid release delays. 'Sixth Prince' [Rodriguez's birth order] and 'Sandrevan' [named after daughters Sandra and Eva] were publishing corporations used for copyright protection.

According to a 2014 court case between Harry Balk (the first to record Rodriguez) and Clarence Avant, however, it was to get around the fact that Rodriguez was still contractually bound to Balk, although that is contested.

At the time of release in America, a number of promotional copies of the album were sent out to radio stations. And on each of these copies was pasted an optimistically worded DJ timing strip, as they were then known:

A radio station mention from THE BUDDAH GROUP
If you don't have time to listen to the whole album, try these*

*Sugar Man	4:40
Only Good for Conversation	2:25
*Crucify	2:24
Establishment Blues	2:05
Hate Street Dialogue	2:30
Forget It	1:50
*Inner City Blues	2:20

*I Wonder	2:30
Jane's Pity	2:38
Gommorah	2:20
Rich Folks Hoax	3:05
Like Janis	3:05

(For muso-pedants, it is interesting to note that the timing of 'Sugar Man' on the US timing strip and the record label is listed as 4:40 compared to the 3:48 that it times out to on the South African release.)

Very little was done to promote the album, apart from one disastrous publicity event where Rodriguez insisted on bringing Brown Berets leader David Sanchez onto the stage with him. The Brown Berets were a pro-Mexico secessionist organisation, and Rodriguez wanted to highlight their political cause. Nevertheless the album received a few short but positive mentions:

Billboard, 28 March 1970
'COLD FACT' LP in 2 page Buddah ad
Words from the city.
'Hard words on a new label with a totally different trip.'

Billboard, 4 April 1970
Page one
'Buddah Records Adding 3 New Labels'
Sussex is a new label launched through a deal with Clarence Avant.
First release is Rodriguez – COLD FACT.
Production by Michael Theodore and Dennis Coffey.

Billboard, 18 April 1970
'COLD FACT' LP
4 Star Review

Billboard, 2 May 1970
'COLD FACT' LP Listed as a New Album Release

The exact sales figures are lost to us today. Needless to say, the record did not do well. This is hardly surprising. Upon its release it was up against competition such as the Doors' *Morrison Hotel* and Van Morrison's *Moondance*. For *Cold Fact* to have been a success without the proper promotion, it would have had to have been a break-out record (which finally it was, but forty years after the fact). In addition, cash-strapped Sussex hardly had the budget to nationally promote an obscure album from a publicity-shy Mexican-American artist.

In comparison, one need only read an ad placed in the 14 March 1970 issue of *Billboard* magazine, the same month that *Cold Fact* was released. A snapshot of Columbia Records' activities (the same Columbia Records that had sent scraps over to Tera Shirma) can be found in the ad copy:

WE MAKE RECORDS
The No. 1 album this week
4 out of the top 7 albums
27 positions on the Top LP charts

The number-one album referred to above was none other than Simon & Garfunkel's *Bridge Over Troubled Water*. The other three releases referred to in the third line were *Chicago*, *Hello, I'm Johnny Cash* and *Santana*.

Very little proof exists of *Cold Fact* receiving much, if any, airplay on US radio. There is some evidence that local independent and alternative FM stations like WABX in Detroit ('the station that glows in the dark') played the album, but this may say more about payola, rampant in the US at the time, than anything else. The practice became less pronounced later when the anti-payola statute was passed, making it a misdemeanour.

The album, with almost non-existent sales in the US, nonetheless quietly made its way across the Pacific, then later the Atlantic, and into several countries as an import. Festival Records imported 400 copies into Australia in 1970, and A&M Records released *Cold Fact* in South Africa in 1971.

8

Have you ever kissed
the sunshine?
(1970–1972)

'How many times can you wake up in this comic
book, and plant flowers?'
— RODRIGUEZ, 'IT STARTED OUT SO NICE'

As the final credits of the 1964 spaghetti western *Gunfighters of Casa Grande* rolled out, the youngest of the five main actors, who had been billed simply as 'Kid', must have let out an audible sigh. At thirty-four, Steve Rowland, son of director Roy Rowland, was already a veteran of the movie business, but he had yet to realise his true calling. At the time of shooting *Gunfighters* in the Spanish city of Jerez, he had been active in the film industry for twenty-one years, having starred (and sung) in his first film, MGM's *Boys' Ranch*, at the age of eleven. He had lived the movie life others only dream of, shooting the breeze with James Dean and Steve McQueen, the three good-looking friends famously taking part in illegal street-car races. He had appeared in famous shows like *Bonanza* and *The Life and Legend of Wyatt Earp*. His circle, or rather his father's extended circle, included his uncle Louis B. Mayer and legends such as Marilyn Monroe, Elvis Presley and Natalie Wood.

In the final chapter of his movie career, Rowland found himself in Spain, acting in a slew of big B-grade movies, including *Gunfighters*, *The Battle of the Bulge* (alongside Telly Savalas, Henry Fonda and Charles Bronson) and *Hallucination Generation*. The actor was, by now, simply tired. He had developed an itch that a life in film couldn't satisfy. There was something else he wanted, something he had always wanted: to be in the music business. His parents had forbidden him until he had – in their eyes – completed his education. So aside from playing in a few solid bands, including the West Coast Twist Kings, and getting a few record deals, one with Fontana Records (whose intention was to turn him into a teen idol), he was bundled off to the Pasadena Playhouse for high school. The Pasadena Playhouse was the West Coast version of the New York High School of Performing Arts, on which the TV series *Fame* was based. Unfortunately for someone who actually wanted to be in the music business, Pasadena led to more film roles and, the next thing he knew, he found himself in his early thirties in Spain, his dream unrealised.

Around this time, Rowland joined a Madrid-based band called Los Flaps. He recorded four songs with them, three in English and one in Spanish, through Hispavox Records. Even before he shot his last frame of film in Madrid in 1966, in the film *Hallucination Generation*, Rowland, the only Anglo-American in the band, met the only Anglo-American in another Spanish band, the Diamond Boys. During his encounter with the Gibraltar-based Albert Hammond, a seed was planted that would later become the British vocal group the Family Dogg. Rowland wiped the stardust out of his eyes once and for all and headed for London, England.

With his dashing good looks and unbridled ambition, Rowland felt right at home in London. He couldn't have chosen a better place to reinvent himself. But his stay was short-lived. After only a few months he was deported back to Spain for overstaying his visa. In order to get back into England, he had to get creative. When asked who finally helped him solve the problem, Rowland explains:

It was Jack Baverstock, the CEO of Fontana Records in London, that thought up the scheme. It was based on the assumption that as an American, my producing UK artists would better help sales in the US. This proved out to be positive, as the first record that I produced was 'Hold Tight' by Dave Dee, Dozy, Beaky, Mick & Tich. It sold 255,000 [copies] and I received a silver disc award.

Rowland applied for and received a work visa and was able to re-enter the UK. Living up to his visa requirements, he went on to produce thirteen top-ten hits for the group Dave Dee, Dozy, Beaky, Mick and Tich. Among these was the million-selling UK number-one 'The Legend of Xanadu', as well as 'Zabadak', a song remembered today for its catchy use of African-style percussion and nonsensical lyrics. (Beyond Britain, 'Zabadak' also charted in the US, Australia, the Netherlands, Germany, Austria and South Africa.) Not many people walk away from a film career, especially those with such strong family ties to the industry. And not many make a success of a second career in their mid-thirties.

Across the Atlantic, at about the same time Rowland was

discovering the likes of Peter Frampton, Rodriguez was in Tera Shirma recording *Cold Fact* with Theo-Coff. Although it didn't do well, the record somehow made its way onto the desk of New York-born music publisher Freddy Bienstock, who was by now living in the UK. Freddy had been the primary song selector for Elvis Presley; rumour has it that Elvis wouldn't listen to a single song unless Freddy had recommended it to him first. One ordinary day, Steve Rowland marched in to see his old friend Freddy for his weekly visit. They chatted for a while before Rowland noticed a copy of *Cold Fact* lying on Freddy's desk. Had the cover not been so very different from all the other albums scattered about, he might not have reached over and picked it up. 'What a strange-looking album . . . a guy sitting cross-legged on the cover,' he thought.

Rowland continues the story:

So I say to Freddy, 'Can I take a listen to this?' Freddy goes, 'Sure.' And I walk over to the listening room and within a few minutes, I go berserk. I am so excited by this album, especially the song 'Like Janis'. I'd had a girlfriend from Australia and the song completely described her and our relationship. And I think, boy, this guy has an insight into relationships. I run out of the office, excited. But Freddy says, 'Steve, relax, it's just a poor man's Bob Dylan.' 'No,' I say, 'it's more like Leonard Cohen.' I tell Freddy, 'Listen, if this guy ever makes a second album, I want to produce it.'

Meanwhile, back in Motor City, Clarence Avant decided to give Rodriguez a second chance, in spite of the bad sales of *Cold Fact*. Mike Theodore and Dennis Coffey set to work immediately. They had already started on arrangements of four of Rodriguez's new songs when they got a call: 'Change of plan, Sussex is not going with you after all. Clarence has decided on a hotshot producer in London for Rodriguez's next album.' Theodore and Coffey were gobsmacked. Theodore later said:

> Neil Bogard, the head of Buddah Records at the time, decided to take Rodriguez to London. For the longest time I thought it was Rodriguez's doing. But later, I found out it wasn't. Looking back, even if it was his doing, I wouldn't blame him . . . a chance to record in London at that stage . . . I would have done the same thing.

Back in London, Steve Rowland received the call: 'So anyway, three to four weeks later, Freddy calls me up and says, "Steve, you got the gig." Never in my wildest dreams did I think this would happen.'

And so, in the late summer of 1970, Rodriguez and Rainy packed their bags and caught a plane to London. Their destination was the famous Lansdowne Studios, founded in 1957 by then producer Dennis Preston. According to Tony Harris and Phil Burns, curators of the Classic UK Recording Studios Resource website (philsbook.com), Lansdowne was built in 1902 by a South African diamond millionaire from Craig's hometown of Kimberley. William Flodthart had wanted to provide a place where struggling painters could work. By the time Rodriguez and Rainy arrived, it had long been used as a music studio. Bizarrely, it was the thick-walled squash courts in the basement that had been converted into studio space, with the old smoking room now the control room. Lansdowne, situated in a leafy upmarket suburb near

Holland Park, was a different world from the urban Tera Shirma Studios in gritty Detroit. Stately and imposing, the building's design harks back to the stepped gables of Amsterdam. Looking at photographs of the building, it's easy to imagine Rodriguez singing the line *'It started out with butterflies on a velvet afternoon'* from such a place. There is something nostalgically English about his second album, *Coming from Reality*. And there is something very 'nice' about the area and the studio. But before one gets too carried away with the 'spirit of place', it's important to remember that the cavernous Lansdowne also played host to the Sex Pistols.

The studio itself produced many fine artists, including Donovan (who would later appear on the same bill as Rodriguez at Sundance), Marianne Faithfull, Gerry Rafferty (another Steve Rowland find), American rock band MC5 (also Michigan natives), Queen, Rod Stewart and Yoko Ono with John Lennon. The Peter Sarstedt song 'Where Do You Go To My Lovely', which reached number one in the UK and South Africa, was recorded at Lansdowne not too long before Rodriguez and Rainy arrived. By the time Rodriguez walked through the door, Lansdowne was equipped with a Cadac console twenty-four-track recorder (a step up from the 'four-track bumped up to eight-track' scenario that Theo-Coff had used to record *Cold Fact*) and, among other newly acquired technology, two Elektro-Mess-Technik (EMT) reverb systems.

Rodriguez brought eleven songs with him, one of which would never be recorded by him. The other ten tracks made it onto the album. Rowland liked what he heard – he thought the songs were very 'Kerouac' – and began to plan out the arrangements in his head. In the meantime, Rodriguez and

Rainy took up residence off Eaton Square in Knightsbridge on Clarence Avant's dime and kept what was described as an uncharacteristically low profile.

Recording began the day after Rodriguez's arrival. Rowland recalls that both singer and producer 'were pensive at first, sussing each other out, but then formed a strong bond that would last for the entire session'. There was a level of mutual respect and that was all that was needed for a period of concentrated creativity. Rowland had a minimalist approach to recording. 'For me,' he says, 'when it comes to music production, less is more. In order of importance, one is the song, two vocals, three instrumentation.'

Typically, the first thing Rowland did was to tune the guitar to G (drums are tuned to G). Then he recorded Rodriguez performing each track on guitar, 'just Rodriguez and his guitar without any other accompaniment'. Rowland is unyielding when it comes to maintaining the sanctity – the honesty – of a song: 'I realised [Rodriguez was] a poet. You don't touch his music. Poets are sensitive. Rodriguez was sensitive . . . I had to respect that.'

According to Rowland, the recordings took place over ten days. Others claim it took about three weeks. The forty-odd intervening years might account for this discrepancy. Rowland again: 'We would record three-hour sessions and then take a break. All the musicians on the album were in their twenties. I purposefully chose young guys . . . I really picked [them], you know. I owe everything to the guys I worked with.'

In no particular order, the musicians were Gary Taylor on bass, who went on to work with Gerry Rafferty; Andrew Steele on drums, who would play with Spilt Milk and Family Dogg; Chris 'Ace' Spedding on guitar, who produced the Sex

Pistols' first demo and would play with Jack Bruce, Roxy Music, Elton John, John Cale and Family Dogg; Phil Dennys on keyboard, who played with the Bee Gees and another Detroit-born musician, Susan 'Suzi' Quatro; Tony Carr on percussion, a future sideman for Mike Batt; and Jimmy Horowitz on violin, whose later claim to fame would be playing with Rod Stewart and Family Dogg among others, but not before nearly outdoing himself on the Rodriguez ballad 'Sandrevan Lullaby – Lifestyles'.

Of this particular song, Rowland says: 'Phil Dennys was the arranger on "Sandrevan Lullaby". I told him, I want you to write the piece, but it must be romantic . . . like a flower opening in the sun.' Dennys did just that. In terms of orchestration, 'Sandrevan Lullaby' is one of the standout pieces on the album. Many agree that the song is bookended by one of the most exquisite, beautiful and melancholic pieces of orchestration ever scored. The loose, broken strumming of Rodriguez's guitar introduces the piece, and then transitions into his arpeggio-style finger-picking in unison with a playful violin pizzicato. A violin melody surges in over that, a tone so exquisite and David Oistrakh-like that it is rumoured to have been played on a Stradivarius. About one minute in, the track warms up (like a flower opening in the sun, or a tide coming in) with a deep, rich arrangement of cello, viola and violin. And then, all of a sudden, the orchestra disappears and the track morphs, Rodriguez's guitar forming the bed for the vocals. With heavy reverb, he begins to sing:

> *The generals hate holidays*
> *Others shoot up to chase the sun blues away*
> *Another storefront church is open.*

On this track, like most others, Rodriguez's lyrics are razor sharp. In concise, finely chiselled sentences, he describes the state of our society, our lifestyles.

Another track that really excited Steve Rowland at the time, and where the maxim 'less is more' was applied, was 'A Most Disgusting Song'. 'Well, that was a song that I could relate to immediately,' he says. 'Anyone who has ever been a musician will relate to that [song].' It's not surprising. In it, Rodriguez describes every gig he ever played. His list of venues includes gay bars, brothels, funerals, workhouses, concert halls and halfway houses. He explains that all the people he performed for were the same, and then comically lists the stereotypes, often using puns to reinforce his imaginative observations. Rodriguez and Rowland made a decision to keep the song sparse, starting out with just Rodriguez's guitar and voice before bringing in the drums and bass to coincide with the line *The local diddy bop pimp comes in*', at the start of the third verse. Finally, with the addition of piano, the saloon-like quality of the song gives you the feeling of actually being there, as if you are sitting across from the '*bearded schoolboy with the wooden eyes*' or next to the '*girl that has never been chased*'. (Or should that be chaste?) Notably, Rodriguez never actually sings in this song. His delivery is spoken; the melody implied.

As with *Cold Fact*, no synthesisers were used in the making of this album. Only a spring echo, particularly prominent on Rodriguez's voice in 'Cause'.

Of all the tracks that were recorded in mid to late 1970 at Lansdowne Studios – and of all the songs that have been prodded, poked and analysed, leaving no word unturned – one hauntingly beautiful song seems to defy analysis. Superficially, 'It Started Out So Nice' seems to be about the arc of love ('*We started out so nice*'). But when one looks deeper, it becomes apparent that the song hides many secrets. At best the song is an allegory for Earth and its trajectory through time and space, one in which the singer sets out his prophecies. At worst it's a puzzle for those of a higher intelligence to solve. Rodriguez never explains his lyrics, successfully sidestepping all questions on the subject, and when he does venture an answer, the response is often designed to put the reviewer off the scent. Words, names – such as Wurs, Genji, Kogi, Ixea, Durock of Avon and Volume – place names and even ideas are never explained, some so foreign that one can't even spell-check them. Whoever has heard of 'flower captains' or 'marble money tunes'? And what about Volume's 'triangle for his thumb'? Perhaps the song is a veiled allegory for the hippie era of enlightenment that crashed and burnt after the Summer of Love, the Sharon Tate murders and the Rolling Stones/Hells Angels concert fiasco at the Altamont Speedway Free Festival that supposedly ended it all. Either way, Rodriguez's prognosis for the future is unnerving:

Now in the third millennium the crowded madness came
Crooked shadows roamed through the nights
The wizards overplayed their names
And after that the Wurs never bothered to have
Summer reasons . . . again.

Like the other tracks on the album, 'It Started Out So Nice' is backed by Rodriguez's guitar. Over that, once again, is a beautifully scored orchestration, this time including a triangle to accentuate certain moments. And, as if to underscore the gravity of the lyrics, his voice receives the tinniest and thinnest of all its treatments, as if it's emanating from a speaker in some futuristic movie, from a time somewhere near the end. Or, as he says in the song:

That eternity was just a dawn away
And the rest was sure to come.

The rest of the unheralded masterpiece that is *Coming from Reality* is made up of rock ballads, personal ballads, love songs, protest songs and songs featuring every conceivable poetic device. 'To Whom It May Concern', one of the first five songs recorded during Rodriguez's first outing at Tera Shirma in 1967, finally makes an appearance, as does 'Silver Words':

But oh if you could see
The change you've made in me
That the angels in the skies
Were envious and surprised
That anyone as nice as you
Would chance with me.

Two significant things happened while the album was being recorded at Lansdowne Studios. The first was when someone in the studio asked where Rodriguez was coming from, and Rainy replied, 'He's coming from reality.' With that, the title *Coming from Reality* was born. There has always been a demarcation, albeit a blurred one, between the two states of reality and non-reality (call it surrealism, if you will) in Rodriguez's life and mind.

The second thing happened like this: Rodriguez knew that Steve Rowland was looking for songs for a proposed album for Family Dogg, his own band. Rowland recalls:

So [Rodriguez] walks in one day just before we start to record and says 'here', and hands me a tape, adding, 'take a listen. If you like it, you can use it. It's a song . . . called "Advice to Smokey Robinson".' So I pop it into the tape player and love it. Later, we would record it for the Family Dogg album, *The View from Rowland's Head*.

With the recording over, Rodriguez and Rainy planned their return to America with justifiably high hopes. *Coming from Reality* was catchy, simple on the surface yet multi-layered with meaning for the thinker, and contained all the elements of a good pop album: rock, reverb, love and reson-ance. The only thing it did not have were backing vocals. Remarkably, and uncharacteristically for the time, there aren't any on *Cold Fact* either, or on the two singles from the Balk sessions, 'I'll Slip Away'/'You'd Like To Admit It'. (Rowland would more than make up for this later with a new version of 'I Wonder'.)

Before leaving London, Rodriguez posed for a series of now iconic black-and-white photographs on the city's streets. In one we see the artist dressed in black jumping over a wall, Big Ben looming large in the background. In a second, closer shot of him we see the recognisable shape of the famous clock tower once more. A third photograph has Rodriguez walking down an alley or side street in a typical London scene. A fourth shows the singer talking to four scraggly young boys, and in a fifth he is seated in front of a brick wall. In all the shots he is wearing the same outfit and carries a small black notebook. All in all, Rodriguez comes across as happy and at the top of his game. But for some reason or another he chose not to use any of these images on the new album's cover.

Before the end of 1970, the couple were back in Detroit and waiting for the finishing touches to be put to the album. Later, in the summer of 1971, Rodriguez and Hal Wilson set out to take a new series of photographs for the album cover. The result of the Wilson shoot was six or seven unpretentious pictures taken in and around Detroit. In the one that made it to the cover, we see Rodriguez seated on a derelict porch, his foot alongside a child's grey shoe. The story behind the small shoe on the cover was explained by Eva:

> The original *Coming from Reality* album cover was a cut-out cover of Rodriguez on the porch. It was taken at an occupied residence in Detroit. The little shoe just happened to be there and my father sat it next to his. I had always wondered if it had any significance but my dad says no. He was also holding a piece of glass, sometimes thought to be a plastic bag of 'something'. The back cover was taken at the Ford Motor Company, the Dearborn automobile factory near River Rouge. It was an employer of many Motor City families, including our own.

What Eva does not explain is the relevance, if any, of the pencil or charcoal drawing behind the photograph in the finished artwork. Also credited to Hal Wilson, the drawing, which is meant to be of Rodriguez, is dark and foreboding. Not surprisingly, when *Coming from Reality* was released into the conservative South African market in 1972, it was without the ominous drawing.

The album was released in the US by Sussex Records and distributed by Buddah in November 1971, once again to little or no fanfare. It had been temporarily held up until a small disagreement could be ironed out. Neil Bogard, the highly influential head of Buddah Records, had requested that certain lines from 'Cause' be expunged. Rodriguez rightly stood his ground, and the offending lines, *'And I talked to Jesus at the Sewer / And the Pope said it was none of his God-damned business'*, remained. The Jesus in question was Rodriguez's brother, and the Sewer was a reference to the dingy bar down by the Detroit River where Rodriguez met up with Theodore and Coffey to discuss the prospects of recording *Cold Fact*. (As an aside, the Pope features in two of his songs: the abovementioned 'Cause', and 'Establishment Blues', where he sings *'The Pope digs population'* – a double sin, one might conclude.)

Coming from Reality contains three credits not often found in the music business. One is for 'Impresario: Clarence Avant' (as mentioned earlier, a credit more often found in films of the fifties and sixties), which speaks volumes about Avant's ownership of and belief in Rodriguez. The others are for 'Creative Co-ordinator: Rainy M Moore' and 'Album Title: Rainy M Moore', suggesting Rainy had a much larger input than that of a manager.

Steve Rowland is clearly proud of his accomplishment as the music producer on *Coming from Reality* and has only the highest regard for Rodriguez and his work. He was astounded when the album went nowhere: 'I was shattered when the album came out and no one would review it. It was for this very reason that I put out the Family Dogg's [*The View from Rowland's Head*] album.' *Coming from Reality* was not reviewed in the UK, and it received only two reviews in the US. *Billboard* magazine singled out 'To Whom It May Concern' as the 'best cut' off the album and recommended 'Cause' and 'Climb Up On My Music' for airplay. *Cash Box* referred to Rodriguez's voice as being 'a pleasantly original amalgam of Jose Feliciano, Donovan and Cat Stevens'.

Back in Detroit, Rodriguez waited for the album to take off. But it didn't. Three sessions (two at Tera Shirma, one at Lansdowne) and, as far as he knew, three failures. As they say in baseball, 'three strikes and you're out'. According to Steve Rowland in *Searching for Sugar Man*, in December 1971 Sussex Records dropped him. Steve is talking about the song 'Cause' at the time, and has tears in his eyes because of the sadness of its prescient first line, *'Cause I lost my job two weeks before Christmas'.*

Rodriguez and Rainy were both devastated by the news. Gradually, Rodriguez put his musical aspirations on the backburner and fell back on the one thing he knew he could trust – working with his hands. He began taking on renovation and restoration jobs in the Woodbridge area of Detroit. Eva and Sandra were now in primary school and needed his attention and support. Left with no choice, the single dad, poet, musician and thinker with two masterworks in the bank was forced to come back to reality. But perhaps the biggest casualty of all was Rodriguez's relationship with Rainy. After being at his side for the most fruitful period of his musical career, they parted ways.

Steve Rowland never gave up on Rodriguez's songs, incorporating six of them into his 1972 *The View from Rowland's Head*. The first album from Family Dogg, *A Way of Life*, had come out at about the same time that *Cold Fact* was being recorded, and featured as session musicians Jimmy Page, John Bonham and John Paul Jones, playing together for the first time (the three would go on to form Led Zeppelin with Robert Plant), and a young Reggie Dwight, who would later jettison his working-class appellation for the more upmarket 'Elton

John'. The Family Dogg's second album, *The View from Rowland's Head*, opens with 'I Wonder' and closes with 'Advice to Smokey Robinson', the only known song that Rodriguez wrote but never recorded or played live himself. Dotted throughout the album are four more Rodriguez songs, all from *Cold Fact*, namely 'Like Janis', 'Crucify Your Mind', 'Inner City Blues' and 'Forget It'.

To Rowland's credit, the songs were all given a completely different treatment on *The View from Rowland's Head*. He did not try to emulate Rodriguez's sound or even his own treatment of the songs found on *Coming from Reality*. 'I Wonder', for example, features a gospel-like choir (backing vocals!) on the chorus that blows the song out of the water, in a good way. But unlike Family Dogg's first album, which charted in the Netherlands and elsewhere, *The View from Rowland's Head* did not do well, although it did receive the long-sought-after British review that Rodriguez never got during his time in obscurity. In spite of it being positive, *Melody Maker* magazine erroneously credited the songs to Rowland, calling it 'a fine, unpretentious album', and stating that 'he's got a good ear for a wry lyric, too'. Not bad for the 'Kid' from *Gunfighters*.

When asked about the name 'Rowland' in the lyrics of 'Advice to Smokey Robinson', the always-affable producer replied: 'When Rodriguez gave me the cassette I don't recall what name was in place of my name. I just remember him saying that the song would be a good one to record with Family Dogg.'

Coming from Reality was released in several countries, but neither Rodriguez nor Rowland received the fame or fortune they had hoped would be forthcoming. Other than the US and the UK, the album was released in South Africa, Rhodesia (now Zimbabwe), Australia and New Zealand. Anecdotally, we now know that certain songs received releases in other countries, too. 'I Think of You'/'To Whom It May Concern' appeared in Brazil around 1972/73 and received a fair amount of airplay. Singles have also popped up in both Italy and the Philippines. When asked about royalties, Rowland said: 'Until Light in the Attic re-released *Coming from Reality* in the mid-2000s, neither Rodriguez nor I saw a single cent from the sales of the album.' Sussex Records Inc. folded in July 1975. It would be years before Rodriguez would receive any acknowledgement (or any kind of financial compensation) for his work.

9

Cass corridor and other escape routes

(1970–1975)

'A revolutionary absurdist? A creative anarchist? A
leftist guitarist? He hasn't quite worked it out yet.'
— *DETROIT: A YOUNG GUIDE TO THE CITY*

In the early seventies, and continuing right through the
decade, we find Rodriguez at his busiest, juggling work,
parenthood, a shaky musical career and several new endeav-
ours, of which three in particular take up most of his time:
namely politics, activism and university. There are no clear
starting points for these new undertakings: ever the
Renaissance man, Rodriguez tackles these various career
paths concurrently.

In the period leading up to *Coming from Reality*, Rodriguez
started telling people about his intention to get into politics.
According to Steve Rowland, the singer was already talking
about running for office during the Lansdowne recordings
in London. It seems that his desire to enter the world of

politics crystallised shortly after recording *Cold Fact*. A 1970 issue of *Big Fat Magazine: The Midwest's Magazine of Rock*, featuring the recently deceased Jimi Hendrix on the cover (he died of a heroin overdose on 18 September 1970), contains an advert with the headline 'Rodriguez for Common Council'. (Interestingly, on another page we see an advertisement for Mr Flood's Party, a club in Ann Arbor that is referenced in 'A Most Disgusting Song', unlocking yet another mystery.) As an extension of his political aspirations, the singer became increasingly involved in grassroots activism. In fact, on every occasion that he surfaces in society in the seventies, he is bouncing back and forth between politics proper and political activism, galvanised by the social conditions surrounding him.

In *DETROIT: A Young Guide to the City*, a well-written and informative young persons' guidebook that, among other things, covers the many different areas in Detroit by ethnicity, Rodriguez features on pages 232 and 233 in the section titled 'Mexicans'. Accompanying the article is a photograph of him in what looks like a field in an urban environment; a tall building looms in the background. Seated on a rock and wearing the same trousers as on the cover of *Cold Fact*, Rodriguez can be seen talking to a small audience of young children who are gathered around him. The segment touches on some of the singer-songwriter's antics and ends with the line, 'At any rate, Rodriguez has announced his candidacy for Detroit Common Council in '73. He's got our support.'

The artist's emergence as a grassroots activist and aspiring politician is not surprising. America was in the middle of a growing period of social unrest, militant vigilantism and, at times, near-anarchism. There were also regular incidences of police brutality towards minorities, particularly blacks and people of Hispanic descent, a fact which gave rise to several militant retaliatory groups across the US.

The first of these was the Black Panther Party for Self-Defense, formed in 1966. Known as the Black Panthers, they were a revolutionary, black nationalist and socialist organisation. The early Black Panther movement took the form of self-defence citizens' patrols with the specific goal of monitoring police behaviour and challenging police brutality. It also developed community social programmes like 'Free Breakfast for Children', which helped shift the perception that the organisation was too militant. Federal Bureau of Investigation (FBI) director J. Edgar Hoover had other plans, however. He thought of the party as 'the greatest threat to the internal security of the country' and would stop at nothing to disband them, including deploying some of the dirtiest tactics ever propagated by the US government. Of course, it did not help that the literature put out by the Black Panthers was so viciously radical. One of the many cartoons in its magazine showed a picture of three black men (so-called Uncle Toms) kneeling over what looks like a white military general bending over with his trousers down, ('kissing up', perhaps the cartoonist was trying to say), and two Panthers pointing guns at them. There are two captions. The first reads: 'The years of Tom are over.' The second: 'The Panthers know who the Toms and the yids are!'

Although the Black Panthers were predominantly an ethnically black organisation, many whites aware of the injustices in the country threw in their support. One was the actress Jean Seberg, who put her career on the line when she backed the civil rights movement by donating money to such organisations as the National Association for the

Rodriguez at the Sewer by the Sea, commonly known as 'the Sewer', the Detroit club where he cut his teeth in the mid- to late sixties

An early publicity still from the days when Rodriguez was known as Rod Riguez, to avoid his name sounding too Hispanic

A promotional flyer for *Cold Fact*

Tera Shirma Studio B, on Detroit's Livernois Avenue, where Rodriguez recorded his first songs and his first album. The studio was named for its owner Ralph Terrana (right) and silent partner Al Sherman

Neica Lee Rompollo, the 'glue holding things together', at the studio's reception desk

Dennis Coffey and Mike Theodore, known together as Theo-Coff Productions, Rodriguez's first producers

Harry Balk, who gave Rodriguez his first break

Steve Rowland was a movie actor and singer before he produced Rodriguez's second album

The cover of *Cold Fact* in the US (left) and South Africa (right)

The US cover of *Coming from Reality* was retitled and redesigned in South Africa as
After the Fact, to echo Rodriguez's first album, which had been successful there

The back cover of *Coming from Reality*

The Italian single release of 'Sugar
Man', official disco entry into the annual
Festivalbar jukebox song contest, 1972

Rodriguez out and about in London after the recording of *Coming from Reality*, 1970

Perhaps an even better example of the kind of politics we may be in for is Sixto Rodriguez. Plain Rodriguez to everyone who knows him.

Rodriguez is a singer, guitarist, and songwriter. And because of the simple truth that he is not a politician, he recognizes that he is probably the BEST kind of politician. A revolutionary absurdist? A creative anarchist? A leftist guitarist? He hasn't quite worked it out yet. At this point he is only sure that his education and childhood on the streets of the Mexican near westside was not fit for children.

It's great knowing Rodriguez personally because he's always brewing and perpetrating SOMETHING. Like his legendary Heikke Bus Tour #2, a guided busload of Inner City wildmen — fueled by the powers of Cadillac Club Sweet Red — who careened out to the Grosse Pointe War Memorial and environs to take snapshots of the natives and to communicate. And then there was Happy Day (more wine). And an insane striptease battle he got involved in with two go-go boys in a gay bar — fans cheering crazily on either side.

Rodriguez featured in *DETROIT: A Young Guide to the City* in 1970

© Ann Kinney

Rodriguez election ad, and an ad for Mr. Flood's Party, a popular club in Ann Arbor, both in *Big Fat* magazine (no. 7), 1970

Rodriguez on campus at Wayne State University, where he studied philosophy, *c.* 1974

© John Hudson

Rodriguez (second from left) at a United Farmworkers Union rally in Clark Park, Detroit, featuring guest speakers councilman Mel Ravitz and union leader Cesar Chavez, 1975

the South End

VOLUME IX NUMBER 40 WEDNESDAY, OCTOBER 22, 1975

today
10/22/75

Sense to you, Too

Bicentennial. If that word hasn't turned you off yet, maybe this will. Another Bicentennial contest. This one's for "Computers with an urge to write marches." We've held one peace at the Bicentennial logo contest, and we didn't even complain about the Bicentennial playwriting contest, so we're going to bear up through this one too, and persevere. First prize is $50, and the deadline is Dec. 3. G.W. Binder has more information at 838-1426. So him.

Trial on Tap

The Wayne County Prosecutor's Office announced on Monday that they would prosecute the Fifth Estate Newspaper on criminal charges for printing instructions in spring, 1974, on how to build a "mute box." The mute box, when connected to a telephone, allows a person to receive long-distance phone calls with no charge to the caller. Bell Telephone instigated the criminal charges through the prosecutor's office and dragged out a five-day trial in August which ended with a deadlocked jury. Members of the Fifth Estate collective claimed a

Student Claims Police Brutality

By JAN B. SANDS
Staff Writer

WSU Monteith senior Sixto Rodriguez is suing the Detroit Police Department for allegedly brutalizing him last Friday during an incident in the 4th Precinct station that left him with four broken cheek bones and four stitches in his face.

According to Rodriguez, a police officer kicked his feet out from under him when he attempted to move away from the officer because the officer was punching his handcuffs behind his back.

"FIRST OF all, I'm getting medical attention," Rodriguez said, "then I'm going to sue all the parties responsible.

"He (the officer who allegedly kicked him) was acting in the capacity of a person representing the city of Detroit, and what he did to me was a question of professional standards," Rodriguez said.

Detective Sgt. Robert Meyers, the officer in charge of the case, said Rodriguez had "slipped" after attempting to push the officer.

"I've never seen a man's eye get so black in so short a time," Meyers said.

Rodriguez said that he had been

Sixto Rodriguez, Monteith student, plans to sue police officers involved in an alleged beating he received last Friday.

The *South End* article about Rodriguez's assault by police, which left him with a black eye

Rodriguez poses for promotional photos at the Michigan Central Station, 1977.

Konny Rodriguez, nee Koskos, Rodriguez's second wife

Rodriguez and a fan during his 1979 Australia tour

An ACE-produced tour guide for the 1979 tour

TANELORN FESTIVAL

LATE FLASH: Mexican-born folk-cult hero Sixto Rodriguez has been confirmed to appear at the Tanelorn Festival.

It will be a rare appearance for the reclusive musician who sells more albums in Australia than any other country. His last tour here was in 1979 when 16 sold-out concerts established Rodriguez as a rivetting performer based in the blues, with stories of the inner city, ghettos and hard times.

He jokes: "You'll see man, I'm gonna get the Grammy Award and I'll stand up there and say thank-you very much everybody for liking my songs but I want to tell you the children of the inner city are starving."

Rodriguez has recorded three albums — "Cold Fact", "Coming to Reality" and "The Best Of" — and a fourth album will be released to coincide with the Tanelorn appearance.

His songs are lyrical portraits, swift and biting, of human suffering and real problems. Sometimes brutal, his material contains humor and hope, confidence that total awareness is half-way here.

**FIVE DAYS OF MUSIC
CULTURE AND
CELEBRATIONS
OCTOBER 1-5, 1981
STROUD, N.S.W.
Syd 712 8863, Melb. 818 0359**

Rodriguez toured Australia for a second time in 1981 and performed at the Tanelorn Festival

Advancement of Colored People, the Black Panthers and various Native American school groups. Seberg, best known for her role in Jean-Luc Godard's French New Wave film *A bout de souffle* (*Breathless*), was living in Paris when the FBI tried to defame her, publicising her pregnancy by means of an anonymous letter sent to a gossip column, planting the seed that she was carrying the baby of a Black Panther. The FBI's underhanded actions and constant surveillance caused Seberg such distress that she went into early labour and miscarried. An open-casket funeral was held to show the world that the baby was in fact white. Such was the level of harassment and discrimination that ethnic minorities in the US faced at the time. And Detroit was no exception.

Another group was the Brown Berets, the pro-Mexico organisation that grew out of the Chicano Movement of the late 1960s. The Brown Berets' initial focus was on returning all United States territory once held by Mexico to Mexico. They eventually extended their activities to organising demonstrations against police brutality and advocating educational equality. (A line from Rodriguez's 'Hate Street Dialogue' – '*The pig and hose have set me free*' – allegedly refers to the police and the rubber clubs they used to break up protests.) Brown Berets leader, or 'prime minister' as he was known, David Sanchez, was the man who Rodriguez brought up onto stage with him during a record-company-sponsored publicity gig. This did not go down well with the company bigwigs and led to a bad review.

The *Oakland North* news project, part of the Graduate School of Journalism at the University of California, Berkeley, explained the social climate in America in the early seventies that formed the backdrop to Rodriguez's actions:

Guided by a socialist perspective, the Black Panthers saw capitalism as the root cause of racial injustice and poverty in the United States. The Panthers' radical analysis rang true for Native Americans still fighting for land rights and the fulfilment of broken treaties, Chicanos familiar with the conditions of farmworkers [. . .] Organizations like the American Indian Movement, the Brown Berets and the Red Guard embraced the Panthers' basic demands for fair housing, employment, health and community control of education and the police.

The full extent of Rodriguez's involvement or sympathies with these movements is not known, but he played his political hand in several creative and unique ways, including running for the Detroit Common Council and supporting the Chicano Movement, the United Farm Workers of America labour union and the struggle of Native Americans. There can be no doubting Rodriguez's socialist attitude towards capitalism, which in the minds of the minorities had lost its way.

The first and probably most unorthodox of his known undertakings as a grassroots activist was with Heikki's Bus Tour No. 2. It all began when a philosopher friend, Heikki Kansa (also referred to by Rodriguez as 'my Estonian Archangel' in the song 'Cause'), was somehow slighted by some rich folks. Rodriguez, in peaceful retaliation, came up with an idea for a bus tour around the affluent Detroit neighbourhood of Grosse Pointe. The story is mentioned in *DETROIT*:

Perhaps an even better example of the kind of politics we may be in for is Sixto Rodriguez. Plain Rodriguez to everyone who knows him. Rodriguez is a singer, guitarist and songwriter. And because of the simple truth that he is not a politician, he recognizes that he is probably the BEST kind of politician. A revolutionary absurdist? A creative anarchist? A leftist guitarist? He hasn't quite worked it out yet. At this point he is only sure that his education and childhood on the streets of the Mexican near Westside was not fit for children.

It is great knowing Rodriguez personally because he is always brewing and perpetrating SOMETHING. Like his legendary Heikki Bus Tour No. 2, a guided busload of Inner City wild men – fueled by the powers of Cadillac Club Sweet Red – who careened out to the Grosse Pointe War Memorial and environs to take snapshots of the natives and to communicate.

The article also mentions Rodriguez's musical career, fixing the story in time:

Rodriguez's first album, 'Cold Fact,' is out on the Sussex label of Buddha [*sic*]. More than any speech, it eloquently expresses his political convictions. Another album is on the way.

Shedding more light on the event, Eva relayed what her father had told her about the genesis of the song 'Heikki's Suburbia Bus Tour':

In the sixties, there were these people called hippies. It can be said that a long-haired, dark-skinned, free-thinking musician like Rodriguez could have been labelled one. In my youth, I recall hearing about how the 'rich folks' (those living in the suburbs), would come down to the inner city of Detroit to actually see these 'oddities' in their natural environment. Maybe even take a picture or two. This happened to be my neighbourhood and some of my people.

Rodriguez had a very good friend named Heikki. I remember a large man with long blond/brown hair. He had a very nice home, a wife named Linda and two huge bullmastiff dogs. Despite stereotypes, Heikki was a mathematician from Estonia [. . .] who rode a classic motorcycle. In fact, one of the places that Rodriguez played, a motorcycle funeral, was for one of Heikki's friends. The motorcycle club was called the Penetrators.

Anyway, someone had made fun of Rodriguez's friend. Protective of Heikki's feelings, Rodriguez organised what I consider to be a peaceful form of retaliation. A bus was chartered, full of hippies, four gallons of wine, etc. The group went to Grosse Pointe, Michigan, and surrounding areas where they visited suburban malls and neighbourhoods on a tour of their own. The rest is in the music. The story made the newspapers in Detroit and also reached Florida.

The track 'Heikki's Suburbia Bus Tour' was recorded at Lansdowne Studios with Steve Rowland and appears on *Coming from Reality*. It is an opportunity to see Rodriguez's mind at work as he translates the prose of the story into the poetry of the song:

Hospitals for flowers
The matron ladies cry
Itchy trigger fingers
as our caravan walks by
Overcrowded laughter

'cause they're all four gallons high
On Heikki's suburbia bus tour ride.

In *Searching for Sugar Man*, daughter Regan provides further evidence of her father's various attempts to run for office. From a box of paraphernalia, she pulls out a bumper sticker – white type on blue, reading 'ELECT RODRIGUEZ' – and an election absentee ballot, which has as the 139th candidate a misspelt 'Sixto Rodriquez'. Out of 169 candidates, nine were elected. Rodriguez was not one of them. In total, Rodriguez would run for political office eight times: for state representative twice, city council three times, mayor twice and senator once.

We do not know the style of his politicking, or the full extent of his canvassing, but it is doubtful that the withdrawn artist would have made public speeches. Judging by his ad placements in small independent music magazines, we do know who he thought would vote for him: music lovers, artists and poets, as well as the common folk and the disenfranchised.

With Rodriguez's unorthodox political career now rolling along, and with *Coming from Reality* on the record-store shelves but going nowhere fast, the artist went back into the studio, once again at the behest of Clarence Avant and despite having been dropped by the label. Avant wanted to give the musician one more chance, remembers Mike Theodore. It was early 1972 when the gentlemen from Theo-Coff were summoned to make magic with three unrealised Rodriguez songs. This time they chose the Pampa Sound Studios inside Pampa Lanes, one of Detroit's oldest and most popular bowling alleys. The main reason for this, says Theodore, was that 'at the time, [Pampa] was better equipped'.

Coffey and Theodore brought in a completely new line-up of musicians, most of whose names unfortunately have been lost to history. Theodore's arrangements differ too, yet are undeniably exquisite – perhaps even more refined than before. He chose to continue his experimentation, this time with flutes, deep throaty contrabassoons and a steel guitar. The result is playful at times, dark at others, with unusual and interesting dissonant intervals and call-and-answer devices. All three tracks, one of which had been recorded in Rodriguez's very first studio session but never released, have 'a pop edge to them', says Theodore. 'Avant really wanted a breakthrough single.'

'Can't Get Away' is a deceptively happy song. But as it progresses, the mood seems to darken, ominous undertones growing with each verse. In the lyrics, Rodriguez alludes to some preternatural thing from which he can never escape, something that seizes him with terror and fright, an undisclosed spectacle that seeps through the floorboards, walls and doorways in Amsterdam, and rings up and down the halls. In terms of the musical arrangement, Theodore plays the instruments up against one another; the low-register guttural contrabassoons and steel guitar interact playfully, yet they underscore the shadowy 'it' from which Rodriguez can't escape:

Scoffed at the prophet's omens
That said I would live to learn
That you can't get away from it.

The song ends with Theodore's trademark swirling string

section, purposely speeded up and then slowed down once more – reminiscent of 'Sugar Man'.

The slow-tempoed, melancholic 'Street Boy', the only Rodriguez release to feature backing vocals of any kind (courtesy of Jim Gold), is simplistic in its arrangement: guitar, percussion and bass. Rodriguez laments the woes of a street boy who can't stay at home because something is always pulling him away. With no clues as to who the boy could be, there seems to be a semblance of truth in the words, almost as if the boy is known to him – perhaps even someone for whom he has great affection.

The third song (and the last that Rodriguez would ever record in a studio setting) is another version of 'I'll Slip Away'. As before, the song opens with Rodriguez's regular guitar strumming and percussion, laying a bed for the steel guitar. Accented throughout are Theodore's well-crafted orchestral harmonies, followed by a great guitar solo by Coffey. And then, as the song ends, we hear Rodriguez's last word on the subject – perhaps even his last word on his music:

> *Maybe today*
> *Yeah, I'll slip away.*

There are two remarkable things about the Pampa recording session. The first is that the very first song Rodriguez ever recorded ('I'll Slip Away') was also the last. The second is that the three songs never made it to vinyl in America. In fact, they would only see the light of day in 1977.

Now in his early thirties and with two daughters approaching their teens, Rodriguez took up his third new endeavour and enrolled as a student at Wayne State University's Monteith

College. Normally it's the other way around: first university, then kids. But nothing Rodriguez ever did was straightforward or the way society would have had him do it. Even his choice of college was different. Monteith was an experimental college within Wayne State. According to academic Jerry Starr, Monteith was established in 1959 and was based on a charter that called for 'an effort to impart to undergraduates, particularly those in training for the professions, that common body of ideas and knowledge that every educated man should possess'.

From the start, the new college was criticised by certain faculties within Wayne State. The English faculty, for example, was troubled by the elimination of a freshman composition course, and the science faculty saw the college as an amateur enterprise. Monteith staff made little effort to interact with their colleagues in the university, preferring to spend their time at the student centre and in their own often crowded and noisy offices. Starr adds:

Most faculty members dressed casually; many called students by their first names and encouraged them to reciprocate. Such faculty saw students as potential allies in creating an oppositional culture, even allowing them to show up unannounced at faculty apartments.

Many of the social science faculty professed radical politics that were deeply cynical about American party politics. Some supported Castro in Cuba. Monteith faculty edited *New University Thought* [. . .] By senior year, students met in seminars to discuss assigned readings and their own papers without a faculty member present. [. . .]

Faculty and students tended to distinguish Monteith from the rest of the College of Liberal Arts, which they referred to as 'Wayne.' This sense of specialness nurtured a separate culture, which flourished through a student center, newsletter and journal, among other activities.

It is not difficult to see why Rodriguez, the commensurate nonconformist, was taken with the institution. The campus, which he frequented even before he was a student, was a hotbed of ideas. Starr describes the situation:

A minority of students – perhaps ten to twenty percent – hung around the student center and faculty offices. [The] faculty, especially in the social sciences, cultivated personal relations with these 'Monteithers.'
Some social scientists emphasized the importance of social criticism and activism. Through them, some students became involved in nuclear disarmament and civil rights issues, linking to groups on campus like the Student Peace Union [. . .] Other faculties emphasized the quest for individual identity and meaning, often through artistic expression.

Rodriguez's involvement with Chicano and grassroots organisations such as United Farm Workers, plus the various Native American pow-wows that he would attend and help organise, are definitive examples of the type of social activism encouraged at Monteith. And as for its emphasis on 'the quest for individual identity . . . through artistic expression', the musician hardly needed any encouragement.

It was on campus that Rodriguez met Constance Koskos, a second-generation Greek immigrant and the woman who would become his second wife and the mother of his third daughter. As she likes to tell it, 'Koskos is my maiden name and was probably changed from a very long Greek name when my father arrived at Ellis Island with his parents in 1920.' A frequent face on the Wayne State University campus, 'Konny', as she was known, worked for the Wayne State University Library System, purchasing and remitting payment for their magazine subscriptions. At the same time she attended school, working towards a bachelor's degree in psychology:

> I was attending and working at Wayne State University in 1972. I was twenty-one years old. I met Rodriguez on campus, quite by chance. I knew who he was and had wanted to meet him. I had seen him walking on campus with his guitar and knew he played around Detroit. I introduced myself, we talked, and the rest is history.
>
> Rodriguez told me about his involvement in the music industry. He showed me his two LPs and said they weren't doing anything. At that point in time, he was really more involved [at Monteith College].

Rodriguez's major interest became philosophy, and he studied Dutch philosopher Baruch Spinoza, a man with whom he shared certain parallels. By all accounts, Spinoza's existence was outwardly simple. He was a lens grinder by profession (a blue-collar job in the seventeenth century), and shunned all rewards and honours in his life, passing the family inheritance on to his sister. When asked about Rodriguez's college life and his interest in philosophy, Konny says:

> Rodriguez studied many philosophers [. . .] The professors at Monteith were mainly doctors of philosophy. The

only classes the students there attended were philosophy lectures.

All other work was done outside the classroom: Rodriguez's two albums were part of his grade, his runs for city council and mayor, the same. There were other examples.

Rodriguez took his time to work his way through college, with projects, activities and the constant struggle to make a living as the breadwinner for his two children taking priority over his studies. He would only officially receive his PhB in 1981.

Rodriguez didn't speak to Konny much about his music, but she does shed some light on his life as a musician during this period:

Rodriguez actually had not played publicly in Detroit at all while he was in [college]. He had his guitar with him a lot and would play when he felt like it at parties or for small gatherings, or just in the halls of the small house called Monteith College, but he had not played for money.

Janice Prezzato, a journalist at the *South End* newspaper at the time, confirms this:

That was typical Rodriguez. My fondest memory of [him] is when I followed him to a local house party at a communal household. He entertained everyone singing fifties and sixties rock 'n' roll on his acoustic guitar. A memorable evening. You always had the feeling that his time was going to come and that people would discover this gentle soul.

Says Konny:

Although he was preoccupied with school and raising his two daughters, Rodriguez played every day at home. He would roam from room to room with his guitar, looking for the room with the best acoustics. Sometimes we were together, and sometimes he would excuse himself, close the door and play for hours.

In his spare time he would read, always eager to learn. Konny recalls:

We both loved libraries [. . .] We both spent a lot of time in the library, and we spent time there on weekends. We all read a lot. The main Detroit library was within walking distance of our house. It's a beautiful building. People there knew him well also.

During his time at Monteith, Rodriguez featured several times in the *South End*, a radical, left-leaning campus broadsheet unpopular with the university hierarchy. The newspaper's offices, situated in a building on Wayne State campus's south end in a working-class area, were a hive of activity and the focal point of leftist politics at the time. In 1968 activist John Watson took over as editor in order to transform the paper into a public resource 'with the intention of promoting the interests of impoverished, oppressed, exploited, and powerless victims of white, racist monopoly capitalism and imperialism' (as stated in Watson's first editorial on 26 September 1968).

What had initially been an ordinary student publication became a radical weekly newspaper with – some would say

– lax standards when it came to editorial accuracy and spelling. A drawing of a right-facing black panther was added to both sides of the *South End* logo, and later, in the interests of symmetry, the panther on the right was flipped. The logo was intentionally meant to link the paper with both the Black Panthers and the League of Revolutionary Black Workers, an organisation founded by Watson. In the late sixties and early seventies, the standing quotation under the paper's masthead read: 'One class-conscious worker is worth 100 students'.

It is hardly surprising that the singer/songwriter/activist was drawn to the newspaper. Prezzato remembers:

I first saw Rodriguez wandering around campus in the seventies. There was a mall that ran through the campus buildings [one of which housed the *South End*]. The apex of the mall was a large square with a flag pole. The centre of the campus was the scene of many anti-war protests in the sixties and seventies. There were tables in good weather with various groups hawking literature and the normal university organisations with information tables. He was always dressed in black and wearing sunglasses with a guitar. He would laugh and joke, but was very humble. He was always popping into the [newspaper], or hanging around the large porch area outside of the *South End* offices. He would normally have someone with him, a woman to help him to organise his time.

One autumn day, he started talking to me, hanging out. I had to coax him into playing [his guitar]. I got to know him well during this time. He was definitely marching to a different drum [. . .] sometimes it was the theatre of the absurd. But always at Wayne State. At the time it really was the ground zero for the Cass Corridor arts community, which still thrives to this day.

One day in April 1974, Rodriguez walked into the *South End* offices and announced that his brother Enrique had secured a meeting with Mayor Coleman Young – Detroit's first African-American mayor – and that the newspaper should cover the story. The mayor, according to the article that resulted, had been 'criticized by Latinos in recent months for being uncommitted to Detroit's Latino community, and to the United Farm Workers' cause'. Prezzato covered the meeting and wrote the story, and staff photographer Joe B. took the photographs. In the meeting, Mayor Young emphasised that he had supported United Farm Workers and its co-founder Cesar Chavez before he took office. 'Any action I make will be on the side of Cesar,' he declared. He believed that corruption in the Detroit Police Department, which seemed to be preventing minorities from entering the force, was the real concern. 'When the new city charter goes into effect, the police situation will be a whole new ball game,' he said.

The article features a photograph of Enrique (referred to as 'the mini-mayor of south-west Detroit') dressed in black with teardrop glasses, locking hands with Mayor Young in a show of solidarity. It is not known how much behind-the-scenes work Rodriguez did, but the meeting seemed to be a success. The article ends: 'As one Latino expressed, "the south-west of Detroit is ready for you (Young) if you are ready for the south-west."'

Just over a month later, Rodriguez was back at the *South End* offices. This time he asked for the newspaper's involvement in an unusual but interesting event that he was helping to host. 'You have to do a story on the Native American pow-wow,' he said, 'about them shining in their culture.' Prezzato's first thought was that there weren't too many Native Americans in Michigan. But Rodriguez explained that there were actually several tribes in the state, including the Ojibwa and the Menominee (there are in fact eleven federally recognised Native American tribes in Michigan). Prezzato eventually agreed, and this time took photographer Carl Ott along. Rodriguez was obsessed with the concept of the pow-wow, but did not want any pictures of himself. He wanted to focus on the people and the children.

Prezzato's finished article is clear and informative. It begins:

Wayne State University, named after Indian fighter 'Mad' Anthony Wayne, hosted Detroit's first American Indian Pow-Wow under cloudy skies this memorial weekend at Matthaei Field. Native Americans came from Illinois, Wisconsin, North Dakota, and Canada to participate in the Pow-Wow and meet for a cultural exchange.

The article is interesting for its cultural insights:

The dances resembled a two-step form of dancing, with many names and variations due to intermarriage between tribes. Dances performed were the Fish, Round and the Grass Dance, sometimes called the Omaha dance. The Omaha dance is a war dance, but according to Pow-Wow moderator Benny Bearskin Sr., 'We dance for friendship and fellowship, due to a shortage of Indian wars these days.'

The photographs accompanying the front-page article are fascinating, showing the dancers in full traditional dress juxtaposed – perhaps a tad soberly and not without irony – against several high-rise buildings where the blue 'plains' sky should have been. Rodriguez's goal was to raise social consciousness, and he succeeded. The Indian war for survival in America is ongoing, and to this day, Rodriguez wears a Native American symbol around his neck. And let's not forget, his first wife Rayma was said to be part Cherokee.

As an aside, among the remarkably few photographs of Rodriguez from this time, there is one that shows him on stage at a United Farm Workers' lettuce boycott rally in which Chavez was headlining. With muscular arms crossed, and in a pink shirt with his trademark black sunglasses, the musician looks on defiantly.

Rodriguez next appeared in the *South End* offices on 17 October 1975 (the date when America celebrates 'Black Poetry Day'). This time, however, the circumstances were less salubrious. Looking dishevelled, he walked in and asked for the city editor. He wanted to run a story on police brutality with himself as protagonist. It was clear he had been beaten up. Prezzato was a bystander on this one, hearing about it as Rodriguez was leaving the building. The subsequent article, by Jan B. Sands, reads as follows:

STUDENT CLAIMS POLICE BRUTALITY

WSU Monteith senior Sixto Rodriguez is suing the Detroit Police Department for allegedly brutalizing him last Friday during an incident in the 4th Precinct station that left him with four broken cheekbones and four stitches in his face.

According to Rodriguez, a police officer kicked his feet

out from under him when he attempted to move away from the officer because the officer was pinching his handcuffs behind his back.

'First of all, I'm getting medical attention,' Rodriguez said, 'then I am going to sue all the parties responsible.'

'He (the officer who allegedly kicked him) was acting in the capacity of a person representing the city of Detroit, and what he did to me was a question of professional standards,' Rodriguez said.

Detective Sgt. Robert Meyers, the officer in charge of the case, said Rodriguez had 'slipped' after attempting to push the officer.

'I've never seen a man's eye get so black in so short a time,' Meyers said.

Rodriguez said that he had been arrested on the charge of malicious destruction of property following an altercation with Latin Quarter storeowner Robert Scott over whether Scott was obliged by law to give change to the public.

Rodriguez had stopped at the store and asked for change for a $5 bill in order to give his two daughters Eva, 12, and Sandra, 10, money for their school's hot lunch program, but Scott refused.

When Rodriguez insisted that it was his right to get change, Scott brandished a shotgun and ordered him out of the store.

Several school children, including his two daughters, were present when the shotgun was pulled out.

During the altercation, a television set was broken.

Scott charged Rodriguez with breaking the television.

Rodriguez said Scott broke the set when he brandished the shotgun.

Although formal charges haven't been filed against

Rodriguez, Meyers said that Scott intended to press charges.

Attorney Alan L. Kaufman, Rodriguez's lawyer, said that he didn't think the police had a case against his client, and called the arrest 'unjustified.'

Meyers promised a speedy investigation into the matter because of future commitments.

'I have seven days of vacation during the last week of this month and I want to have the matter cleared up before then,' Meyers said.

The story made the front page of the *South End* on the following Wednesday, 22 October 1975. In a tightly cropped photograph, taken by Millard Berry, Rodriguez's beaten face is clear for the world to see.

The news on the front page of the *South End* the very next day, 23 October, would have come as a further blow to Rodriguez. The article was written by staff writer Tom Panzenhagen:

U. COUNCIL COMMITTEE TO RECOMMEND MONTEITH COLLEGE CLOSING

A committee of the University Council will recommend Nov. 5 to the entire council that Monteith College no longer be funded by the university for monetary reasons [. . .]

The ad hoc committee, a nine-member subcommittee of the University Council's Policy Committee [. . .] voted unanimously Monday to recommend that further university spending on Monteith be ended.

The experiment was over. And, sadly, Rodriguez was never elected to political office.

10

Where women glow
and men plunder

(1979–1981)

'My understanding was that Clarence [Avant] was happy to sell the Australia and New Zealand rights to all of the songs for anything he could as no one in the world was interested in Rodriguez.'
— PHIL BIRNBAUM, BLUE GOOSE MUSIC

To all intents and purposes, Rodriguez gave up his ambitions of becoming a recognised musician in 1972 after the Pampa Studios recording session. He spent the following years studying philosophy, working as a community activist, running for office, and playing and writing very little music. He was, to borrow a phrase from the conventional workplace, retired from music. To keep the wolf from the door, he continued with construction jobs on the side and started participating in child development programmes for the city of Detroit. 'I saw some things I thought people should be made aware of, but I was unable to do that with my music,' he said. He also wasn't getting any younger. If you haven't made it by your mid-thirties in the music business, then you probably never will. Indeed, some of Rodriguez's contemporaries – Janis Joplin, Jimi Hendrix, Jim Morrison and Jim Croce – had burnt through entire music careers before their deaths in their late twenties. The music business certainly wasn't a place for late starters.

And then one day in 1979 the phone rang. It was a tour promoter in Australia. Apparently, Rodriguez's albums had been selling steadily, and in increasing numbers, in that country over the years. He had become a cult artist Down Under. 'Would you consider touring Australia?' the promoter asked. Needless to say, Rodriguez was surprised. How had this happened? Was he even up to it? Playing at home and gigging in familiar places is one thing, touring multiple cities in a strange land with a strange band is quite another. At that stage, Rodriguez had never played for audiences larger than a couple of hundred people. Just how had his two forgotten albums gained traction on this continent in the far corner of the world?

Australian music company Festival Records released *Cold Fact* in Australia in 1972. It is not known how the record company discovered the album, but it was probably part of the Sussex rollout. As is the case with most cult albums, it began at grassroots level. Glenn Baker, the Australian editor of *Billboard* magazine, would later write:

One LP from the original small pressing was purchased by Sydney radio announcer Holger Brockman, who began dropping the track 'Sugar Man' into his 2SM evening shift around 1972. Three years later, having moved over to the freeform 2JJ he was regularly playing the entire Rodriguez repertoire.

2SM was a Sydney AM pop station owned, surprisingly, by the Catholic Church. Due to the restrictive policies at the time, Holger Brockman (whose name was considered 'too foreign-sounding') worked under the pseudonym Bill Drake. By 1975 he had moved over to a new station, 2JJ (also known as Double J, and later Triple J) and began working under his own name. And so it was that the man with a 'too foreign-sounding' name was the first to give the man with a 'too Hispanic-sounding' name his first extensive airplay. It was this that led to the groundswell. Baker again:

> The buyer demand generated by this airplay simply could not be met. Sussex had long gone bankrupt and, after warehouse stocks in America and South Africa were exhausted, import stores were turning away hundreds of willing purchasers. As word of mouth enhanced the popularity of the singer/songwriter and his bleak observations of hopelessness, a giant cassette network sprang up with friends taping their taped copy for friends.

Sometime in the late seventies, Israeli-born entrepreneur Zev Eizik discovered Rodriguez. Eizik had immigrated to Melbourne after completing his schooling. He attended university and got involved in the student council, helping run an on-campus flea-market stall that sold all kinds of things, including records. When the couple who ran the stall went out of business, Eizik took over. He soon noticed that a lot of people were coming over to ask if he had any albums by Rodriguez. He had never heard of the artist, but eventually managed to track down a copy of *Cold Fact* and took a listen. He saw the potential and decided to see if he could locate more copies. He discovered that Festival Records had brought in a few hundred LPs in 1972, but no longer had stock and had given up their licensing rights.

Sensing an opportunity, Eizik unsuccessfully attempted to buy stock from Fontana Records in the UK. He then made some enquiries and finally tracked down the source of the album to a man called Clarence Avant, the erstwhile 'impresario' from Sussex Records. In July 1975, with unpaid federal and state taxes, the US Internal Revenue Service had padlocked the Sussex offices and auctioned off all its assets. Many of the label's master tapes were assumed missing or destroyed after that. The closure of Sussex Records led to a quagmire of record deals and secondary deals between foreign licensees and other entities with little accounting of royalties. When Eizik finally caught up with him, Avant was living in Los Angeles, quite a distance from Melbourne. But Eizik, who by now owned his own label called Blue Goose Music, was determined and flew to the US for a meeting with the former studio head. Avant was impressed with the young man from Australia, and a deal was struck. According to Phil Birnbaum of Blue Goose, Avant 'was happy to sell the Australia and New Zealand rights to all of the songs for anything he could as no one in the world was interested in Rodriguez', but Baker gives a slightly different version, claiming that Eizik only secured the licensing rights for a 'Best Of' album.

Either way, in June 1977, Blue Beat, a subsidiary of Blue Goose, released *Rodriguez: At His Best* in Australia. Six of the eleven songs on the album were off *Cold Fact*, two were off *Coming from Reality*, and the remaining three – 'Can't Get

Away', 'I'll Slip Away' and 'Street Boy' – were from the Pampa sessions and, until now, had never seen the light of day. Surprisingly, with little or no publicity the new Rodriguez album reached number twenty-eight on the Australian charts, seven and six years after the release of *Cold Fact* and *Coming from Reality* respectively in the US.

Boosted by the success of *Rodriguez: At His Best*, Eizik released *Cold Fact* through RCA Records in May 1978, and in January the following year he released *Coming from Reality* on Blue Goose records. The latter received a positive Australian review:

A NEW LOOK, NEW SOUND RODRIGUEZ
COMING FROM REALITY by Rodriguez.
(Blue Goose MLF269)

Quite a change from Rodriguez's first album Cold Fact. On Cold Fact Rodriguez sang bitter, disillusioned songs about slums, drug abuse and broken love affairs. Something in between the two albums obviously changed his point of view because Coming From Reality consists mainly of love songs. And not the cynical odes to past affairs of Cold Fact – these ones are full-blown, sentimental Paul McCartney-type love songs. And even the social comment songs on the album seem less bitter and more resigned. The strings have been laid on with a heavy hand, on some tracks providing the only backing to Rodriguez's guitar and voice. But the voice shines through and the clever poetry on some tracks is as incisive as ever. But don't expect the same Rodriguez as you heard on Cold Fact.

— Roger Crosthwaite

Eizik claimed at the time that *Cold Fact* sold 100,000 units. If true, this is a rare feat for an album that was already seven years old. *Coming from Reality* seems to have done well, too. Baker writes:

> With no commercial airplay whatsoever and certainly no hit singles, [*Rodriguez: At His Best*] shot to platinum status. This feat was echoed by *Cold Fact*, and in 1979 *Coming from Reality* helped to move Rodriguez past the collective double platinum mark, a seemingly impossible achievement for a non-chart entity.

By now Eizik had become more involved in the Australian music business as a tour promoter, later handling such acts as the massively popular Australian band Midnight Oil, fronted by the charismatic Peter Garrett. With *Cold Fact* and *At His Best* selling well in Australia, Eizik – in his capacity as a director of Australian Concert Entertainment (also known as ACE) – decided to see if he could get the artist to come out, to capitalise on the album sales. He picked up the phone.

After careful consideration, Rodriguez accepted the offer to tour. Baker recalls:

> When contacted by Australian Concert Entertainment, the retired singer who had never performed before more than a few hundred people at [any] time was understandably apprehensive at the thought of flying 12,000 miles for a concert tour. After lengthy contemplation he decided, 'I owe it to those people who have taken time to find my music.'

Rodriguez, Konny (pregnant with Regan), Eva and Sandra flew to Australia in March 1979. Eizik and his team from ACE then travelled with them around the country. The touring schedule was hectic, involving thirteen flights in six weeks and numerous time-zone changes, but Rodriguez was treated like a rock star for the first time in his life. As in South Africa, most people Down Under believed he had died (of a heroin overdose in a New York City gutter, to be exact). It is still a mystery how these rumours originated in the southern hemisphere.

Baker describes the singer's initial trepidation and how it eventually gave way to gratitude and excitement:

Rodriguez arrived in Australia with his family. He readily admitted his difficulty in relating to the press attention, which surrounded him, and early interviews were awkward and unproductive. He did manage to make plain that his social conscience had not dimmed. 'These are new times and there are different answers that we are trying to seek out. There has to be an end to violence but the answers are not as easy as they were ten years ago.'

Gradually his trepidation gave way to a realisation that the interest in his music was sincere but still he walked the streets late at night unable to sleep and he sat nervously shaking in a taxi for fifteen minutes before taking the stage at Melbourne's Dallas Brooks Hall for his first concert. Slim, in a conservative beige suit, he merely ventured on stage with a sheaf of lyrics to songs he had long since ceased to perform, and entered into a form of holy communion with the entranced audience; the majority of which was young and working class. The opening chords of most of his seventeen songs were greeted with whoops of recognition and joy, while some followers of this unlikely Messiah were obviously transported into the realms of ecstasy. Rarely has an audience been in such accord with a performer; never has the youth of one generation found such empathy and identification in the street poetry of an alien era of consciousness.

In all, Rodriguez played to sixteen sold-out concert halls in Sydney, Melbourne, Perth, Brisbane, Adelaide, Newcastle and Canberra. In the Queensland capital he filled the cavernous Festival Hall, a feat beyond many high-profile rock acts. Having heard of the huge popularity of his music on the inmates' radio station, he asked to perform at Melbourne's Pentridge Prison, an event which had a profound effect upon him. By the end of the tour the man brimmed so full of confidence and excitement that he pleaded to be able to make record-store autograph appearances. He left Australia, buoyed by the love and devotion of a following that neither his dreams [nor] aspirations had prepared him for, pledging to return.

During the tour Rodriguez recorded a live album, released as *Alive*, at the Regent Theatre in Sydney on the evenings of 17 and 18 March. For some obscure reason, he only agreed to a one-year licensing deal, which meant that the album became something of a collector's item. A far more valuable item today, however, would be Konny's suitcase containing all the smaller tour souvenirs, which was stolen at LAX when the family landed back in the US.

Very few photographs exist of the 1979 tour. News of the six-week slog across Australia doesn't seem to have made it to Detroit, in spite of it being a remarkable story: from blue-collar worker to rock star. Nevertheless, financially speaking things were looking up for Rodriguez on his return. The tour of Australia had been a lucrative one. For the first time, his music had paid off. Konny left her job at Wayne State University to welcome daughter Regan into the world in May 1980. The following year Rodriguez's eldest daughter decided to enlist in the military, but as a seventeen-year old, she needed the permission of her parents. Rodriguez, a staunch pacifist, refused to sign the forms, leaving the task to her mother. Eva would go on to serve first in the medical corps and later as a helicopter pilot.

It was also in 1981 that Rodriguez received his degree. It had been a long time coming.

In late 1981 Rodriguez received a second request from Eizik's ACE to tour Australia. The request came at short notice. He agreed, and this time travelled with an additional family member, one-year-old Regan, who almost didn't make the trip. Delays in processing her passport meant that mother and daughter had to wait in Los Angeles for the required travel documents to be issued while Rodriguez went on ahead. On arrival in Australia he received the itinerary for the tour. The front cover of the information guide features an amateurish illustration of Rodriguez holding a banner bearing his name. In the background is a sign with the words 'ACE PRESENTS'. This time around, fifteen shows were planned spanning ten cities, namely Adelaide, Launceston, Hobart, Sydney, Canberra, Perth, Melbourne, Brisbane, Lismore and Newcastle. Once again the Rodriguezes were accompanied by Eizik, and also tour manager Andrea March, on their flight to each destination, while the band took a bus.

Although the tour officially kicked off on 12 October

1981, with the last show planned for 2 November at the Civic Theatre in Newcastle, the high point for Rodriguez was his inclusion in the line-up for the Tanelorn Music Festival held on the Labour Day holiday weekend (1–5 October) before the tour. He was one of a long list of acts to play over the five-day period. Others included Split Enz, Midnight Oil and Men at Work. Tanelorn was a one-off camping festival on a farm in New South Wales not unlike Woodstock, with all the goings-on of such classics as Altamont, Woodstock and the Isle of Wight. Super-8 footage from the time shows hippies, tents, nipples, motorcycles and even a tepee. It is not known if any babies were born. So taken was Rodriguez by Peter Garrett from Midnight Oil that in a 1998 interview he said:

> I feel that Midnight Oil is the top band. I first watched them perform in '81 from about 30 feet and witnessed their powerful stage performance at past two in the morning in the freezing cold temperature of the Australian wind. It was so cold that as Peter Garrett performed, steam was rising from his head. It was almost phantom-like. He is musical, political and international.

It was Rodriguez's biggest gig to date. A flyer advertising his inclusion in the festival reads:

TANELORN FESTIVAL
LATE FLASH: Mexican-born, folk cult hero Sixto Rodriguez has been confirmed to appear at the Tanelorn Festival.
It will be a rare appearance for the reclusive musician who sells more albums in Australia than any other country.

It includes a quote from Rodriguez that shows his musical aspirations in spite of his late blooming in a foreign country, mixed with his aspirations for the city of Detroit:

> You'll see man, I'm going to get the Grammy award and I'll stand up there and say, 'Thank you very much everybody for liking my songs, but I want to tell you, the children of the inner city are starving.'

Press clippings from the day after, however, imply that his performance did not go down that well:

> The Mexican singer took the stage at Tanelorn solo and having seen him both solo and with backing, I'd say the Capital Theatre show [in Sydney, scheduled for 18 October] will be an improvement on his low-key and sometimes shambling Tanelorn set.

Alongside the article is a photograph of a smiling Rodriguez with the caption: 'Rodriguez . . . shambles.' By all accounts, however, the shows improved from that point on. On 4 November, after a long tour, the singer and his family departed Sydney International Airport aboard Pan Am flight 812 for Los Angeles. The last words on the information guide and itinerary read: 'Goodbye and good luck.'

Many critics have pointed to the fact that director Malik Bendjelloul left out the two tours of Australia in *Searching for Sugar Man*. When asked about this, he said that he was sure that neither Craig nor Sugar was aware at the time that Rodriguez was touring Australia. The primary focus of his film was the story and journey of the two

South African fans, which did not cross to Australia at all.

It is true that the two detectives knew nothing of the tours that had taken place nearly twenty years before they began their search. Craig only learnt that Rodriguez had toured Australia in his first conversation with Mike Theodore in August 1997, when he discovered Rodriguez was still alive. And Sugar only heard that part of the story when Rodriguez told him about it in their first conversation a few weeks later.

There is another possible reason for Malik's decision. As the teller of a cohesive story, the director was posed with the problem of a double arc. It's a little like telling the story of Cinderella, but then discovering that in the real story she attended two balls, losing a slipper twice. Malik's focus was on the second ball: Rodriguez's 1998 tour to South Africa.

PART III

THE MUSIC

11

When your swans have turned to geese
(1998–2001)

'He's not dead, he's just late.'
— Unknown journalist, Westcliff Hotel,
Johannesburg, 2001, after Rodriguez's
no-show at his own press conference

More than 25,000 adoring and ululating fans at six sold-out shows in Cape Town, Johannesburg and Durban, a platinum record awarded backstage after the first concert at Johannesburg's Standard Bank Arena for sales over 50,000 copies (someone in the crowd yelling: 'Where's the money?'), and not a step closer to being recognised in his native Detroit, let alone the United States. Not even as a character in a sensational, one-of-a-kind story. No airplay. No write-ups. Nothing. Ultimately, the tale of the 'failed' musician who discovered he had been famous for the better part of his life on another continent turned out to be nothing more than a curiosity, a regional Cinderella story. 'I guess

you can say the carriage turned back into a pumpkin,' Eva
Rodriguez said later.

The transition from workman on a building site to headlining rock star must have been daunting to say the least, a
pinch-me moment. It was almost as if the plane that brought
Rodriguez to South Africa not only passed through a series
of time zones, but also an invisible barrier into an alternate
reality. Although he had done it before, to Australia in 1979
and 1981, it is still a difficult concept to fathom. Imagine, if
you will, that a painting you did at school becomes an iconic
image in Brazil, appearing on stamps, posters, everywhere.
Or a poem that you wrote becomes the lyrics to a top-selling
song in Egypt, and you only find out about it a quarter of a
century later. And in both scenarios, everyone knows your
name and has a story to tell about how your genius formed
the backdrop to one or other meaningful life experience – a
proposal, a break-up, the birth of a child – while you were
'carrying fridges on your back', as Rodriguez's third daughter
Regan would later say.

These fictitious scenarios are hard to imagine, harder still to
fathom. There are simply no parallels. Yet it happened, and the
setting for this implausible scenario is even more unbelievable:
the last stand of a white minority government in a changing
world, a land of violence and killing and police brutality, a
police state functioning with a 'detention without trial' policy,
a country that tried desperately to validate a system under-
pinned by Calvinist beliefs, a system known as apartheid.

The thing about life, as Rodriguez would be the first to tell
you, is that it goes on. Another thing he says is that 'nothing
beats reality'.

It would end up taking a surprisingly long time for

Rodriguez to get paid for his first South African tour. For those closest to him, who were keen that he should finally get some financial reward for his music, it was a real concern. Then, in September 1999 when all the excitement was over, the Universal Music Group, the distributors of Rodriguez's back catalogue (except for *Live Fact*, a live album recorded during the 1998 South Africa tour on the Sony label), confirmed that they would no longer be pressing or distributing his CDs in South Africa. No reasons were given for this decision.

In the meantime, on 27 January 1999, Brian Currin and Sugar Segerman brought out the first issue of *SA Rock Digest*, an online blog – before the word existed – of all things rock- and pop-related from a South African perspective. In no time at all, the blog amassed 5,000 subscribers. But then, amid the glory of reinvigorating a lost singer's career, Sugar's own career took a nosedive when he was retrenched from his job. Stoically, he took it on the chin, imagining he would find work quickly. Despite having a law degree, nothing substantial came his way, apart from a part-time opportunity to lecture media-related law at Varsity College, a small tertiary institution in Cape Town. But it wasn't enough to support his family, and he became anxious as time went on and nothing full-time materialised.

In early 2001, when Sugar started hearing rumours of a second Rodriguez tour to South Africa, he spoke with Eva and tried to arrange it himself through people like David Marks, the music producer. But once Rodriguez finally received his full fee for the first tour, he handed the task of arranging what was to be a far more extensive tour, with sixteen dates planned around the country, once again to Zev Eizik and Magnus Erickson.

In August 2001, just after Rodriguez's fifty-ninth birthday and a month before the scheduled second tour, Sugar flew to America with a special gift concealed in his suitcase. After the singer's first tour of South Africa in 1998, Tonia Selley had produced a fifty-two-minute documentary called *Dead Men Don't Tour*, using the footage of the concerts and interviews with the main players. Rodriguez's wife Konny explains the title:

> We were sitting around, talking about how people thought he was dead, killed by his wife on stage, or dead of a heroin overdose. Someone asked how they could get people to believe he was alive or something to that effect, and I said, 'Dead men don't tour,' and Tonia, the director, liked that.

After paying the costs for a three-person camera crew to cover the shows on Betacam, Tonia and her associates had exhausted their miniscule budget, and it took a whole month to edit the film in a garage in Emmarentia, with render times so slow that Tonia would have to lie awake all night babysitting the unreliable early digital edit machines. The documentary finally aired on SABC 3 on 5 July 1999, more than a year after the tour was over. But Tonia failed to get clearance from the publishing company that owned the rights to Rodriguez's music, and so the film had to be shelved after its one and only broadcast.

Before Sugar headed out to the US, he had the idea to take a specially made NTSC copy of *Dead Men Don't Tour* with him to present to Rodriguez as a birthday gift. It would be a way for the musician to prove to the non-believers back home that he had just toured South Africa and played to thousands of screaming fans. Most of his fellow Detroitians had never heard him play, and even doubted that he could. Jerome Ferretti, Rodriguez's animated bricklayer friend, paints this picture in *Searching for Sugar Man*:

> He was really quite famous. He'd be, you know, tearing down this old shack, or he'd be sweeping up filth or dirt and he started to show me one day and I didn't believe him about the album and how it got to be so popular. Somebody [in South Africa] had a bootleg copy of this thing and it spread around [. . .] It got to be so popular that children could recite it and sing the songs word for word, all the songs word for word, and I had never heard of the album and I said can you get me an album and he couldn't even get me one. I mean, that's how obscure of a thing it was, but he had all these, you know, photos and stuff, with these giant crowds, 20,000 people, like Woodstock or something . . . Are you kidding me, that's you? I thought it was photoshopped or something, I didn't believe him. But he had all these giant crowds and he was quite content to just go and sweep up people's lawns or clean up and do manual labour.

Sugar felt it necessary to give Rodriguez proof of his other life; proof of his dreamlike interlude of glitz and fame so he could mollify the cynics around him. Pleased with his idea, Sugar flew to Detroit from New York one morning, soaring over Manhattan, the whole island stretching out before him, the Twin Towers clearly visible. From the airport, he caught a cab into the city, and along the way noticed a sign on the highway pointing to Dearborn, which gave his little excursion a nice opening ring. The taxi took him straight to Rodriguez's home, a double-storey house the singer had bought near the Wayne State University campus for $50 around forty years earlier. Rodriguez lived on the ground floor and Regan upstairs.

They were keen to see the film and immediately went up to Regan's living room to watch it. Tonia's documentary captured the spirit of the historic tour, and so enraptured was Rodriguez that he and Sugar immediately watched it again. A friend of Regan's who was present was completely amazed that Regan's dad, the guy who she knew worked on construction sites, was actually an international superstar. 'Watching her trying to reconcile that fact was very funny indeed and a sign of things to come,' said Sugar afterwards.

The next day Rodriguez drove his South African guest around Detroit and introduced him to some of his friends and fellow artists, musicians and workers. Later they attended Rodriguez's birthday party at Sandra's house, where Sugar met up with the family – first wife Rayma, second wife Konny, and daughters Sandra and Regan. Curiously, Rodriguez's wife and ex-wife seemed capable of coexisting harmoniously. It was a surreal moment for the boy from Emmarentia. Sugar took the opportunity to discuss the upcoming tour and agreed to meet Rodriguez on his arrival in Johannesburg to help him settle in and prepare.

When Sugar flew back home that August, he once again saw Manhattan spread out before him, unaware of the great tragedy that was about to unfold at the World Trade Center. Rodriguez's tour would already be under way when the 9/11 terrorist attacks occurred, and it would have a great effect on the singer as well as the trip.

The problem with getting a taste of rock stardom in your late fifties is that there is no rock-star handbook, no *Rock Star*

101. The second tour to South Africa was to have its fair share of drama and ups and downs. As time went by, Sugar became increasingly involved as a facilitator. Erickson had recruited Johannesburg-based events company Authentic Ideas to handle the basic details of the tour. A few days before Rodriguez was scheduled to arrive in South Africa, Sugar flew up to Johannesburg to be there for the singer's arrival as per their agreement. He met with Nancy Hillary and her Authentic Ideas team, but Nancy seemed unfriendly towards him and he didn't feel at all welcome or useful, so he left. Somewhat bizarrely, given it was for a musician who eschews extravagance, Erickson had planned a massive media launch to be held on the pool deck of the Westcliff Hotel, a signature Orient-Express Hotel, and a lavish setting for a man who sings about poverty and the dire conditions of inner-city Detroit. The only grounding aspect was the sight of elephants in the zoo below. Waiting for the press conference to start some time after leaving the airport, Sugar was both amused and taken aback by the evening's ironies. Little did he know that things were about to get really weird.

The pool deck boasts a magnificent view of Johannesburg, and the early-evening city lights twinkled below as the assembled journalists and other media folk waited for the star's arrival. The problem, however, was that Rodriguez had missed his connecting flight from New York to Johannesburg and was, at that very moment, wandering around JFK International Airport. The story being spun at the launch was that this behaviour was typical Rodriguez – slack, casual. 'He's not dead, he's just late,' one wag suggested.

Erickson was determined to have his press conference, however, so from the pool deck of the Westcliff Hotel he managed to get someone at JFK to put out a public-address announcement over the airport's intercom system requesting Rodriguez to present himself at the desk of the airline he was flying. Rodriguez heard the announcement and went to the counter, where he was handed a phone. It was Erickson, who put his mobile to the microphone so that everyone at the Westcliff could hear his conversation with the musician. Erickson then asked the backing band, which was set up and waiting, to play 'I Wonder', to which Rodriguez, standing at the airline counter more than twelve thousand kilometres away, sang along for a few verses. In spite of the bizarre nature of the launch, the press got the message: Rodriguez was coming.

Later, the singer gave his audiences a whole host of alternate reasons why he was not able to make the press conference that night. Eizik, in turn, blamed FedEx for not delivering the airline ticket in time. Sugar later found out that the real reason Rodriguez had missed his flight was because he had insisted on an advance payment from Erickson and Eizik, based on his earlier experience, and had refused to leave the US until he had been compensated with the agreed-upon amount.

The backing band Eizik had chosen for the tour was the Big Town Playboys, a jazzy R&B group from Britain who had never even heard of Rodriguez or his music. The Playboys were session musicians under the leadership of the band's bass player, an on-and-off bassist for Van Morrison. At the time, Erickson managed Van Morrison's European tours, which was how he came to put the band together, and why they now found themselves at what can only be termed the strangest tour launch of their lives. Little did the Playboys know that this was just a taste of things to come.

Rodriguez arrived in Johannesburg a few days later and

the tour management checked him into a lavish suite at the Westcliff Hotel. The plan was for him to meet the band and have a few rehearsals before the opening concert. When Rodriguez and the Big Town Playboys finally got together for a short one-hour rehearsal, he discovered that there were no strings on his guitar. The rehearsal couldn't go ahead and so they were far from ready when the time came to play in front of an audience. As a result of this, things were slightly frosty between the band and Rodriguez going into the first of the two opening concerts at the Carnival City entertainment complex near Johannesburg.

Rodriguez always got a rapturous welcome when appearing on any South African stage, and that night was no different. But the crowd soon realised that the backing band was not familiar with his songs and was playing in more of an R&B style, which wasn't what they had come to hear. Another problem was the recently promulgated ban on smoking indoors, which had only recently taken effect in South Africa. Without cigarette smoke to mask the smell, people were reluctant to light up a joint, as one does at a Rodriguez concert, which seemed to have a negative effect on the crowd in the auditorium. Ultimately, the concert fell a little flat.

The second night went better thanks to the fact that Rodriguez and the band had had some time to practise. But that was not the only reason. When Sugar escorted Rodriguez onto the stage to begin his set, he noticed a large fan behind the drummer, the purpose of which was to keep the band cool. Inspired, Sugar lit up a spliff and blew the smoke into the fan, which had the effect of dispersing the herb around the room and seemed to give everyone in the venue tacit permission to go ahead and light up. As a result, the auditorium soon had the correct vibe, not to mention the correct aroma, for a Rodriguez concert. The crowd from the second night went home a lot happier than the first.

After that, the Rodriguez show hit the road and rolled around Gauteng Province, even stopping for a concert at a game lodge near Pretoria. Unfortunately, this was the site of yet another fiasco. Either the lodge or the advertising and/or ticket-sales company got the start time wrong, so half the crowd only arrived as the concert was ending. Sugar watched in horror as a long line of paid-up customers drove in for a show that was technically over. Authentic Ideas had to do a lot of smooth-talking, as well as find a way to compensate the irate crowd. Nancy and her crew were not having a good day. And if that wasn't enough, a group of heavy, mulleted Hells Angels arrived on the scene, insisting that they wanted first dibs on any cash Erickson received.

As the tour ground on, things only got worse.

It all came to a head during the first of two concerts at the 3 Arts Theatre in Cape Town. Sugar was in the audience when Rodriguez came onstage that first night. Even from a distance, he could see that the singer looked a little out of it and was being supported by some crewmembers. Rodriguez immediately let everyone know that he was tanked up and, as the concert began, it was clear that he was in no condition to perform properly.

From the outset, it was a shambles. Rodriguez stopped songs midway, slurred into the microphone and constantly harassed the band. Many in the audience simply walked out in disappointment. Thirty minutes in, the crowd was half the size it had been when Rodriguez first came onstage. Then it all broke down when the band responded to something Rodriguez had said by putting down their instruments and walking offstage en masse, leaving him alone to face his audience. Sugar could do nothing but look on with dismay. After so many years in the wilderness, waiting for his time to come, now that it had, Rodriguez was blowing it in style. For a moment there was just an awkward silence. Then someone threw what looked like a joint onto the stage. It landed near Rodriguez, who picked it up, lit it and inhaled deeply, to the audience's obvious delight. Whatever he was smoking seemed to sober him up and he resumed playing, really well. The audience responded positively, and after a little while the band filed back onto the stage, picked up their instruments and began to play. Rodriguez almost blew it all over again by asking the audience – rhetorically – if they thought the show was better without the band. Thankfully, the Playboys stayed onstage and finished the set with a strong performance that hadn't seemed possible an hour earlier.

As if finding Rodriguez the first time hadn't been hard enough, Sugar was relaxing at home the next day, a Saturday, when he got a call from one of the singer's minders to tell him that Rodriguez had gone missing from his hotel in Sea Point. They had no idea where he was and he had to be ready for his second concert in Cape Town that evening. For the first part of the tour, Sugar had acted as Rodriguez's direct minder, but during the Johannesburg leg he had been gradually pushed into the background because the tour organisers felt he was a bad influence on the singer. In Sugar's opinion, it was the complete opposite. So when he got the call to help find Rodriguez, he felt slightly vindicated. In addition, it was his son Rafi's thirteenth birthday and the whole family planned to be in the front row for that evening's concert. This made Sugar even more determined that they would not be made to witness the previous night's spectacle.

So off he went to look for Rodriguez. He drove around Sea Point, and after a while and by complete chance came across the resurrected rock star. He was with two local girls who had found him wandering around and had recognised him and taken him under their wing, with the idea of showing him the city before delivering him safely back to his hotel. Rodriguez was in no great shape, but there was still some time before the concert, and so Sugar put him to bed, closed the door and watched a rugby match on TV while the singer slept it off.

The second Cape Town concert was a wonderful evening for all concerned. Rodriguez made up for the previous night's dramatics by playing one of the finest sets Sugar had ever seen him play. The band responded with a great all-round performance, and the whole audience, including the Segerman family in the front row, had an absolute treat and a night they would never forget. Afterwards, Rodriguez came out and signed the line; he was kind, generous and gracious to everyone who had waited to meet him.

Rodriguez was in South Africa on 11 September 2001. Like countless other Americans back home, his wife Konny drove down to New York to help out in any way she could. Rodriguez felt very uncomfortable being in a foreign country with a tour to complete and no way to get back to the States, with all the flights in and out of the US being suspended.

As a sign of allegiance, he started wearing a small American flag that protruded from the top-left-hand chest pocket of his black leather jacket. One day he and Sugar took a walk around downtown Cape Town and found themselves at Greenmarket Square, a large flea market in the middle of the city. Many people in the square recognised him. Some kept a respectful distance, while others approached him and politely introduced themselves. Rodriguez, as always, was civil and kind to them. But a small gang of street kids came into the market looking for hand-outs from the locals and tourists alike. Noticing the Stars and Stripes on Rodriguez's jacket, which singled him out as a foreigner with money to give, they mobbed him. The singer, unaware of the ferocity of these gangs of children that roamed the city centre, generously pulled out a roll of banknotes and started distributing them to the kids. This set off a wild response from the children, who swarmed all over him, forcing Sugar to intervene. Rodriguez was visibly shaken by the incident and asked to leave immediately. Back at Sugar's house in Oranjezicht, Rodriguez took his guitar and sat with the Segerman kids out in the garden, where they played songs to one another until he had calmed down from the whole experience. Sugar's daughter Natalia had just recently begun playing the guitar and Rodriguez's compliments were warmly welcomed.

The rest of the tour went off smoothly. By the end, Rodriguez and the band were getting on much better and feeling a lot tighter with the songs they were playing. Soon it was time for the singer to head back home. Unfortunately, rumours circulated later that he hadn't received a cent from that sixteen-date tour. Authentic Ideas had a miserable time trying to keep the whole affair going and suffered substantial losses too.

At nearly sixty, Rodriguez was experiencing all the teething problems that a tour musician thirty to forty years his junior would have to go through. His records were no longer being pressed in the country that had most whole-heartedly embraced his music. With each bad performance he seemed to be alienating his core fan base. And you still could not find a single copy of a Rodriguez album in the United States. Without some kind of drastic impetus, it looked as if his future was panning out to be a series of on-and-off gigs in South Africa, strung together by the reality of backbreaking menial labour in Motor City, performed in quiet obscurity.

Of course, what Rodriguez could not know was that this trickle of recognition would build into a tsunami that would take his career to places beyond his wildest dreams. Elsewhere on the planet – in different countries – three curious individuals were waiting in the wings to take his career to a whole new level: an Irishman, an American and a Swede.

12

Come get it I got it
(2002–2005)

'This film's crap, let's slash the seats.'
— DAVID HOLMES, MUSICIAN AND COMPOSER

It would take an Irish former hairdresser and chef, who once ran a nightclub coincidentally called Sugar Sweet, to give Rodriguez's music the next push it needed. Belfast-born DJ and producer David Holmes is nothing if not musically enterprising. He is also something of a 'genre agnostic'. This is not surprising: with nine siblings, he was exposed to the full gamut of musical styles from an early age, including Motown, R&B, Latin jazz, punk rock, film scores and disco. His creative streak has led to albums with titles like *This Film's Crap Let's Slash the Seats*, *Let's Get Killed* and *Bow Down to the Exit Sign*. When not composing music film scores for the likes of Danny DeVito (*Out of Sight*) and Steven Soderbergh (the *Ocean's* trilogy), Holmes produces remix albums. One, released in 2002 and titled *Come Get It I Got It*, featured a reinvigorated remix of none other than Rodriguez's 'Sugar Man'.

Come Get It I Got It is described on Amazon.com as 'an eclectic mix of Northern soul, funk, blues and electronica'. After a short intro, the album opens with a melancholic version of 'Sugar Man' and also includes 'Tom Cat', a bluesy Muddy Waters rarity. 'Sugar Man' is presented almost entirely in its original form as recorded by Theo-Coff, with the exception of minimal audio overlays at the beginning and the end of the track to help with the segues. Besides appearing on the LP, the remixed 'Sugar Man' was also released as a limited-edition seven-inch single along with Holmes's version of 'Tom Cat'. Only 500 copies were pressed, making it a collector's item today.

It just so happened that Craig Strydom was reading in a hotel bar while on a stopover in London on his way back to the US, when he heard the newly released track playing and impulsively called out, 'That's Rodriguez!' He was greeted with bemused looks. Craig had moved to St John's, Newfoundland, in June 1999, and a year later he took a job in Baltimore, Maryland, where he would stay for the next twelve years. For now, his involvement in the Rodriguez story was a thing of the past.

In July 2002, a local South African music company called PT Music (as in 'Phase Two') announced that it had acquired the South African rights to the Rodriguez record catalogue – the one inexplicably dropped by Universal a few years earlier – and that it would soon be re-releasing *Cold Fact* and *After the Fact – Coming from Reality*. In a previous business incarnation, PT's managing director, the charismatic Terry Fairweather, had pulled off an enviable coup by picking up the South African licence to press and distribute a largely unknown Sheffield band called the Human League, at the time on the Virgin Records label. His timing couldn't have been better. The first single to appear by the newly licensed band was the world number-one hit, 'Don't You Want Me'.

How PT Music acquired the Rodriguez catalogue is quite remarkable. The Copyright Group sent Fairweather a list of artists that were up for licensing. Scrolling through the publishing company's catalogue of largely unknown and no longer relevant acts, he came across a listing for a 'Rod Riguez'. As a South African, the name rang a bell. Surely this wasn't the same Rodriguez that he had grown up listening to? As it turned out, it was. When he asked what albums he would acquire if he bought the rights to the package, Fairweather was told that there were two albums under that name, *Cold Fact* and *Coming from Reality*. He could not believe his luck. Business sense told him that he had no option but to buy the package lock, stock and barrel, which he did. To write the liner notes and correct the lyrics (which were riddled with errors), Fairweather turned to Sugar and his partner, Brian Currin, who by this stage had merged Sugar's Great Rodriguez Site and Currin's Climb Up On My Music websites to form one site known as Sugarman.org, and who were fast becoming the custodians of various Rodriguez ephemera. The merger had two distinct advantages. Firstly, over the next decade it became the single most comprehensive resource for everything Rodriguez-related. Secondly, it allowed Sugar to become the official gatekeeper for anything pertaining to the singer's music.

Shortly thereafter, the albums *Cold Fact* and *After the Fact – Coming from Reality* were reintroduced to South African audiences.

*

In the meantime, on 10 July 2002, Rodriguez celebrated his sixtieth birthday. A few days later, an article by English music journalist Tim Forster appeared in the UK music magazine *Mojo*. In the 'Buried Treasure' section, devoted to forgotten classics, the article, a review of *Cold Fact*, begins:

> Ask the question 'Who is Rodriguez?' of any Australian or South African music fan and there will probably be more than a glimmer of recognition. Ask any American and you'll almost certainly draw a blank.

The write-up, the first full-scale positive review of a Rodriguez album by a bona fide music publication outside of South Africa or Australia, is informative and engaging, and perfectly describes the particulars of the lost gem.

> Establishment Blues, a soapbox rant of rhyming couplets, almost parodied the protest song ('Gun sales are soaring/ Housewives find life boring/Divorce the only answer/ Smoking causes cancer') while Inner City Blues – a title that pipped Marvin Gaye by six months – pitched the runaway girl in the city against her suburban parents ('The curfew's set for eight/Will it ever be straight/I doubt it').

There is no doubt the article piqued the interest of music enthusiasts everywhere. The forum messages that Sugar and Currin received at Sugarman.org – by now an accurate barometer of Rodriguez activity and sentiment – confirm this. And then, to cap off a good year for the artist, the December 2002 issue of *Mojo* ranked 'Sugar Man' at number thirty-four in their list of '100 Greatest Drug Songs Ever', beating fellow Detroit band MC5's 'Kick Out the Jams' by ten spots. (The number-one spot went to Jefferson Airplane's 'White Rabbit'.)

Then, in 2003, Sugar helped arrange for Rodriguez and Regan to drive up to New York to meet and work with David Holmes at Avatar Studios (formerly known as the Power Station). Here Rodriguez added backing vocals to a new version of 'Sugar Man', which was recorded by Holmes's recently formed band, the Free Association, with Petra Jean Phillipson on lead vocals.

It's a catchy version of the song. If anything, the Free Association took the drug inferences quite literally when recording and mixing the track. Theodore and Coffey's original analogue-born, ethereal arrangement is still present, but is heightened by the addition of layers of electronica. Phillipson's vocals are 'druggy', for lack of a better word, and purposely *desafinado* (off-key). All in all, the recording is reminiscent of the treatment a seventies film director would give to a drug scene – the audio equivalent of double exposure – in order to underscore the moment. And, oddly, the song closes with a London-style rap.

Phillipson was the natural choice for 'Sugar Man'. She says of herself:

I rebelled as a child. I'd write songs to myself about Paddington Bear. Lost in London. I had a very natural instinct for music, in later years I have found I have a photographic memory of lyrics, but was very shy. None of my teachers recognised my talent. I was put in remedial English only to be moved to the top set the next week. They couldn't work me out.

It was the first time in thirty years that Rodriguez found himself back in the studio. Slowly but surely he was breaking into the American music scene, one small step at a time.

Back in Cape Town, aside from running Sugarman.org with Currin, Sugar continued to review albums for *SA Rock Digest* and teach at Varsity College. One day while exploring the neighbourhood between lectures, he came across a small record store forming part of a bigger bric-a-brac concern on Kloof Street. DJ and vinyl enthusiast Jacques Vosloo ran the record section – or record room, for that's all it was at first – which he had named Mabu Vinyl, after a stance in kung fu. Happy to meet a kindred spirit, Sugar offered to promote the record store by giving it a weekly spot in the *SA Rock Digest* newsletter, where he would list all the new vinyl records that came into Mabu each week. He knew he was onto something when well-known music producer Patric van Blerk, the man behind the band Rabbitt, popped in one day after reading about it in the *Digest*.

After a while, Vosloo struck out on his own, moving Mabu Vinyl to a prominent intersection at the top of Long Street. In the meantime, Sugar, in his job as album reviewer for the ever-growing *SA Rock Digest*, had amassed a large number of new CDs, mostly samples that had been given to him to review, and for which he now had little use. He needed to find a place to trade them, and that's when the idea came to him. Visiting Mabu one day, he had noticed that a section of the sidewalk right outside the store – a triangular piece of real estate measuring around six-by-six-by-four feet – actually belonged to the store but wasn't being used. Sugar asked Vosloo if he could rent the space, and on 1 November

2003 Sugar resumed work as an entrepreneur, albeit with a postage-stamp-sized CD stall.

Over time, Vosloo's love for surfing meant that Sugar found himself running the whole store more and more, eventually almost every day. Finally, they agreed to combine the two businesses and become equal partners in a concern that Sugar would run for their mutual benefit. Over time they built the iconic record store and tourist destination that Mabu Vinyl is today, first on the busy corner at the top of Long Street, and then, several years later, at Rheede Street, near where they first started. Mabu would come full circle.

At last Sugar had a well-stocked business that was paying his bills and keeping him happy and busy. His other unofficial job, that of publicist to Rodriguez, continued, but with no obvious direction, until one day the singer received another invitation to return to southern Africa.

Rodriguez's eldest daughter Eva had developed other reasons for visiting South Africa after her father's first tour in 1998. She had obtained leave from her air-force base in Kansas to join Rodriguez for the tour, and during those three weeks she began a relationship with Juan Introna, the South African driver and bodyguard assigned to Rodriguez. The romance went from strength to strength, with the result that when Eva returned to her base in the US, Juan went with her. On completion of her military duties, Eva received a large pension and she and Juan returned to South Africa, where they bought a piece of land on one of the hills above the sleepy seaside village of Wilderness along the Western Cape's Garden Route. Coincidentally, their purchase was a stone's throw from Craig Strydom's brother Adrian's house in Wilderness Heights, where Craig did a lot of his initial

Rodriguez research. Eva and Juan built a house on their land and settled down to a life on the South African coast. The couple's only son, Ethan, was born soon after.

With a grandson in South Africa, Rodriguez was eager to visit. An opportunity presented itself in 2004 when he received an invitation to perform a one-off concert in a city called Otjiwarongo in Namibia. Meaning 'a pleasant place where fat cattle graze', Otjiwarongo has roughly 70,000 inhabitants and is located about 400 kilometres from the capital Windhoek in the former South African protectorate. The concert was to form part of the Cheetah National Arts Festival. On 10 July 2004, on his sixty-second birthday, Rodriguez landed in Windhoek where he was met by Eva and a few other South Africans who had travelled there to see him perform. The concert was largely unexceptional owing to the fact that, once again, Rodriguez had to play with a completely new set of musicians with whom he'd had very little opportunity to rehearse. After the show, Rodriguez travelled to Wilderness and spent some time helping Eva and Juan with the construction of some buildings on their property. He enjoyed being with his new extended family, spending downtime in such a beautiful area, working hard and hanging out with his grandson Ethan.

During his visit, Rodriguez read about a local band called Garden Root, who were performing a series of concerts in the nearby coastal town of Knysna. They had several of his songs in their repertoire and, intrigued at the idea, Rodriguez, Eva and her family headed off to watch them. The trio consisted of Graeme Sindall on lead guitar and vocals, his brother Heath Sindall on drums, and Neil Lord on bass. It was a particularly memorable night for the young band when after the show they discovered that Rodriguez was actually in the audience. A journalist caught wind of the story, and a week or so later a feature appeared in the nationwide *Sunday Times*.

This seemed like an opportune time for some shows, and so a brief tour was quickly arranged, with Garden Root as Rodriguez's new backing band. Together they put in some lengthy rehearsals and played three sold-out gigs in the middle of August. The first and largest was in nearby Mossel Bay at a venue called the Barnyard, and the two smaller gigs were in Wilderness Heights at a community centre called Back of the Moon. The concerts were pretty raucous, the mostly local audiences spilling onto the small stage and Rodriguez struggling to stay in the groove with his young band. But, as with any Rodriguez concert in South Africa, regardless of the venue, the crowd or the band *du jour*, the three gigs were momentous and layered with maximum nostalgia, joy and respect. His South African fans were more than happy simply to be in the same room as their idol and to hear him sing their favourite songs. Like Bob Dylan, another performer who never seemed to give his fans exactly what they were looking for, Rodriguez left his devotees satisfied by just showing up and playing a few tunes.

After the tour, it was back to the anonymity of Detroit, where the singer settled back into his working and family life, and waited for the next unexpected stop on his journey. That would come in 2005, when Terry Fairweather announced that PT Music were about to release a remastered version of *Cold Fact*, as well as a new Rodriguez compilation called *Sugarman: The Best of Rodriguez*, which would include most of the best tracks from *Cold Fact* and *Coming from Reality* and the final recordings from the Pampa sessions with Theo-Coff: 'I'll Slip Away', 'Street Boy' and 'Can't Get Away'. The album also included as a bonus track the original Harry Balk recording of 'I'll Slip Away', a version of the song never before heard in South Africa.

Once again, Sugar was tasked with writing the liner notes, chronicling the whole Rodriguez story up to that date. In addition, he and Currin wrote short descriptions for each of the tracks on the album. Fairweather was keen to organise some kind of promotional event to launch his two new releases, but flying Rodriguez out to South Africa would be too costly, and no other option presented itself.

13

London calling

(2005)

'Yes, London. You know, fish, chips, cup o' tea,
bad food, worse weather. Mary fucking Poppins.
London!'

— DENNIS FARINA AS COUSIN AVI IN *SNATCH*

It started out so nice. But it didn't end that well. London is a
long way from home when you're no longer wanted.

It all began when Sugar received a call from Josh Georgiou,
a Johannesburg club owner and music promoter. Josh and
Sugar shared a history, having both grown up in the same
area: Sugar in Emmarentia, Josh on the Greenside side of
Barry Hertzog Avenue, the road that divides the two suburbs. Josh's parents ran a convenience store called the Milk
Bar in the local shopping centre. Sugar remembered the
younger boy from the days when they used to spend their
time playing pinball and reading comics in Josh's father's
store. The two had lost touch until Sugar realised that Milk
Bar Kid, the DJ from Johannesburg who he and Brian Currin

had been mentioning and promoting in *SA Rock Digest*, was actually Josh playing under the moniker of his dad's old shop. Besides being a top DJ, he had been an A&R man for Sony, signing the Springbok Nude Girls, South Africa's biggest rock band of the nineties.

In 2005, when Josh called Sugar, he and his partner Alan Freeman were the co-owners of the hippest underground music club in Johannesburg, the legendary 206 on Louis Botha Avenue in Orange Grove. But Josh and Alan were looking to add some new business opportunities to their already successful and thriving venture, and they wanted to take Rodriguez on his first tour of London. They asked Sugar to help arrange the trip and act as the singer's manager/ minder for the duration. He accepted, and over the course of a few weeks the whole thing was arranged. One of the strongest motivators for the London tour was David Broido, a South African bass player living in London. For the longest time, David had nurtured a fervent desire to play a gig backing Rodriguez at the famous Kentish Town Forum, primarily so that he could walk to the venue, which was close to where he was living. He had suggested to his good friends Josh and Alan that they arrange the tour.

Ultimately, it became a 206 Productions (Josh and Alan), Sugar Music (Sugar and Currin) and PT Music (Terry Fairweather) co-production. The plan was for Rodriguez to fly to Cape Town, where he would stay at a guesthouse next door to Sugar's house in Oranjezicht and play four warm-up gigs, before heading to London for two concerts at the Forum. With the contractual details out of the way, a three-piece backing band was selected. David Broido got his wish and flew back to South Africa. Officially known as the Blue Coins, the band eventually featured David on bass, the talented and experienced multi-instrumentalist Sean Ou Tim on drums, and Sasha Sonnbichler on guitar. As soon as Rodriguez arrived in Cape Town, rehearsals began in a designated downstairs room in Sugar's house. As with most South African musicians who end up backing Rodriguez, the songs were already part of their musical DNA, which meant that in no time at all they developed a rapport with the singer.

The four concerts planned for the Cape Town leg of the tour were after all also an opportunity to promote the new *Sugarman: Best of Rodriguez* album. There would be two events at the Independent Armchair Theatre in Observatory, a small music venue that held around 250 people; a short promotional gig at the CD Wherehouse, a music megastore down at the V&A Waterfront; and one in Stellenbosch, a student town near Cape Town, where Sugar's daughter Natalia was to be the opening act. (Yes, Sugar admits it was a case of nepotism.) The week of rehearsals was a success and Rodriguez and the band gelled, forming a good working relationship that boded well for the upcoming tour. When not rehearsing, the singer enjoyed walking around the city where he was recognised and greeted by loyal Capetonians. Typically, he would take the time to speak to his fans when approached.

Eva, Juan and Ethan travelled to Cape Town from Wilderness to visit and ensure that everything went off smoothly. Although Sugar had been officially tasked by Josh and Alan to keep Rodriguez happy and in good shape for the shows – both in Cape Town and in London – and was being paid to do so, it didn't take long for Eva and Juan to slip back into their respective roles of manager and bodyguard-cum-driver. Sugar felt this was having a negative effect on his role, as Rodriguez always had the highest regard for his daughters' abilities and opinions, and after a while it became clear that he preferred having Eva look after his affairs. Without a massive budget for the tour, the places Rodriguez stayed at, both in Cape Town and in London, were never going to be five-star. But they were still, in Sugar's opinion, adequate. However, Eva wanted better for her father and Sugar sensed that the singer wanted to find a way to get Eva back in charge. His suspicions were soon confirmed.

The date was 29 September 2005, and Eva and Juan insisted on picking up Rodriguez from Sugar's house. In terms of the contract, Sugar was meant to take Rodriguez to every venue, but he let it pass. The Independent Armchair Theatre, known to locals simply as 'Armchair', was a low-brow rock venue in the mostly student suburb of Observatory, close to the University of Cape Town. Situated on Lower Main Road, this gem was surrounded by grungy bars, second-hand shops and liquor stores. There were only 250 tickets available for each performance and they sold out quickly. The opportunity to see Rodriguez in such a small, intimate venue was too good to be true. With Armchair filled to the brim, however, it was a crazy, sweaty and chaotic evening. The band had to work hard to stay with Rodriguez and conquer the inferior sound at the same time, but the crowd lapped it up and it was a huge success.

Not for everyone, though. The backstage 'dressing rooms' were situated upstairs and contained just a few old chairs and tables scattered around, not really befitting a rock star. Rodriguez and Eva were not happy to begin with, and then it really all fell apart. Already disgruntled, Eva drew attention to a bare electrical wire lying in one of the rooms. Shortly afterwards, there was an electrical short in the room and the lights went out. Rodriguez saw this as proof of his daughter's vigilance and wisdom, and became more determined than ever to have her as his manager. Sugar began to feel increasingly uncomfortable from that moment on.

After a few days' break, the planned promotional gig at CD Wherehouse rolled around. Scheduled for two o'clock in the afternoon, Rodriguez, Sugar and the entourage arrived early to walk around the V&A Waterfront and grab some lunch. Many passers-by recognised the singer in his black outfit and trademark hat. When they arrived at the venue, Rodriguez was feeling nervous, so Sugar asked the store manager if there was a private room where the singer and band could have some quiet time and possibly smoke. The manager showed them to a small room just off the main shop floor. Rodriguez began tuning his guitar and lit up. Suddenly there was an urgent rap on the door; it was the store manager. He was freaking out because he thought they meant cigarettes when they asked for a place to smoke. A joint was simply out of the question, as the smell, aided by the air conditioning, was permeating the store.

Rodriguez and his entourage gathered their collective wits and entered the large shop, which by then had completely filled up with fans. The singer charmed the crowd with four or five of his best-known songs before stepping down from the small stage to sign CDs and other paraphernalia for a long line of admirers. All in all it was a fun promotion and the Rodriguez road show could have stayed there all day, but they still had to get across to Stellenbosch for that evening's concert at the Dorp Street Theatre.

An hour's drive from Cape Town, Stellenbosch is a beautiful and historic town. It is surrounded by some of the Cape's finest vineyards, having been settled and farmed since the late 1600s by both the Dutch and the French. It is also a well-known student town, home to the highly regarded University of Stellenbosch. The Dorp Street Theatre is one of a row of semi-detached old Cape Dutch–style double-storey buildings. The venue is on the ground floor and is a medium-sized restaurant with long tables and a stage at the far end. The performers were housed in rooms next door.

There was an unfortunate incident before the gig when Sugar told Eva's son to quieten down because he was disturbing Natalia's practice and relaxation. It was Natalia's first major gig and she was very nervous. Eva and Juan did not like Sugar telling Ethan what to do and reprimanded him. The incident created an unpleasant atmosphere and, in Sugar's mind, further undermined his official standing. But he avoided confronting the couple, as he knew they wouldn't be going to London.

The venue filled up quickly and Natalia played a solo set with just her guitar, performing six of her songs. She had written some strong songs over the years, and had even released a CD called *Long Street Lullabies* featuring the best of them. She received an enthusiastic response from the audience. But the man they had all come to see was up next and the crowd rose to give him a standing ovation. Sugar remembers it as a wonderful show, noticeably less raucous than the Armchair concert that preceded it, owing to the fact that everyone was seated at tables. The audience responded ecstatically to every song. Sugar was standing off to the side of the stage when Rodriguez played 'Crucify Your Mind'. As he sang the line '*As a tear rolls down your cheek*', Sugar turned to the waitress standing next to him, to see a tear rolling down her cheek.

The next afternoon, Clem Leech, who was handling the London side of the tour for 206 Productions, arranged interviews for Rodriguez with two UK newspapers, the *Guardian* and the *Telegraph*. Well-known South African writer Rian Malan would conduct the interview for the *Telegraph*, while the highly respected music journalist Alexis Petridis would write for the *Guardian*. The team was thrilled to have two such distinguished journalists doing a story on Rodriguez. Sugar invited Rian to his house for the interview. In 2000, Rian had written the acclaimed two-part exposé for *Rolling Stone* on the late Solomon Linda, the Zulu musician who wrote the song 'Mbube', later immortalized as 'The Lion Sleeps Tonight' and who had been cheated out of a lifetime of royalties. Rodriguez was in a talkative mood that day, and the interview took an unusual turn when Alexis got put through on the speakerphone while Rian was in the room. In the end, Alexis interviewed Rodriguez over the phone with Rian observing and listening in. The South African then wrote his piece based on that conversation and what he witnessed in Sugar's den. Both esteemed journalists lived up to their reputations and wrote excellent pieces, which greatly helped 206 Productions spread the word about the tour around London.

The second Armchair concert was just as hectic as the first, the place packed once again to capacity. The main purpose of the series of small Cape Town gigs was not to make a ton of money for Rodriguez, but rather to get him and the band tight and confident for the more important London shows. Not only would the latter be more lucrative, but they were the first concerts that Rodriguez, in his new incarnation, would play in a country other than South Africa. A few days later, when the time came to depart, the singer seemed happy with his band, and was relaxed and ready for the trip. The Rodriguez show hit the road once more, this time boarding a plane for London.

*

While waiting at Heathrow for Konny to fly in from Detroit, Sugar walked over to the newsstand and bought the latest issues of the *Guardian* and the *Telegraph*. Alexis and Rian had written positive articles, both solid inducements to anyone who had even the vaguest idea of Rodriguez's existence to buy tickets for one of the two performances before they sold out. As it happened, neither concert sold out, despite some innovative marketing by 206 Productions, including the printing of hundreds of long rectangular flyers in black, the size of a large knife blade, with lines from Rodriguez songs on one side – '*I wonder how many times you've had sex*' or '*A monkey in silk is a monkey no less*' – and details of the two Forum gigs on the other. These were widely distributed in places where South Africans and Australians were known to congregate.

On arrival in London, the group settled into their hotel. Because Rodriguez and the band were already well rehearsed, there was time to do some sightseeing and shopping before the two live gigs on Friday 7 October and Saturday 8 October. The support slots had been given to two deserving and emerging South African artists: Laurie Levine, a talented singer-songwriter with a beautiful voice, and Jim Neversink, a Durban musician, singer and songwriter whose eclectic musical style spanned indie rock, country, Americana and punk.

Accompanying the team was Josh and Alan's friend Justin Cohen, a young film student who in 2002 had co-created a half-hour short about the search for Rodriguez as part of his film degree. The film, *Looking for Jesus* (the title of Craig Strydom's first article on the search before it was changed by *Directions* magazine to 'Looking for Rodriguez'), had been screened at South African movie theatres and on the satellite TV network DStv. Local actors played the lead roles and, while mostly based on fact, some 'creative' fictional plot twists were added. The film concludes with the Strydom character travelling to Detroit, knocking on Rodriguez's door and then sitting on the porch while his idol sings 'Cause'. Once viewers got past the title and realised it wasn't a Christian film, word spread and it became increasingly popular. With that success in mind, Justin decided to get a decent camera and join the tour with the goal of filming it for a follow-up documentary.

It wasn't long before the earlier frictions and tensions between Sugar and Rodriguez returned. Mindful that 206 had tasked him with keeping Rodriguez content and in good shape for the concerts, Sugar made sure that access to alcohol was controlled. (The promoters had, however, ensured that there was plenty of weed around.) Even though Eva wasn't in London, Sugar felt her presence and was aware that things were not right between him and Rodriguez because of it. Nevertheless, they carried on, and after a few rehearsals at the Forum Rodriguez was ready for his London debut.

Although the promoters had put in massive effort to publicise the concerts, the venue was far from full on the first night. Nonetheless, it went off well. The crowd was made up predominantly of South African and Australian expats, who knew Rodriguez's music and appreciated the fact that they could see him in London. Laurie Levine and Jim Neversink received warm and hearty responses for their polished sets, and Sugar felt the pre-tour in Cape Town had done its job, as the ecstatic audience was treated to as good a Rodriguez performance as he had ever seen. The promoters were thrilled, and pleased with Sugar for keeping their star in shape. In what had become tradition, Sugar waited until at least two-thirds of the concert had passed before going out on the stage with a full glass of wine for Rodriguez, who then used it to toast his audience, to their great joy.

There was a celebratory atmosphere back at the hotel after that first concert. Everyone partied until late, in what Sugar refers to as 'the appropriate manner'. Team Rodriguez had to rouse themselves early the next morning, as the promoters had arranged for the singer to appear on BBC's Radio 4. Feeling a little worse for wear, the group jumped into a taxi and headed off to the studio. The programme turned out to be a round-table talk show with special guests discussing the art, music and film events occurring in London that weekend. Among them was Matt Lucas, one half of the popular UK TV show *Little Britain*. Everyone waited outside the studio, Rodriguez sitting quietly on a chair in a corner. No one paid much attention to the gentleman in the dark suit and hat holding a guitar. When his turn came, the host introduced their special musical guest and invited him to play a song. Rodriguez launched into 'The Establishment Blues' as the panel looked on, entranced. When the song ended, there was a long silence and then a collective releasing of air. They had just had their first taste of Rodriguez.

'Wow,' said the host, 'is this off your new album?'

When Rodriguez told them that the song was in fact off his debut album, *Cold Fact*, released some thirty-five years earlier, the panel was astounded at how the lyrics had retained their relevancy. Once the ice was broken, everyone seemed to get on really well and, in keeping with tradition, most of them retired to the nearest pub for a drink after-wards. Matt Lucas was warm and friendly, and enjoyed meeting Rodriguez. He promised that he would try his best to make the evening's show.

By the time that night's concert rolled around, word had spread among the South African and Australian expats that Rodriguez was indeed playing live at the Forum. As a result, the Saturday-night gig was close to full and the anticipatory buzz in the auditorium was even greater than before. The man they had all come to see was on top form and gave the best show of the whole tour. The audience sensed they were witnessing a special concert and responded accordingly with a mass sing-along and rapturous applause, plus a great reluctance to let Rodriguez leave until he had performed a second encore, a repeat of 'Sugar Man'.

The tour had been a great success, and so what happened next took the wind out of Sugar's sails completely. The next morning, 206 Productions called a meeting in a hotel conference room to discuss the possibility of Rodriguez playing one more concert in Johannesburg on his way back from London to Cape Town, where he was due to catch a flight back to Detroit. Sugar had joined the tour as Rodriguez's manager, but strictly speaking, according to the contract he had signed, his managerial mandate officially ended after the second and last concert in London. Rodriguez was aware of this.

As the first item of business, the singer asked if there was anyone who had no reason to be there and, if so, to leave the meeting. No one was quite sure what he meant at first, but then, looking at Sugar, Rodriguez announced that he no longer required his services as manager and that he should leave the room. Sugar was pretty shocked by this, but had no option other than to make an embarrassed exit. Sitting in his hotel room later, Sugar thought about what had transpired and realised that the storm between him and Rodriguez had been brewing for some time. It had its roots in the fact that he had always accompanied the singer on his South African tours as a friend and occasional minder. Now he was a manager, being paid to do a job. Sugar fully appreciated that, as a man of over sixty, and after all he'd been through, Rodriguez didn't need someone like Sugar telling him what he could or couldn't drink or smoke, or when. Having to 'police' the singer had definitely changed their relationship. Another contributing factor was most likely the emergence of Eva as a potential manager for her father, and the rivalry it seemed to create between her and Sugar.

Sugar spent the remaining day in London feeling very down and keen to get back home to Cape Town. The next day, while the group waited outside for their transport to Heathrow, it seemed to Sugar that Rodriguez was making a point of avoiding him and being unfriendly. They drove to the airport in an uncomfortable silence, which only got worse when they discovered they'd been seated next to each other for the eleven-hour flight back to Johannesburg. To make matters worse, both Rodriguez and Sugar had caught colds since leaving the hotel. Comically, the two sat side by side in their aeroplane seats, going through stacks of tissues and feeling pretty miserable. They didn't speak to each other for the entire journey, and on arrival at O.R. Tambo International Airport they said their frosty goodbyes.

It started out so nice. But it definitely didn't end that way.

14

Light at the end of the tunnel
(2006–2009)

'It's criminally insane that this classic material
isn't available in the United States.'
— Matt Sullivan, Light in the Attic Records

It took monumental effort to get Rodriguez's two studio
albums finally re-released in the United States. And like
most important things that occurred in the singer's career
post 1998, the email that started it all travelled around the
world and landed in Sugar Segerman's inbox. The date was
7 February 2006 and the missive read:

Hi Stephen:
Like lots of us, I'm a huge Rodriguez fan and wanted to get
in touch with you. I run a Seattle based label called Light
In The Attic Records, specializing in the reissue of long
lost gems. I'm curious if you might be able to put me in
touch with Rodriguez in regards to a long overdue reissue
of his catalog in North America? It's criminally insane

that this classic material isn't available in the States.

I imagine that Rodriguez could be earning a decent amount of publishing royalties with a U.S. domestic release. And of course musically, this is a record that must be heard and properly distributed here in North America. All of us here at Light In The Attic would love to release this in the right fashion as well – including new expanded notes, unseen photos, an enormous 24 page CD booklet, etc.

Light In The Attic is distributed worldwide, including North America, Asia, South Africa, Europe, and Australia, while recent press on the label has been featured in MOJO, The New York Times, Rolling Stone, Spin, and Q Magazine.

I look forward to hearing from you. Thank you for your time,

Matt Sullivan

Sugar sat back in his chair and wondered how in the world the owner of Light in the Attic had discovered Rodriguez's music. As it turned out, Matt had come across the singer through David Holmes's *Come Get It I Got It* remix album. Matt said that, in 2002,

I picked up the comp at a great (but sadly now defunct) record store in Seattle called JAM Records. The comp was a nice mix of David's favourite cuts and 'Sugar Man' was track number two. To say it blew my mind would be a massive understatement. That started my Rodriguez reissue quest, which led me to Sugar by simply emailing his website, saying, 'How can I find Rodriguez and reissue his music?' If my memory serves me right, Sugar responded within a day or so, saying that he had a few of our records in his shop and thought we'd do a good job on the reissues, put me in touch with Regan and off I went.

Actually, Sugar's email went like this:

Hi Matt,

I was standing in a CD store in central Cape Town yesterday just up the road from the second hand CD and record store that I run nearby. I was looking through the racks and saw the new double-CD, 'Last Poets' re-release that I had been looking for.

As I took it off the racks a voice behind me said 'Light In The Attic.' It was a record industry friend standing behind me who was trying to tell me that it was in fact your company that had released this. But as your company had been on my mind since we received your email regarding Rodriguez, and a possible Cold Fact CD re-release in the US, it was quite a strange, but welcomed, coincidence.

I have been working with and for Rodriguez for around 10 years now and I am as eager as you are to get him and his music into the broad American musical consciousness. I have no doubt that when the many Americans who do not know Rodriguez's music get to hear it, he will become as massive in the US as he should have been many years ago.

There have already been a few movies and documentaries made about him, and last October we got him onto a London stage which raised his international profile even more after some excellent press.

We are currently talking to a major movie director who is keen to make a feature film about Rodriguez and his story. All it would take is a film like that (with its built-in soundtrack), or the use of a track like Sugar Man in a major movie to finally kick-start Rodriguez's US career. A film in Australia last year [*Candy*, directed by Neil Armfield] featured the song 'Sugar Man,' and his following in Australia is massive.

So I am supportive of anyone who can help us get Rodriguez the US exposure he deserves. But there is one major stumbling block and that is Rodriguez himself. Despite putting many offers from many different sources in front of him, the past 30 years of 'nothing' from the music industry has made him reluctant to consider 'any' offers. We have been trying for years to unravel his copyright, publishing and royalties situation because they are all over the place. But nothing has moved forward.

This makes it very difficult for us as we regularly get approached from people all over the world asking about potential tours, CD re-releases, possible documentaries and features about him, interviews, and even gigs in the US in New York, San Francisco, San Diego, Seattle, and Canada.

He is very difficult to contact (he doesn't own a phone, a cell phone, a car, a TV or even a computer) and it is therefore difficult to discuss these things with him unless we leave a message for him to call us back from a pay phone. I can contact him, and get messages to him, through his family, but we are always reluctant to give out their contact info as he is a very private person and very protective of his family's safety and privacy. Often, it is just a fan wanting to meet him for personal reasons (which I know you are definitely not).

So your email reaches me just as I am almost ready to admit defeat here. From what I've read about 'Light In The Attic,' I'm sure you would do a great job re-releasing his albums, but I felt it necessary to give you the background info so that you are under no illusions as to how hard it would be to achieve this.

Still, one can only keep trying, and I strongly believe that his fame in the US is still coming. I will help anyone who can help us achieve this. I'm suggesting you send me a short proposal as to what you are considering and I will pass it on to him and ask him to contact you directly (or through me) if he is interested in taking this further.

Please understand that Rodriguez is a thoroughly decent gentleman from the old school, but he is very cautious of anyone from the industry with an offer to help. But balanced with that is the fact that although he lives a very modest existence, and really does work freelance on building sites for around $10 an hour, he has a large family and grand-children and he would be very happy if a deal were to be put in place that could secure his and his family's financial future.

So that is where we are at present. I'm only telling you all this because it is important you know this before moving forward.

Regards,

Sugar

The 'major movie director' mentioned in Sugar's email to Matt was none other than Phillip Noyce. But he was just one of many over the years who had made enquiries as to the possibility of turning Rodriguez's story into some kind of film project. At that stage, the Australian film director's attempt seems to have been the most serious. He was a big-time player, responsible for films such as *Dead Calm* (one of Nicole Kidman's first features), *Clear and Present Danger*,

Rabbit-Proof Fence and *Catch a Fire*, not to be confused with the Wailers album of the same name.

Noyce's 2006 film *Catch a Fire* is a biographical thriller set against the backdrop of apartheid. It was while filming in South Africa that Noyce and actor Tim Robbins visited 206 – the club owned by Josh Georgiou – and first heard the Rodriguez story. The veteran director had immediately recognised the potential for a strong feature-length plot and had contacted Sugar in Cape Town. By that stage Sugar was used to these kinds of approaches, but so far nothing had materialised. He was a little wary, and recalled an incident with a Dutch filmmaker the previous year during that fateful London tour.

Willemiek Kluijfhout had been working on a documentary about Rodriguez and had made contact with Sugar, asking to be put in touch with the singer. Sugar had agreed to help facilitate the process, and knew that Willemiek had gone to Detroit to film Rodriguez shortly before the London tour. He did not hear anything further until Willemiek let him know that she was in London to continue filming. When Sugar mentioned this to Rodriguez, the singer stated that if he found out Willemiek was anywhere near the Forum, never mind filming inside the venue during the concert, he would refuse to perform. Sugar was taken aback, as he was unaware that there'd been any problems. When he told Willemiek before the first concert, she was as surprised and seemed to have no idea why Rodriguez was behaving this way towards her. She was visibly distressed by the news, but there was nothing Sugar could do. To this day, Willemiek still has no idea what she may have done to offend the Rodriguez family. In light of this experience, how could Sugar ever be sure that Rodriguez would be willing to cooperate with any filmmaker? Yet he also always kept in mind the words of his late father-in-law, Lionel Benjamin, who would often say that when opportunity knocks, you must jump. When asked how one knew if it was a good opportunity, he would answer, 'I don't know, you just keep jumping.'

Film project aside, Matt wasted no time in replying to Sugar's email:

Hi Sugar,

WOW! It's wonderful to hear from you and a great surprise to know that you stumbled upon our 'Last Poets' re-release. So much love went into that project. And yes, a very strange coincidence indeed!

I definitely understand the sensitivity regarding Rodriguez and his fears of the music business. I've read it time and time again, but it continues to blow my mind that he still has not received proper royalties for his success in South Africa and Australia. As you know, that's just not right. This brings up a big issue … in regards to copyright ownership, who controls the publishing and master-rights for the albums Cold Fact and Coming From Reality, or, in other words, who do you believe controls these rights? Last week, I spoke with the US division of Sony-BMG regarding the ownership of the master rights for both albums, and was informed that [...] they do not own the material and do not know who does. (I suspected that it might be BMG, as Sussex Records was originally distributed/controlled (?) by Buddah, which is now owned and operated by Sony-BMG. Considering that, I'm imagining that Clarence Avant, the label's original owner, may still control Sussex.) I'd be more than happy to send over a proposal, but if at all possible it would be ideal to have a better understanding of what rights Rodriguez even slightly controls (or may control) and who the other parties involved might be. Any light, which you can shed on this subject, would be greatly appreciated.

I can tell you that we're honest people with good intentions and if we can turn this project into a reality then Light In The Attic would do everything in its power to ensure that Rodriguez receives a strong advance and royalty rate. No question [that] the man deserves some much overdue respect in such places as North America, Europe/UK, and Asia. We're huge fans of his work and strongly believe in this re-release. I plan to remain positive and [to] persevere. We can't be defeated. You made it happen in South Africa, you took the man to London, and you've done so much. All of us need to continue what you've started. That may sound cheesy, but it's the absolute truth. We're in this for the long haul.

Thanks again for getting back to me. It's a great pleasure to be speaking with you.

All the best,

Matt.

Sugar was intrigued by the idea of a potential re-release, but he knew that nothing was a shoo-in when it came to Rodriguez. Nevertheless, over the next two years Matt worked diligently to put a Light in the Attic version of *Cold Fact* – on both CD and vinyl – on record-store shelves. Sugar was patient because he knew it would make a big splash in the various international music media outlets. He also hoped it would expose a whole new audience to Rodriguez's music.

The Light in the Attic story is in itself an interesting one. According to writer Josh Young, the record label began with a car crash in Madrid, Spain, and a rather bad one at that.

After finishing high school, the teenaged Matt Sullivan travelled around Europe. Writes Young:

This particular sunny day in Madrid, was to have lifelong consequences for young Matt Sullivan. Aside from the site of the totalled Fiat [. . .], something of even greater interest immediately caught Matt's eye. The unlucky car he had just hit was filled to the brim with records – Stooges, Love, Suicide, MC5 – in other words, REALLY GOOD records. Matt introduced himself to his unwilling-yet-amiable 'crash mate', Iñigo Pastor, who just happened to own the stellar Spanish labels Vampi Soul and Munster Records. The shock of the accident suddenly took a proverbial back seat in the scheme of things as the two immediately began to talk music. Within an afternoon's time, a transatlantic bond based on the love of music was formed.

Matt immediately ditched his plans for the rest of his European sojourn and soon began camping out at the Vampi/Munster headquarters in Madrid. [. . .] He soon discovered that the thrill of finding a long-lost gem and reissuing it to a grateful public was often tempered by the more loathsome side of the music business – endless unpaid orders, flaky artists, and threats of lawsuits from hustlers and frauds of all sorts. But Matt remained undeterred, and with guidance from his Spanish mentors, began making plans for a record label of his own.

Once back in the States, the Master Plan began at once. The idea was to build a label which placed as much emphasis on releasing quality reissues as it did developing new talent. In the late '90s, the dot-com boom provided much-needed funds for Light In The Attic's humble birth in a basement in Fremont, Seattle. Ironically, though, it was the dot-com bust that really got LITA going. Suddenly unemployed, Matt wasted none of his new-found free time. Instead, he began building LITA from scratch. His tools? A little savings and a lot of tenacity.

In Seattle, Light in the Attic started producing live shows by up-and-coming artists, but the plan was always to be a record label first and a production company second. So, according to Young:

Armed with much-needed funds that the shows provided, the company began to focus on the business of making records in late 2002. [. . .] Matt soon called upon lifelong friend Josh Wright for help with the business.

Light in the Attic's mission was simple: put out great music, wherever it may be found, however it may sound. In the years to come, Light in the Attic would be responsible for releasing rare treasures such as the funk-rock maverick Betty Davis, proto-punk band the Monks, and folk singers Karen Dalton, Jim Sullivan, Michael Chapman and Serge Gainsbourg. But it would be the re-release of music by a Detroit construction worker that would leave the most indelible mark on the company.

As the name suggests, the albums that Matt and Josh chose to release on their innovative independent label were the dusty relics that everyone else had seemingly forgotten. Releasing them therefore involved a lot of slog, research and rights- and publishing-related hassles, which in Rodriguez's case were often even more convoluted than usual.

Matt recalls how he bugged Clarence Avant for over two years trying to license the Rodriguez catalogue:

But guys like Clarence were used to dealing on the big label level, the level of Motown, of which Clarence had been its head, and not some little kid from a start-up label in Seattle. He's a very busy guy. Thankfully we had *Cold Fact* producer Mike Theodore on our side. Mike was rooting for Rodriguez. He was passionate about the man and felt incredibly disappointed that Rodriguez's career did not take off. Anyway, I'd sent Avant samples for years and then one morning I got a call from Clarence to say that he was going to be in Seattle to celebrate his wife's anniversary, and if I wanted to, I could join him for breakfast. So I headed out to the Marriot, a fancy hotel, and handed him a beautiful press kit. 'How the fuck did you get all this press?' he asked. He realized that I wasn't going to go away and we made a deal. If he hadn't gone to Seattle, this may not have happened.

Matt was so close to a deal, but then something happened that nearly scuppered the agreement. The Copyright Group is a British publishing company that, through the convoluted world of music publishing, owns the licensing rights to the Rodriguez catalogue in the UK. How they obtained these rights is unknown, but it was through them that Terry Fairweather and his PT Music got the licence to release both *Cold Fact* and *Coming from Reality* in South Africa after Universal had let the licence lapse. With Clarence Avant's signature on paper and his dream almost a reality, Matt found out quite by accident that Munster, his old company in Madrid, was just about to sign a deal with the Copyright Group to distribute Rodriguez's catalogue. Matt went into panic mode. Years of flirting with Avant on the fringes had come to this? In sheer desperation, he picked up the phone and called his old mates in Spain, and through sweet-talking and a cash offer of $1,000, he managed to get Munster to drop the deal.

Interestingly, Matt Sullivan wasn't the only person to become interested in Rodriguez's music in the wake of the David Holmes album. In 2006, a young Scot from Paisley with an Italian name, Paolo Nutini, released a cover version of 'Sugar Man', adding to a growing list of Rodriguez covers. Aside from the countless times Rodriguez's music has been sampled, notable covers include 'Sugar Man' by both Stella One Eleven and South African band Just Jinger, and 'I Think of You' by Susan Cowsill.

In the meantime, after an absence of twenty-six years, Rodriguez found himself back in Australia in April 2007. He played several gigs, including one at the Byron Bay Bluesfest and one at the Tivoli in Brisbane. A fan named Phil Buckley filed an eyewitness account of the latter on the Sugarman. org forum:

> I just got home from tonight's show in Brisbane. A lovely little venue called the Tivoli, crowd around 1,500 maybe (I'm no judge of numbers). The first thing that struck me was how many young(er) people were there (I'm 50) – lots of my generation with kids, and lots of kids by themselves. Talking to a few of them, most said they recalled the music 'on dad's records.' The man has a whole second generation of fans. As for the show, personally: brilliant!!! – played all the faves, the voice is superb (guess that comes with years of NOT singing) and the band of local Australian players was excellent – all the flourishes in the right places. Opened with 'I Wonder' (surprisingly) followed by 'Only Good for Conversation' then one great song after another [. . .]

As for the crowd, almost every song was a sing-along (he even complemented the crowd on their lyrics) and it was such a good vibe. The woman singing to 'Forget It' and 'Like Janis' was pure joy. The whole crowd shouting out 'that's a concrete cold fact' and 'frankly I couldn't care less' was superb.

Cold Fact was finally re-released in the States on 19 August 2008, putting Rodriguez and his music into every major music publication, both off- and online, and giving him the kind of international media exposure about which he had only ever dreamt. Another major benefit of the Light in the Attic re-release was the love and maintenance given to all of Rodriguez's songs, as the album was remastered and beautifully packaged with full liner notes and extras (in contrast to the shoddy quality of the earlier South African releases, which were badly pressed, replete with typos and scant information). Plus the legalities seemed to have been finally tied up to everyone's satisfaction. According to Matt, Avant told him that the Sussex label never actually went bankrupt in the seventies, but instead a tax lien was placed on the business. Record label CBS Records then rode in and paid the lien on Avant's behalf, and six or seven years later, he got his masters back. It was during this six- or seven-year period that certain sub-licensing deals were made that perhaps resulted in the later royalty quagmire.

Sugar once again contributed to the liner notes – which were mostly written by long-time Light in the Attic contributor and Canadian DJ Kevin 'Sipreano' Howes – and during the process discovered the surprising fact that not one Rodriguez single had ever been released in South Africa, 'so we are not sure how much radio play Rodriguez actually got in the seventies, or on which stations, particularly the pirate radio stations that existed in the so-called "homelands", which had been established within the borders of South Africa as a way to get around apartheid'. To find out more, Sugar contacted Chris Prior, an influential DJ from the early eighties known as the Rock Professor, but he didn't have any information either. The two records were 'cult' albums in every sense of the word.

As Sugar had predicted, the Light in the Attic release of *Cold Fact* started garnering some attention and positive reviews in various music publications across all platforms, from *Pitchfork* and *Uncut* to *Rolling Stone* and *Mojo*. Joe Tangari, one of *Pitchfork*'s most respected reviewers, wrote:

> It's not difficult to hear why so many South Africans placed [*Cold Fact*] on the shelf next to Black Sabbath and the Beatles and figured that's what the rest of the world was doing, too. It is one of those rare lost albums that turns out to be a genuine classic.

For the moment, the spotlight was back on Rodriguez, even if, once again, it was like preaching to the converted. With no reason to wait, Light in the Attic went to work and released his second album, *Coming from Reality*, on 4 May 2009. Although stylistically different from its predecessor, it too received positive reviews.

Not too many precedents exist for this kind of scenario: two 'flopped' seventies albums re-released nearly forty years later, primarily on vinyl. Precedents or not, Matt and Light in the Attic knew that a successful re-release didn't necessarily mean people would flock to buy the albums. Life is mercurial. They couldn't rest on their laurels. In yet another unprecedented move, Matt decided to get the now sixty-plus singer on the road. For the US leg of the 2009 tour Rodriguez played with an emerging indie band from San Francisco, the Fresh & Onlys. In the spirit of an up-and-coming act, the band toured in a van with Matt, who was in charge of the whole expedition. The tour dates included:

Friday 10 April: High Noon Saloon, Madison WI
Friday 24 April: Beachland Ballroom, Cleveland OH
Friday 8 May: Schubas Tavern, Chicago IL
Saturday 9 May: Magic Stick, Detroit MI
Wednesday 13 May: Rock and Roll Hotel, Washington DC
Thursday 14 May: Johnny Brenda's, Philadelphia PA
Friday 15 May: Bowery Ballroom, New York NY

Then it was over to Europe for a quick series of one-nighters:

Friday 29 May: Paradiso, Amsterdam, Netherlands
Saturday 30 May: Whelans, Dublin, Ireland
Monday 1 June: Nouveau Casino, Paris, France
Wednesday 3 June: Circolo Degli Artisti, Rome, Italy
Saturday 6 June: Barbican, London, UK

Then they were back on North American soil for a further stint of stand-alone gigs:

22 June: Richard's on Richards Cabaret, Vancouver BC
23 June: The Triple Door, Seattle WA
24 June: Doug Fir Lounge, Portland OR
26 June: Slim's, San Francisco CA
27 June: El Rey Theatre, Los Angeles CA

The crew then continent-hopped once more to perform on Sunday 12 July 2009 at the Les Ardentes festival in Liège, Belgium. In an email report on the tour to Sugar, Matt wrote:

Hey Sugar,

I've been meaning to email you both since I got back home earlier this week from California. Rodriguez was AMAZING in his U.S. West Coast debut. Absolutely breath-taking shows, especially San Francisco. In Los Angeles, he had an 8-piece band with a three-piece horn section, while in San Francisco it was a 10-piece band with flute, French horn, clarinet, etc. The SF show was at the Great American Music Hall – a classic old theater built in 1907 (the first building built after the big 1906 SF earthquake. It's a gorgeous room with incredible sound). The bands re-created the record like nothing I could ever even imagine, along with playing some great songs from Coming From Reality. The shows brought me to tears. Los Angeles sold out and SF was a great turnout as well, 500 people in a 600-person venue. I must say that the SF show was literally one of the best days of my life. He also played some special live session perform-ances: the first being at dublab.com in LA and then an in-store performance at the legendary Amoeba Music in SF (on Haight Street, near the intersection of Haight & Ashbury!). Much of the shows were filmed so we'll be seeing some clips on YouTube soon. [...]

Thank you again for everything. None of this would be happening without your kind support over the years.

It's been a beautiful journey and it's far from over.

Cheers,

Matt.

'It's been a beautiful journey and it's far from over.' Matt could not have known then just how prophetic his words would turn out to be. If touring your own country and playing to your fans in cities like Los Angeles, Chicago and San Francisco is a dream in the minds of most rock musicians, then Rodriguez was at long last living the dream. But it was still only a minor breakthrough to a niche audience of independent music lovers. To the masses, Rodriguez remained completely unknown. For now.

PART IV

THE MOVIE

15

The boy who painted the chair
(1977–2007)

'I have never met anyone with such an engine.'
— MARTIN VÅRDSTEDT, PRODUCER, *KOBRA*

In one scene in the 1990 Swedish TV mini-series *Ebba och Didrik*, a young boy, known in the show as Philip Clavelle, paints a chair in a shed in the woods. The chair, which in a previous scene appears to be broken, has now been glued back together and the boy is painting it red. One of the show's two protagonists, a young girl named Ebba, arrives at the shed and a long conversation ensues. Ebba, played by the twelve-year-old actress Lisen Arnell, is animated and chatty. Her best friend Philip, however, says little. All he does for most of the scene is listen and paint. Watching, one cannot help but see the parallels between the laborious task of painting the chair over and over again, and the insular and arduous process that making the film *Searching for Sugar Man* would become – editing on the kitchen table, learning the craft of animation because there was no money to hire animators, writing and recording music at the same table because there was no money for that either, and later functioning as cinematographer and soundman when there was nothing left with which to hire a crew. The boy painting the chair, Philip Clavelle, is none other than twelve-year-old Malik Bendjelloul in his first role. Eighteen years later he would begin work on the Oscar-winning documentary, *Searching for Sugar Man*, a 'handmade' film if ever there was one, and the movie that would give the music of Rodriguez the impetus it needed to finally break into the United States, forty-three years after the fact.

Malik was born in Ystad, Sweden, to Algerian-born physician Hacène Bendjelloul and Swedish translator and painter Veronica Schildt Bendjelloul. From a young age, Malik nurtured a lively imagination and would often speak animatedly, in melodic English – 'Swenglish' – of his Ali Baba-like ancestry in the country of his father's birth. He also loved to tell how his father had wooed his mother by writing her long but labyrinthine love letters in an almost unreadable small hand. Stockholm-born, Veronica translated comics such as *Isabelle* and *Lucky Luke*, as well as books by Agatha Christie. She was also responsible for giving the clueless prison dog in the *Lucky Luke* series its Swedish name, Ratata (Ran Tan Plan in the French, Rin Tin Can in English). Hacène and Veronica had two sons, Johar born in 1975 and Malik in 1977.

Television, theatre and film were a constant presence in the Bendjelloul home. Veronica's father, Henrik Schildt, was a notable actor, and his brother Jurgen, Veronica's uncle, was one of Sweden's foremost film critics before his death in 1990, writing for *Aftonbladet* and also for Swedish radio.

Malik's two uncles on his mother's side, brothers Peter and Johan Schildt, were also both heavily involved in the Swedish film and television industry: Johan as an actor, and Peter as an actor and director. One of Peter's first roles was in *Ådalen 31*, which was nominated for an Oscar and won the Grand Jury Prize at the 1969 Cannes Film Festival. Later, in 1982, Peter served as assistant director under Ingmar Bergman on the Swedish drama *Fanny and Alexander*, which went on to win four Oscars. In fact, it was Malik's uncle Peter who gave him his first part in *Ebba och Didrik* in 1990, which also starred Malik's grandfather Henrik. 'We used to joke that it was nepotism and cronyism,' Peter told Emelie Henricson of *Expressen*, one of two evening tabloids in Sweden, 'but it was like any other screen test before we decided [. . .] then it turned out that he was fine. He had never been involved in something like this.' Peter directed the series, which was so popular in Sweden that it was rerun four times. In the show, Malik's big brooding brown eyes were already a distinguishing feature of his persona.

Malik was educated at the Rönne Gymnasium in Ängelholm, an area known for its clay cuckoos and a famous flying saucer memorial dedicated to a UFO landing that was supposed to have occurred on the site in 1946. After school, Malik studied journalism and media production at the Kalmar University, today the Linnaeus University, renamed in honour of botanist Carl Linnaeus. It was during his time at Kalmar that he got the idea to start making documentaries. Malik later told the LNU alumni website: 'I knew at an early stage that I wanted to work with telling stories in some way. During my internship I decided to make a music documentary. That's when I realised that it doesn't necessarily need to be as hard as you think. A great idea and a camera will get you far.' It was also at Kalmar that he came across a posting on the noticeboard announcing that Barracuda Films, a Stockholm-based production company, was hiring. He sent in his application and got the job.

His tenure with Barracuda Films began after his graduation and lasted for three years, during which time he worked on music documentaries and features on Elton John, Björk, Sting and a long-form piece on the pioneering German electronic band Kraftwerk. Unbeknown to Malik at the time was the fact that with their ground-breaking 1978 album *The Man-Machine* (which included the hit 'The Model'), Kraftwerk had forged a connection with Detroit. Because of the complexity of the album, Detroit sound engineer Leanard Jackson was flown over to Düsseldorf to help with the mix. Malik's work on the Kraftwerk documentary is solid and mature for someone only starting out, and still holds up today. In the feature we see hints of the techniques that would later define Malik's style in *Kobra* and, even later, in *Searching for Sugar Man*.

If Barracuda was where Malik cut his teeth, it was on the show *Kobra*, produced by SVT, that he was able to hone his newly acquired skills and turn his natural 'instinct' for storytelling, and particularly the art of interviewing people, into a razor-sharp talent. SVT, or Sveriges Television, is Sweden's largest network and the national public TV broadcaster, modelled on the BBC. *Kobra*, which first aired in 2001, is a weekly avant-garde lifestyle magazine programme that has hosted many luminaries since its inception, including Woody Allen, Madonna, Norman Mailer, Jeff Koons, Isabelle Huppert, Bruce Springsteen, Nick Cave and Ingmar Bergman. Malik's tenure as a freelance reporter for *Kobra* (he was never officially on their books) was like a whirlwind. With his inherent level of contagious energy, and his fearlessly pragmatic take on projects, the senior producers at *Kobra* must not have known what to do with him at first. Evident from the start was his ability to take a holistic approach to whatever subject matter he was working on. Once he was locked onto an idea, it was all-consuming. He let nothing stand in the way of him and his goal, especially not trivialities such as budgets. Money was but a means to an end. Time meant nothing to him either. He was known to disappear into the bowels of the editing suite and not emerge for days. And unlike the youth from his generation who were fascinated by the special effects that could be created digitally, Malik was fascinated by the special effects that could be created through analogue methods (here there are echoes of Mike Theodore's analogue experiments on 'Sugar Man'). Where many young filmmakers of today have as their first stop Photoshop or AfterFX, Malik would first pull out a piece of paper and a pair of scissors, and see if the particular effect could be achieved 'in camera' – without moving pixels around. Unsurprisingly, he was fascinated by the work of French film director Michel Gondry (who appeared on *Kobra* too). Other influences were David Lynch and the German filmmaker Werner Herzog.

One of the many things Malik did at *Kobra* that demonstrated his unconventional thinking was the opening sequence of the show, made in 2005. Where myriad digital options were available for the thirty-second sequence, Malik chose to do it all on camera. To do so, he sourced several wooden frames in the outline of a TV set, and set each of these up in the studio on stands. Then he choreographed moments, each of which would occur behind one of the various screens – people playing cards, a man and woman in conversation, a woman in a phone booth, a car scene with an old-school back-projected road film clip, a band playing, a couple arguing. But what makes the sequence so interesting is that the whole clip is filmed in one long take (a film-maker's dream), without edits. Ultimately, the camera pushes through the final wooden TV frame to reveal the word 'KOBRA' in neon blue. An Indian-influenced track – tablas, sitars and singing – forms the charged underscore of this fast-moving title sequence.

Perhaps more remarkable than the actual filmic qualities of this opening scene was Malik's power of persuasion, a quality that would later serve him well in the making of *Searching for Sugar Man*. Single-handedly, he was able to corral the upper echelons of Swedish culture to star in the sequence. Present in the scene are no less than Benny Andersson from ABBA, musician Eagle-Eye Cherry, *Girl with the Dragon Tattoo* actor Michael Nyqvist, and literary historian and ex-president of the Swedish Academy Horace Engdahl.

As his confidence grew, Malik had no compunction taking on large jobs for *Kobra*. His homage to the Fatboy Slim music video featuring Christopher Walken was one such feat, copied scene for scene with Swedish actor Mikael Persbrandt playing the role of Walken. (Persbrandt would go on to take a small part in the second and third instalments of Peter Jackson's *Hobbit* trilogy as the shapeshifter Beorn.) Another coup was a 2004 segment featuring Danish artist Thomas Altheimer, who, in an act of extreme amateur activism, travelled to Guantánamo to scare the Americans away by blasting them with classical music from a pitifully ineffective, hand-held portable sound system. (Altheimer had been inspired by the US army's trick of irritating Panama's dictator Manuel Noriega into submission by blasting heavy doses of Guns N'

Roses in his direction.) Later, Malik did a segment on Iranian refugee Mehran Karimi Nasseri's nearly two-decade-long stay in the transit area of Paris's Charles de Gaulle airport, using a mixture of film and overlaid hand drawings, carefully distilling the story down to the red plastic couch on which Nasseri had lived. Another segment that utilised clever editing of a mixture of filmic devices, including drawings and cardboard cut-outs, was titled *Paul Is Dead*. This piece analysed an urban legend from the late sixties that suggested that Paul McCartney had died in 1966, only to be secretly replaced by a lookalike. But perhaps one of Malik's most impressive creative segments was a piece on the Swedish-Hungarian artist Gábor Palotai. In this complex work, Malik plays with visual perspectives and shifting realities by means of trick photography, the analogue kind (such as moving screens and mirrors to create the illusion). This and *Paul Is Dead* are – when one considers the six-to-eight-minute time constraint put on all of *Kobra*'s segments – two of Malik's most complete and cohesively perfect pieces. But the list goes on:

Another documentary I did dealt with how the American Defense in the 1980s tried to teach its soldiers to become invisible and walk through walls. I also made a documentary on a man who was teaching language at Oxford – a language that didn't really exist, a language he was making up as he spoke. I came to realise that a good story is irresistible in a way that few other things can be. I've read newspapers and scrutinised the web, for months in a row sometimes, in the search for a great story. The searching became an additional part of work in itself.

Many of the film techniques found in *Searching for Sugar Man* are evident in the inserts and stories Malik created for *Kobra*. In fact, some would say that the level of filmmaking to be found in his work for the show is far more experimental than that in the documentary. Interestingly, while each of the many segments he made for *Kobra* appear to be stylistically cohesive, some would argue that the opposite is true in *Searching for Sugar Man*, where filmic devices that were used in the beginning, for example, do not feature again, making the film less cohesive. It's a minor criticism.

Besides his obvious talent, many people on the *Kobra* team also remember Malik for some of his eccentricities. How he ate the same breakfast for months; or the day he took a friend out to dinner to celebrate the fact that he had been alive for 10,000 days. Such was his thinking, always out of left field.

Ultimately, Malik's involvement in *Kobra* was all-encompassing, his enthusiasm unbridled. And the results are proof. There's no doubting the fact that he had found a canvas for his unlimited palette of ideas. In 2006, however, after nearly ten years spent creating an impressive body of work, he developed an itch. He needed to spread his wings. After all, he was still under thirty and had already achieved more than some do in a lifetime. He decided to embark on a grand adventure, and backpack around Europe, South America and Africa with his camera to 'find the best story in the world', as he liked to put it. There was never anything small about Malik's aspirations. He identified six stories that would take him to ten different countries, and pitched his idea to *Kobra*. Although sad to see him go, the show agreed to support him by funding his airfare.

Malik had never heard of Rodriguez, but when casting his net he came across an article in the UK edition of the *Guardian*

Quiz-master, Paddy O'Byrne, with the "Quiz Kids 1969". Left to right: Michael Mendelowitz, Jenny Hill, Jeffrey Glass, Barbara Piazza and Stephen Segerman.

The Quiz-Kids—1969

By Paddy O'Byrne

Stephen Segerman's first brush with fame as a quiz kid on South African radio. He is on the far right

Stephen in the air force, where he first discovered the music of Rodriguez, 1972

80341795/4
C.B. STRYDOM

Craig Strydom's army ID from 1983, the year he vowed to find out what happened to Rodriguez

© Dean Hutton

Voëlvry veteran Willem Möller alongside Rodriguez during the first South African tour in 1998

© Stephen Segerman

Sugar, Brian Currin, Eva Rodriguez, Craig and David Viljoen during the 1998 tour

Craig with his wife Philippa Berrington-Blew and Rodriguez at the Standard Bank Arena, 1998

In Sugar's den: Ronit Segerman, Sugar and Rodriguez, 2005

Sugar and Rodriguez outside Mabu Vinyl

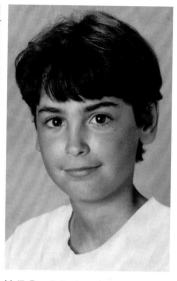

Malik Bendjelloul aged eleven

'Malik's childlike naivety made him extraordinary': Malik and brother Johar at the UFO monument in Ängelholm, spring 1983

HD Söndagen den 21 januari 1990

"Philip" i Ebba och Didrik:
Slutet en hemlighet

ÄNGELHOLM (HD)
Såg ni Ebba och Didrik på Kanal 1 i går kväll? I så fall såg ni också Ängelholms färskaste och yngsta tv-kändis. Philip (Ebbas pojkvän i pjäsen) spelas nämligen av 12-årige Malik Bendjellourl. I konkurrens med 1 000 jämnåriga fick han rollen.

Att sedan hans morbror är identisk med filmens regissör Peter Schildt är ingen fördel.
– Nej, snarare tvärtom, säger Malik, och intygar att släktrelationen gjort det ännu tuffare.
Författaren Christina Herrström har också anknytning till trakten. Föräldrarna är bosatta i Skälderviken, där utescenerna spelats in.
– Jag har tillbringat varje sommar där, säger den 30-åriga manusförfattaren.
– Ebba och Didrik handlar lika mycket om vuxenvärlden. Det räcker bara vara barn i huvudrollerna.
Christina Herrström har alltid

Här intill pirarmarna i Skälderviken träffas Philip och Ebba i tv-serien. Mötesplatsen, telefonkiosken, finns inte kvar. Den tog filmteamet med sig.

'The Ending is a Secret': Malik Bendjelloul as Philip in *Ebba Och Didrik*

Shooting starts: Sugar, cinematographer Camilla Skagerström and Malik Bendjelloul in Cape Town, 2008

Sugar, Craig, Rodriguez and Malik on stage for a post-screening Q&A at Sundance, 2012

'Butch and Sundance', Malik with producers John Battsek and Simon Chinn, Park City, Utah, 2012

Rodriguez playing with his back to the audience in his hotel room, Sundance, 2012

Malik, Michael Moore and Craig at the Tribeca Film Festival, 2012

The night *Searching for Sugar Man* took home the Oscar: Sugar, Malik, Craig and Simon Chinn at the 2013 Academy Awards

Rodriguez addresses fellow graduates at Wayne State University after receiving an honorary doctorate, 2013

written by journalist Alexis Petridis. The piece, titled 'The singer who came back from the dead', told the story of two South African Rodriguez fans who went on a hunt to discover more about their dead idol and found him alive. It was the piece that Petridis had written to promote the London tour in 2005. When Malik started planning his journey around the world, one of the six stories in his mind was the search for the long-lost singer. At this stage, he decided to track down Craig Strydom and Sugar Segerman.

Craig had by now moved on from the story and was trying to make a mark in advertising in Baltimore, Maryland, the city he had lived in since 2000. Sugar, however, was working hard at building up Mabu Vinyl and, along with Brian Currin, maintaining Sugarman.org, which involved, among other things, answering the slew of emails that came in daily (a labour of love that they have kept up since the inception of their various websites). One morning, an upbeat email from Sweden caught Sugar's eye. The date was 15 September 2006, seven months after Matt Sullivan's first email to Sugar.

Hello,

I'm a reporter on Kobra, the biggest culture TV show in Sweden. We would very much like to make an interview with you concerning the amazing rediscovery of Sixto Rodriguez. We are coming to South Africa in November and it would be a true honour to meet you.

Kobra is the premiere arts and culture feature program and runs every Monday primetime on SVT, Swedish National Television – the equivalent of BBC in England. Among previous editions are features about Stanley Kubrick, Woody Allen, Bret Easton Ellis and Madonna. SVT broadcasts nationwide and reaches a potential audience of

20 million viewers all over Scandinavia. Kobra's rating is
around 10% of the population.
  Best regards
  Malik Bendjelloul

Sugar replied, telling Malik that he was welcome to contact him when he arrived in Cape Town. Just over a month
later, a second email appeared in his inbox:

Hello Sugar,
This is Malik from Swedish Television. Today I will start my
journey and make TV features from around the world. First
Italy, then Ethiopia and then South Africa, arriving in
Johannesburg on the 15th of November. After that I'm quite
flexible, but the best thing would be to meet you sometime
early December. Are you available?
  Really looking forward to meet you!!
  Best regards
  Malik

Sugar can't remember the exact date that Malik arrived
in Cape Town, but he will never forget meeting him for
the first time. At that stage, in early December 2006, Mabu
Vinyl was still in its old premises at the intersection where
the city meets Gardens at the top of Long Street. That day,
around mid-morning, a tall, thin and friendly-looking guy
approached the shop, marched inside, and with his open
hand raised in greeting, said, 'Hullo, I'm Malik!' Anyone
who has ever known Malik will recognise his trademark
effusive greeting, which was not only reserved for hello.
When saying goodbye he would repeat the same open-
handed wave, accompanied by an equally effusive 'Farewell!'

Sugar's first impression of Malik was that the Swede reminded him of Tintin, the well-known character created by Belgian cartoonist Hergé, whose crazy tales of exploration formed a big part of Sugar's early reading and education. It was thanks to *The Adventures of Tintin* that he learnt about the moon and the countries and peoples of the world. Malik had Tintin's open, welcoming and inquisitive demeanour.

Sugar took Malik to his house, where they talked about Rodriguez and *Kobra* and Malik's mission to travel the world to find stories that he could turn into interesting segments for the programme. Malik told Sugar about how he had discovered the *Guardian* article on Rodriguez quite by chance while researching something completely unrelated online. The story had so fascinated him that he had added it to his list of subjects that he wanted to find out more about on his journey. Malik filmed their conversation on a small camera and then asked if they could go somewhere scenic so that he could film more of the story with the beauty of Cape Town as a backdrop.

They headed up to Tafelberg Road – the road that runs along the foot of Table Mountain and where the Lower Cable Station is situated – in Blue Thunder, Sugar's trusty old Opel Ascona. There wasn't enough time to go up the mountain, so they drove along Tafelberg until they found a spot where there were no other cars. With a wonderful view of the city behind him, Sugar sat on the bonnet of his car and talked about Rodriguez while Malik filmed. The filmmaker seemed to be able to work quickly and get what he wanted with a minimum of fuss, which wasn't something Sugar was used to after having worked with a lot of the prima-donna commercial directors in Cape Town. Afterwards, when the two said their goodbyes, Malik assured Sugar that he would send him the segment he planned to make for *Kobra*. When Sugar told his wife Ronit about Malik and what they had filmed, her first comment was that he was going to be on Swedish TV in a very old, faded and misshapen blue T-shirt! But he wasn't too concerned. He had been filmed on numerous occasions over the years by potential filmmakers all promising to turn the Rodriguez story into a documentary, but so far nothing had materialised. The interest shown by Phillip Noyce had fizzled out, with the director telling Sugar in an email that he wasn't 'able to work out how to take this remarkable story to a wider audience'. Why should this time be any different?

Then, six months later, while Sugar was moving Mabu Vinyl into its new premises, he received another email from Malik:

14 June 2007

Hi Sugar!
So nice to hear from you! I've been thinking a lot about Rodriguez and your story lately. You were so kind and it was such a great pleasure to report the story and you treated me so well!

The situation is as follows: I came home a month ago from my journey around the world and started [to] edit the stories. The show I work for, Kobra, will broadcast Rodriguez when their new season starts this autumn. It's a normal Kobra feature, between 5–8 minutes long. But I've tried to convince the bosses on the network that the story is good enough for a longer documentary. And I think that it's not impossible that they will agree. I spoke to one of the bosses only yesterday and he said that my pitch was one of the few they'd put in the 'very interesting' file.

So maybe we could do something bigger! Of course

nothing is decided yet, and sometimes decisions take time, but wouldn't that be great?!

Do you know how Rodriguez himself is doing these days? Any planned concerts in South Africa or anywhere else? Anything else that happened?

By the way – I've just started reading the Paul Auster novel, 'Book of Illusions'. Have you read it? About a man who tries to find an old silent movie film star who mysteriously vanished. A good story, but your story is even better. And true!!

Hope you're very good!

All the best

Malik

A few months passed before Sugar heard from Malik again. By now the eager young filmmaker had made contact with Rodriguez's daughter Eva, too:

24 September 2007

Hi Sugar!

Although I haven't got the final decision yet it really looks like the documentary will take place. The man who takes the decision has said yes, only that it's still informal.

That means that it most certainly will be an hour long documentary on prime time Swedish Television sometime next year! (The slot is Fridays 8 pm). And quite a lot of work to do! But extremely fun work! We will need to make a lot of more interviews and go again to South Africa and to Detroit (to meet Rodriguez himself). Probably the filming will take place January–March 2008. Isn't that fabulous? I'm very happy to have stumbled across the story and I'm so happy to have met you. I've made a short test film that the bosses

at SVT have seen and everyone thinks you (and Eva) tell the
story in such a charismatic way!

Let's talk on the phone soon. Are you home or at work?

All the best!!

Malik

Judging from his email, Malik had aspirations of moving
quickly with the making of the documentary. Of course, the
universe had other plans.

16

The only one who didn't know
(2008–2009)

'Half of the time you feel like a prostituted beggar,
half of the time you feel that you're actually doing
something that will be quite good.'
— MALIK BENDJELLOUL IN CONVERSATION WITH SUGAR
SEGERMAN

There is a scene in *Grey Gardens*, arguably the greatest documentary ever made, in which one of the subjects of the film, Edie Bouvier Beale, humming a military tune and drunk with infatuation for filmmaker David Maysles, implores, 'Darling David, where have you been all my life?'

This scene reveals an inherent difference between fiction filmmaking and documentary filmmaking. In the former, the contract between the filmmaker and the subject (the actor) is based on a trade of money for services, while in the latter the contract is based on a very different currency altogether, one that involves flattery, persuasion, an emotional give-and-take, and the belief that you are both part of some greater good, something without which society would be poorer. The documentary subject, working for free, is happy to have this intrusion into his or her life in order to be a part of something 'bigger than themselves' and, inevitably, a relationship develops. In the documentary format, the director and subject enter into a social contract as opposed to a monetary contract.

Besides the directorial tasks of finding storylines, choosing camera angles, and deciding on editorial in-and-out points, the documentary filmmaker's biggest job involves persuasion. He or she has to convince the subject not only to agree to being filmed, but also to give up his or her time for little to no compensation. Ultimately, it becomes a question of how much the documentary filmmaker is willing to give of him- or herself in order to get the story from others. The 'giving of oneself' becomes proxy for the lack of hard currency (dollars and cents). Often, by the time mountains have been scaled and dragons slain, the documentary director finds himself a hollowed-out husk, having given of himself so completely in the service of the story that he or she has very little left to give. One of the primary tasks of a successful documentary filmmaker, therefore, is to continuously inject vitality into the story, validity into the subject matter, and importance into the featured people. It is a labour of love and up to the director to turn his subjects into foot soldiers for the cause.

Very often in the documentary format, subjects will offer up their homes for accommodation in lieu of hotels, their cars for transport in lieu of production vehicles and their time in spades. Contrast that with traditional filmmaking – a Screen Actors Guild production, for example – where a hefty penalty is placed on even the smallest infringement:

the lack of a footstool, say, at the door of the star's Winnebago. Pulling off a documentary therefore requires not just someone with an eye and ear for storytelling, but the kind of person with the ability to cajole, coax and motivate. It requires someone with the ability to surmount the daily challenges of balancing budgets and egos, as well as all the variables that come up during filmmaking and at which one cannot simply throw money. The young Swede from Ystad was one such person.

Malik Bendjelloul wasted no time celebrating the arrival of 2008: on 1 January he was ready to go. The first and most important item on his long list of deliverables was to make positive contact with Rodriguez through his daughters, because, as Sugar had explained, without their buy-in, there would be no film. As Sugar saw it, Rodriguez could be difficult, but Regan and Eva in particular had a big influence on him and he valued their opinions. At this stage the gatekeeper appeared to be Regan once more, but it would ping-pong back and forth between Rodriguez's daughters over the years. As Rodriguez was notoriously shy and unforthcoming with regard to interviews, Sugar figured it was unlikely Rodriguez would be the main talking head in a film – he would more likely remain as mysterious and removed as he was in real life – and the bulk of the story would be told by those around him. But to ease the filmmaker's fears, Sugar said he was sure that as soon as things got going and Malik was there speaking to everyone and being his charming self, Rodriguez would warm to him and would be happy to assist with the film and speak to the camera. To get the ball rolling, Malik composed a letter of introduction to the Rodriguez family, which he planned to send to Regan.

He sent the following draft to Sugar for counsel:

Dear Regan!

My name is Malik Bendjelloul and I'm a Swedish filmmaker, maybe your sister Eva or Sugar Segerman might have mentioned my name ... I work for an international culture TV show on National Swedish Television and last year I went down to South Africa to make a story about your dad's fascinating story. I interviewed your sister and Sugar with the purpose to make a small piece for Swedish Television. But when I showed the material everyone around (including myself of course) were like – hey this should be a full documentary! So I went to the National Swedish Television documentary department and asked them for funding and they said YES! And then I went to one of Sweden's most renowned film producers with lots of contacts in South Africa, the US and Australia and he also said yes wanting to help produce and distribute the film. So it has really quite high potentials, the idea is to travel all over the world and interview all the people involved in the story and the ambition is to make a brilliant documentary film aiming at the cinema screen.

So my question to you is if it would be possible to meet Rodriguez? And also to meet you? There's no hurry, the filming won't start until mid-March, and will probably continue for almost two months.

Best regards and a really happy new year!

Malik Bendjelloul

Sugar wrote back to Malik, saying that 'today is the first day of what will be a great and rewarding year for us all'. He continued:

Your letter is fine, but with a few additions. Firstly, you should tell her that you have been in contact with Matt Sullivan and that everyone is hopeful that the documentary will tie in perfectly with the 2008 (Light In The Attic) reissue of *Cold Fact* and give it extra international attention. I know that Rodriguez is not that happy doing documentaries, but if he understands that this is all connected and for his benefit, then he should be willing, especially if Regan is happy. Secondly, I think you should also mention that you understand that Rodriguez's privacy and that of his family is very important to him and that it will be respected at all times. I'm sure that should smooth the way for future plans.

Malik's email to Regan did the trick. On 12 January, he passed on the good news to Sugar:

Just got word from Regan. She seems to be happy and interested in the project and will ask Rodriguez. I had a meeting with the producers yesterday, and they are very enthusiastic. They said they had five projects going on at the moment and that Rodriguez is their highest priority, the one they believe has the greatest potential and the one that really should be aiming at a theatre release. The process of [obtaining funding] for projects of this size is slow. They will have to do a lot of pitching at international film forums and most probably the film won't be ready this year. One and a half to two years is quite normal for projects like this.

Malik was moving fast. In a short space of time, and with Sugar's help, he had not only identified the key players in the Rodriguez story, but had also contacted and received tentative agreements from most of them. Sugar was excited about how quickly matters seemed to be moving. He was sure Mike Theodore would come on board, as he had been trying for ages to make something like this happen, and he had co-writing credits on two Rodriguez songs, so he stood to gain financially in the long run. Justin Cohen, the director of *Looking for Jesus*, was located in Cape Town and easily accessible. Tonia Selley was in the Cape too, with her husband Willem Möller, the well-known and respected South African guitar player and producer who had been the guitarist in Big Sky, the band that had backed Rodriguez on his first tour to South Africa in 1998. As mentioned previously, Möller was also one of the original Afrikaans musicians to be inspired by Rodriguez during the apartheid era, and was subsequently involved in the Voëlvry (Free as a Bird) movement, which saw a group of prominent Afrikaans alternative musicians tour South Africa to speak out against apartheid.

One noticeable absentee was Craig Strydom, who had become increasingly ambivalent over the years about participating in the whole saga. He was trying to build a career in advertising in America and did not want the story of Rodriguez to define his life, but no matter what he did, the conversation always turned to the singer and Craig's role in finding him. In 2002, while living in Baltimore, Craig had been surprised when he began to receive emails about a film called *Looking for Jesus* that was playing on South African TV screens and that supposedly featured him as a main character. He had neither received word that a film was being made nor been consulted at any stage. He was especially perplexed, because the title of the film suggested the filmmaker, Justin Cohen, had used Craig's first article on Rodriguez, 'Looking for Rodriguez', as a jumping-off point. It was becoming clear even then that the Rodriguez story had a life of its own and would barrel along with or without all of its key players.

In spite of Craig's ambivalence, however, the first documentary made of the Rodriguez story in North America had come about before that, after he met Mark Blackburn, a freelance journalist with CBC Canada, at a cocktail party in St John's, Newfoundland. Blackburn was so spellbound by the story that he promptly got Craig into the studio and produced a half-hour radio programme about the Rodriguez phenomenon. It aired in 2000.

When Craig received Malik's email in early 2008, he didn't reply immediately. He assumed that Malik was a young film student who would be wasting his time, and time was the one thing he didn't have at that stage in his career. But the filmmaker persisted and managed to track him down to Baltimore. Craig soon realised that his assumption about Malik was wrong, and it didn't take much to convince him to participate. It had been his obsession for so long, after all.

Malik was also working hard to track down Clarence Avant in Los Angeles. Matt Sullivan had told him that Avant was tricky to get hold of and that it had taken him over two years to get sign-off to license Rodriguez's music. Sugar's advice to Malik was to approach the ex-Sussex boss with kid gloves. He had, after all, paid for and still owned the masters and publishing rights of the first two albums. Of course, we now know that Avant paid not only for the album recordings, but also for two further sessions, one of which resulted in three additional songs. Avant was, in truth, an impresario – Rodriguez's *only* impresario. With the exception of the early 1967 Harry Balk session, and the David Holmes remix in New York, every single song Rodriguez ever recorded in a studio had been on Avant's dime. Sugar also warned Malik that, as far as he knew, Rodriguez and Avant had had a falling-out after recording *Coming from Reality*. At that stage no one knew about the additional sessions, the occurrence of which suggests that their relationship blew hot and cold. Malik was curious about Avant's relationship with Rodriguez and about whether Avant, who owned the publishing rights for all of Rodriguez's songs, knew anything about the South African sales of *Cold Fact* and *Coming from Reality*. According to the singer, he had not received any royalties for either of the two albums. If he had, he would have known that his music was selling in South Africa.

By all accounts, Avant was still a big shot in the US music business and could lay claim to some important friends. Sugar had it on good authority that when former president Bill Clinton visited Israel, he contacted Zev Eizik on his good friend Clarence's instructions. Given this, Sugar suggested that Malik not ask Avant directly about any 'missing royalties'. He also recommended that the filmmaker talk with Eizik, who had been an important source of information about Rodriguez's early period and who might facilitate access to Avant. Malik was learning fast about selective duplicity and the fancy footwork required to make a documentary, especially when egos come into play, which is practically all of the time. When Malik finally made contact with the elusive music producer, Avant indicated a willingness to speak on camera. This was an interesting and wholly unexpected development.

In mid-February 2008, on the advice of SVT producer Hjalmar Palmgren, Malik contacted Hysteria Films, a Stockholm-based documentary-film production house, where his script and film treatment landed on the desk of producer Malla Grapengiesser. As fate would have it, a few days later the Swedish cinematographer Camilla Skagerström walked into Malla's office. Curious about the treatment lying on the desk with a picture of a Hispanic man on the cover, and just as Steve Rowland had done in Freddy Bienstock's office almost forty years earlier, Camilla asked who this person was. Malla told her it was Sixto Rodriguez, the subject of a proposed documentary by a young TV journalist named Malik Bendjelloul. Camilla's interest was piqued. 'Would you like to meet Malik?' asked the producer, handing her the treatment and the script.

Later that month, Malik relayed the exciting news to Sugar that he had secured the services of none other than the talented cinematographer Camilla Skagerström, who he felt would be perfect for the job. What he did not tell Sugar was that he now had a production company behind him, with Malla Grapengiesser as the film's new producer. Sadly, the agreement with Malla and Hysteria Films would sour very quickly. But Malik was just thrilled to have Camilla on board. As she was working on a documentary in Cuba at the time, the shoot had to be postponed by a few weeks. So Malik planned to arrive in Cape Town in mid-April 2008 to set things up and find locations, and then begin shooting upon Camilla's arrival a week later. They would set up base camp at Sugar's house. The plan was to film in South Africa for two weeks and in America for two weeks, and then to return to the US in the summer to cover the release of *Cold Fact* on the Light in the Attic label. The air tickets were booked and it was all systems go.

The movie was fast becoming a reality, and Sugar made himself completely available for the period that Malik planned to shoot in Cape Town. He had been tasked with finding film footage from the so-called 'old' South Africa of the 1970s and 1980s, a time of civic unrest and white minority denial. Footage from that era existed mostly in the Super-8 format. Sugar made a sign, which he put up in the window of Mabu Vinyl, asking for historical film footage. Within a week or so he hit the jackpot when a young woman named Michaela Kedian brought in a packet of canisters containing old films that her grandfather had shot in the sixties and seventies all around South Africa. Sugar took down her contact details in case they decided to use some of the footage in the documentary. As it turned out, these were the only Super-8 films he received in response to his notice, and they turned out to be exactly what Malik was after.

Malik in the meantime scripted a first draft of the outline for the film and emailed it to Sugar, explaining that because it was a documentary, it was impossible to write an actual script,

> so this is just a small start, just a way and an order in which the story could be told. A LOT is certainly completely wrong and apart from a couple of quotes from you and Eva the rest is just imagination. I have no idea if people would really answer like this, and if people are willing to do things in the way I describe. It's just a small start to start thinking on how the plot could be written.

Sugar thought the script was wonderful, and admitted to Malik that it had left him a little damp-eyed. He passed on the information he had written for the upcoming Light in the Attic *Cold Fact* reissue and offered up two boxes of Rodriguez memorabilia from the various South African tours, including in some cases the actual newspaper cuttings and reviews. When the time came, Malik emailed Sugar:

> Packing my bags! Leaving Stockholm tomorrow afternoon and getting to Cape Town around 8 am on Tuesday. Should I get to your shop after arrival at 2 Rheede Street? Wow, now we're starting!

Malik arrived in Cape Town on Tuesday 8 April 2008. He moved into the Segermans' spare room and immediately went to work discussing locations with Sugar, reviewing script options and watching hours of Super-8 films from the young woman who'd come into Mabu Vinyl. Luckily there was an old eight-millimetre film projector wasting space on a shelf at the record shop. Malik and Sugar dusted off the relic and spent a couple of evenings in the dark, viewing jumpy footage on the dining-room wall. The films were perfect. They included footage taken at the Kruger National Park, at the old D.F. Malan Airport in Cape Town (in which one could see the old South African Airways livery – a flying springbok – on the tails of aeroplanes), and on the top of Table Mountain in the days of the old cable car. The next day Malik contacted Michaela and agreed on a price for the lot. He also promised to convert all the footage to DVD so that she could take home a copy for her family, which he did after the standard release had been signed.

Camilla Skagerström arrived a week later and she and Malik took rooms at a nearby B&B. Shooting started in earnest the following day, mostly interior scenes at the Segermans' home. Sugar's pride and joy is his den, a room filled to the brim with books, records, photos, CDs, cassettes and magazines. It's pretty much what Mabu Vinyl would

look like if shrunk down to one-twentieth of its size. It therefore provided plenty of relevant backdrops and negated the
need for a stylist – not that there was money for one anyway.
The room, crammed as it was with sound-absorbent material, was also great for audio. Sugar spent the better part of
two days speaking into the camera, telling sections of the
story based on the rough script from which they were
working. This time he wore a clean shirt. They filmed several
scenes at Mabu after hours, but at that stage Malik hadn't
fully figured out his vision for the documentary, so shooting
was pretty much at random. Remarkably, a lot of what was
shot in that first week ended up in the final edit.

Malik and Camilla headed to Wilderness next, where they
filmed Eva, and then on to Johannesburg to cover some of
the other players: Robbie Mann, Steve Harris and Terry
Fairweather, all in the record business and all in some way
linked to the sales of Rodriguez's music. It was the first stop
on the so-called 'money trail'. Matt Mann, Robbie's father,
had been one of the pioneers of the South African recording
industry and the founder of RPM Records, which had been
responsible for releasing Rodriguez's music in South Africa
at some point. Steve Harris had been the managing director
at RPM at the time. Terry Fairweather's PT Music was the
current distributor of Rodriguez CDs in South Africa and
was paying royalties to the Copyright Group, which Malik
made a note to check out.

Shortly before leaving for the States, Malik managed to get
a call through to Clarence Avant. Avant seemed extremely
amiable and offered to collect Malik and Camilla from the
airport and take them out to lunch. When Malik told him he
was calling from Johannesburg, Avant said, unprompted,
'Oh, I heard [Rodriguez] is big over there. It's so strange, I

never received any money from them.' A few days later, the Swedish filmmaker and his cinematographer flew to Los Angeles.

Malik emailed Sugar after his interview with Avant:

> Met Clarence two days ago, a very special man. He invited us out to lunch and was very kind all the time. He constantly repeated how cool and weird it was that I did this story, and what a nutcase I must be to do so, but that he liked nutcases and that's why he gave Matt [Sullivan] the rights to re-release the records. He thought Matt and I were, like him, passionate nutcases and that's why he wanted to help us. [. . .] I asked him how many records he sold in the US, and he answered without hesitation, 'Six. I bought one, my wife bought one and a friend of mine bought one.' I showed him the 25-min pilot and it seems he actually understood the potential of the story. By the way, he wanted me to help him get in contact with Rodriguez again.

It's interesting that Avant asked for Rodriguez's contact information. If he owned the publishing rights to Rodriguez's music, you'd expect he would know how to contact him.

The next stop on Malik's trip was Palm Springs to meet Steve Rowland, the producer of Rodriguez's second album. He reported back on this too:

> Steve Rowland was also fantastic. A real Hollywood actor (he really was you know, he had pictures of him and James Dean on the wall. He'd tried to pick up Marilyn Monroe and been dating Natalie Wood). He was extremely passionate about Rodriguez and said many beautiful things about him.

Then it was off to the most important place of all, Detroit. When he heard that Malik and Camilla were on their way, Sugar became anxious, recalling again what had happened with Willemiek Kluijfhout. He could not predict how Rodriguez and his family would react, but this film at least had a secret weapon: Malik's charm. A few days passed before he heard from the filmmaker:

We're in Detroit now and have been hanging out with Rodriguez for two long days now. He's extremely happy about the film and has sat for hours in front of the screen seeing the interviews we've made with Clarence Avant and Steve Rowland with tears in his eyes. I arranged for him to call Clarence whom he hasn't spoken to for a long time and they had a long conversation and tonight we're gonna call Steve who he hasn't spoken to for decades. It's amazing to hear those interviews. Steve said 'He's my most memorable artist ever,' and I asked him 'You've been working with Jerry Lee Lewis' and he said 'Yes, Jerry Lee Lewis is a fantastic artist, but Rodriguez goes beyond that.' We haven't filmed more than a small interview with R[odriguez] in a car.

The car interview didn't make it into the final cut, but Malik was ecstatic at this stage of the shoot:

Most of the time we've just been hanging out. He's been playing the guitar (but is more interested in hearing me play...). He is such a wonderful man. It's going to turn out so sweet. Still, he's super sensitive to everything and I'm not sure if we're really going to film him much more. Regan has been super helpful and been driving us around everywhere. A real sweetheart. Helping us out in every way possible.

After filming some of the other family members, Malik wrote to say that

we did see R more, we really came quite close in the end, he wanted to see us every day. Mostly just hanging out, eating dinner and talk and talk and talk. We did very little filming, only the essential parts. But it was an extremely fascinating time we spent with him, I'm longing back a lot to Detroit.

And then it was nearly over. After seven weeks on the road (the trip took longer than initially expected), Malik and Camilla began their journey back to Stockholm. But first they had two more important stops to make on the US East Coast. They spent close to three hours in New Jersey with Mike Theodore, who told them lots of interesting things, including the fact that the three tracks that appeared exclusively on the *Best Of* album had actually been recorded in the seventies almost straight after *Coming from Reality* and that the session had somehow fizzled out. He also told them that it was his idea to put a crystal ball on the cover of *Cold Fact*.

Their last interview was with Craig Strydom, who was visiting New York City at the time and had planned to attend the Dada exhibition at the Museum of Modern Art with South African jazz musician Graeme Sacks. Craig met Malik and Camilla somewhere near Columbus Circle in Manhattan and the trio headed to a record store called Westsider Records on 72nd Street to film. (Westsider Books, just down the road on 80th and Broadway, and owned by the same couple, would later feature in John Turturro's 2013 film *Fading Gigolo*, co-starring Woody Allen.) However reluctant Craig had been to appear on camera at the time, he has fond memories of the day. He enjoyed meeting the Swedish filmmakers and seeing Malik's interview style. They filmed for around two hours and it turned out to be harder than he had initially thought it would be. Firstly, because of his advertising job, Craig was far more comfortable being behind the camera himself, and secondly, he had to rack his brain for facts and information that he had not thought about in over a decade. Malik asked questions to establish the storyline, but then, through extensive repetition, carefully re-crafted the answers so that ultimately the story was told in catchy bite-sized snippets. Malik knew the time limitations of a feature documentary and understood the value of sound bites. When the shoot was over, Craig asked Malik to say 'hi' to Sugar. In spite of their close kinship after what they had achieved together, the two fans who had helped reignite Rodriguez's career had not seen each other in over ten years. Craig stepped out onto 72nd just as the heavens opened. It turned out to be a wet walk to MOMA to see a moustache on the *Mona Lisa*.

With hours of footage in the can, there was no time to waste. A few weeks after returning to Sweden, Malik headed off to the north of Italy where he attended one of the biggest international pitch forums for documentaries in Europe. Around 120 projects were sent to the forum and only twenty-two were chosen. The Rodriguez film, at this stage under the working title *The Only One Who Didn't Know*, was one of the favourites. Malik was jubilant. 'It's absolutely amazing,' he told Sugar, 'we won the award for most interesting project and best pitch.'

A piece in the May/June 2008 edition of *Crawdaddy!* was the first mention in the media of the documentary's existence. The article stated that Hysteria Films was hoping to release the feature in early 2010.

In an attempt to capitalise on the upcoming Light in the Attic reissue of *Cold Fact*, in July 2008 Rodriguez played a Saturday-night gig at the Surf Lodge in Montauk on Long Island. Malik flew over to film the show, and recounted the event: 'Everything went really well and it was a great gig. Two sets, 45 minutes each, wonderful to finally hear him play live.'

By making the effort to be there, the filmmaker had finally succeeded in gaining Rodriguez's trust, which resulted in the whole family accepting him, especially Regan. Malik spent some time with Rodriguez and Regan in New York, and actually convinced them to visit Sweden for a week-long holiday with a gig thrown in. He was one step closer to actually having Rodriguez in the film as a fully fleshed-out character.

The singer's trip to Sweden was a happy one in every way. In the words of Malik:

Rodriguez was here for a week with Regan. We had a good time, he even played a very successful gig. I got an eight-piece band together with strings and horns – it sounded great and the venue was packed, maybe 300 persons who all were there to see him. I showed R+R some of Stockholm and they went for a boat ride and saw the Old Town and stuff.

It was around this time that the Light in the Attic reissue of *Cold Fact* finally made its appearance in record stores and created a mini-storm of positive publicity in the music press. In the meantime, Malik was logging air miles as he flew back to New York to film Rodriguez's first-ever Manhattan show, which formed part of the tour to promote the album. It was a small gig in front of 180 people at Joe's Pub in Lower Manhattan. From New York, Malik followed Rodriguez to Detroit, where he filmed the singer's first-ever official gig in his hometown. Malik wrote to Sugar:

It went great, a wonderful show and it was very interesting to hear the locals' stories about this man they've seen walking the streets for years who they didn't know was a great singer. All is well with Rodriguez, he seems very happy with his American adventure!

Back in Stockholm, Malik began editing his footage with an eye on hopefully being accepted to some of the upcoming film forums in Europe. He sent out a new, longer trailer and was accepted to three of the biggest: the Sheffield Doc/Fest in the United Kingdom (where D.A. Pennebaker, the director of Bob Dylan's *Dont Look Back*, was about to pitch his new film), CPH:DOX in Copenhagen and the International Documentary Film Festival Amsterdam (IDFA). Malik also received word that the Swedish Film Institute had come on board. Things were looking good. Back from his travels in the UK and Denmark, he was once again full of good news:

Just came home from Copenhagen after a couple of days of pitching. Before that we were pitching in Sheffield. Everything is going great, we have had meetings with a lot of big guys, the BBC's Storyville, American film distributors Transit and Magnolia (who just had a big documentary hit with what seems to be the documentary of the year, a film called 'Man On Wire' about Philippe Petit, a guy who walked on a [tight]rope between the WTC-towers in 1974, a really great film, worth to check out if you have the chance) and a couple of other interesting names.

We've gotten a very good response, everybody is really keen on to continue to talk to us. But especially the Americans are very hard on contracts, they want to see that Rodriguez gives us the story exclusively so that there won't be any other documentaries coming out on him. We're going to try to get that, hoping that Rodriguez won't be too scared of written agreements ...

But it's an exciting time, when you meet those people who have been involved in all these famous films, your ambition levels just increase. In December, we'll hire a very good screen writer for feature films who will work with us for a couple of weeks to develop the story. After that the idea is to go to Detroit again in January and then probably to South Africa in February, both for some filming and to go through film-archives to find old clips. What I'd really love to find are old Apartheid-clips. Do you know if they ever did any propaganda films?

The next stop was Holland. During his stay in Amsterdam, Malik met with Willemiek Kluijfhout, who had ultimately abandoned her quest to make a Rodriguez documentary. Over coffee, the two discussed the challenges of filming the story. On his return to Sweden, Malik reported:

Came back from IDFA in Amsterdam a couple of days ago! It was quite a nice pitch, IDFA is (they claim) the biggest documentary film festival in the world, and we've had a lot of interesting meetings. We've made our pitch just after a woman who won the Academy Award last year who pitched together with [director] Joe Berlinger who made the 'Metallica: Some Kind of Monster' and our pitch was considered to have been more well made!

Malik and Camilla returned to Detroit in February 2009, by which time the filmmaker had established a very good relationship with the Rodriguez family:

Came back from Detroit a couple of days ago after two weeks of shooting. It all went well. We filmed a lot with Rodriguez, we went with him to a gig in North Carolina and we also filmed at his house, before he didn't even want to show it to us. What a place! Cold!! We also met with a lot of his friends, some really good characters, you know the cool old people that hang out at the Brewery (did you ever go there, Rodriguez's favourite bar?) And we did a lot of filming in Detroit – in the day, in the night, from the ground and from up above. It's an extremely cinematic place. We were there during the coldest winter in ten years, −20°C, white snow everywhere, quite beautiful.

Malik was still searching for a title for the film. So far they had come up with plenty, but none that seemed 'just right'. The working title used in the pitch forums, *The Only One Who Didn't Know*, was a tad too long. Rodriguez preferred *The Man Who Found Out*, but Malik felt it revealed too much of the story. Other suggestions included *Deconstructing Fame*, *Sugar Man*, *The Cold Facts*, *I Wonder*, *Inner City Blues* and *The Man from Detroit*. Title or no, the Swedish Film Institute was very happy with the new footage from Detroit and gave

Malik more funding so that he could continue to film. It was clear he was having financial problems, but at that stage he was so committed to the project that he would have done just about anything to make it happen.

Sugar wrote to Malik to tell him that Rodriguez was returning to South Africa that September for another tour of the country. Malik replied:

Everything is going really well with the film. Last Friday we got a yes from a big American film fund (who recently co-produced the Oscar-nominated documentary 'Waltz With Bashir'). That's the biggest individual contributor to the film so far, we're very happy! Later this week we're going to join Rodriguez on a part of his European tour, in Paris, Rome and London. This spring I almost only focused on Rodriguez. Not only creative work, as a lot of work is just writing different treatments and synopses and storyboards to satisfy all the strange requirements from the different funders.

The process seemed to be wearing him down somewhat:

Half of the time you feel like a prostituted beggar, half of the time you feel that you're actually doing something that will be quite good. I guess it's worth it though, if you want the big guys in it takes so much time it almost drives you crazy, but it gives you so much more possibilities when you actually get the go-ahead. Right now we got more than 50% of the budget in place, and according [to] the producers of the film who've done this before, the first half is the tricky one, the second half often comes much easier.

In June 2009 Malik attended Rodriguez's London gig at the Barbican Theatre. Two of Sugar's children, Daniell and Natalia, were in the audience. About 60 per cent of the 1,000-strong crowd was South African. Having just spent some more time with Rodriguez, Malik again wrote to Sugar about his experience with the singer:

Rodriguez is not the easiest guy to be friends with. Someone told me something that might be true: Rodriguez likes new people and to make new acquaintances but the closer you think you get to him, he'll react in the opposite way. You never know Rodriguez better than the first day you met him. It's a strange thing, it was a bit like that for us, he was never as willing to co-operate in the film as he was the first time we met him.

Sugar agreed with Malik's observations, but added, 'Hey, who are we to tell him how to behave? He's the legend; we are just in service of the legend.'

About the film, Malik reported:

The film is going really good. I'm sitting editing all day long. It's great fun. It's fascinating to see how the material takes different shapes when you just alter some small music piece or use some other interview parts. It's quite creative and fun to sit and experiment and see how the film takes new forms.

Ultimately, Malik decided not to film the 2009 South African tour, saying:

I don't think we're going to go to South Africa for the

Rodriguez shows. He's so afraid of being filmed and feels so uncomfortable when he's having a film crew around that we told him [we won't] film anything that we don't absolutely need. Better to wait until the film is almost finished and try to get him in front of the camera if there [is] some crucial gap somewhere. Fortunately the parts with Rodriguez are quite powerful already.

Perhaps because of bad blood from the 2005 London tour, for the first time ever Rodriguez didn't contact Sugar while in Cape Town or pay his customary visit to Mabu Vinyl to say hello. Sugar was disappointed; nonetheless, he attended the concert on 13 September as a fan. It was about the sixteenth Rodriguez gig that Sugar had seen to date, and it was good. As had become usual, Rodriguez was helped onto the stage because of his poor eyesight. He was wearing about five layers of clothing, which he slowly removed until he was down to his customary black shirt with the collar and sleeves cut off. He played really well and had a decent backing band. The crowd loved it as always. There were no surprises, apart from Rodriguez's choice of opening song, Paolo Nutini's 'Last Request'. Its inclusion was perhaps in recognition of Nutini's 2006 cover of 'Sugar Man'.

Then, on 30 September, Sugar got a call from Eva, completely out of the blue. She was at the airport with her father, about to leave for the US, and Rodriguez wanted to say a quick hello. They had a really friendly chat and Rodriguez sounded very happy and excited about the documentary. After all that had transpired, it was a pleasant surprise, to say the least.

Ultimately, however, it turned out to be a good thing that Malik did not film the South African tour. A fan wrote on the Sugarman.org forum that Rodriguez wasn't on top form at

The Barnyard in Plettenberg Bay and that the show was musically weak, with some indifferent performances from the backing band.

Nevertheless, Malik, ever positive and prepared to see only the very best in every human being, forged ahead with his documentary, using ingenuity and charm in the absence of budget, and forging friendships with every character . . . *Darling Malik, where have you been all my life?*

17

A slowdive off
Chapman's Peak
(2009–2011)

'When I see three oranges, I juggle; when I see two
towers, I walk!'
— PHILIPPE PETIT, TO REACH THE CLOUDS: MY HIGH
WIRE WALK BETWEEN THE TWIN TOWERS

*Imagine it is the evening of October the fourteenth, 1988.
Imagine you are Christopher White, driving home. You are
extremely tired and not watching the road properly.'* So goes the
voiceover for one of South Africa's most iconic television
commercials, as we watch a white Mercedes-Benz driving on
what seems to be a perilous, winding coastal road with a
yawning drop to the right. Suddenly, at a particular bend,
the car swerves off the road, plunges down an impossibly
high cliff – rolling, bouncing and pounding the cliffside –
and finally crash-lands on the rocky beach below. *'In some
accidents, no car can save lives,'* the voiceover continues, *'in
others only the safest car would. Christopher White survived this*

100-metre plunge for two reasons: he was wearing a seatbelt, and he was driving a Mercedes-Benz.' True story. A short while later, a commercial aired featuring a blue BMW driving along the same stretch of road. This time, at the point where the Mercedes-Benz plunged off the cliff, the BMW effortlessly navigates the bend. *'Doesn't it make sense to drive a luxury sedan that beats the bends?'* asks the narrator, with obvious play on the homophones 'bends' and 'Benz'. Clever comparative advertising aside, many would argue that the real hero of these two adverts is the remarkable, and now iconic, road that the vehicles are attempting to navigate.

Chapman's Peak Drive is a breathtakingly beautiful nine-kilometre route with 114 potentially perilous curves skirting the rocky coastline of Chapman's Peak on the Atlantic coast of Cape Town. It is a world-renowned attraction and so it came as no surprise that on one of Malik Bendjelloul's first location scouts in 2010 with Sugar Segerman at the wheel, they ended up driving along this cliff pass. Fast-forward a few weeks, and Sugar, driving his daughter's grey Volkswagen Passat for the day, has been asked to circumnavigate this treacherous stretch of road once more, this time while talking into a camera. It is blisteringly hot outside. Director of photography Camilla Skagerström sits in the back, while Malik fiddles with his iPhone in the front passenger seat. Mounted on the bonnet is the camera that will film the whole sequence from the exterior. Playing on repeat on the car's sound system was Malik's favourite album *Souvlaki* from the English rock band Slowdive. *Slowdive off Chapman's Peak*, Sugar thinks, recalling Christopher White's now-infamous plunge off that very cliff.

Those familiar with the film will recognise this as the opening scene of *Searching for Sugar Man*.

*

By January 2010, it was clear that Malik had high hopes for his film, as he wrote to Sugar about the documentary *Man on Wire*, which had won the 2009 Academy Award for Best Documentary Feature:

> I love 'Man on Wire!' It's a good inspiration. It's a narratively well-told story about a spectacular event that happened in the past, just like the Rodriguez film. But the Rodriguez film will be better! Haha! No, I don't know, but I've really looked at them very closely and compared them, and I do think that the Rodriguez film will have in many ways a couple of more exciting scenes. But, it's hard to tell. 'Man on Wire' is really a great film. (And it won the Oscar!)

As previously mentioned, *Man on Wire*, directed and produced by Brits James Marsh and Simon Chinn respectively, chronicles French tightrope-walker Philippe Petit's daring, and illegal, high-wire walk between the Twin Towers of the World Trade Center in New York on the morning of 7 August 1974. Malik could not help comparing his film with *Man on Wire*, even though his was far from finished. While Marsh's film covered what was hailed as the 'artistic crime of the century', Malik's covered an artistic crime of a different sort: the crime of a world robbed of the music of a creative genius through circumstance (plus the fact that Rodriguez wasn't paid royalties). In addition, both films make use of fictional devices – surprise, suspense and good old-fashioned story-telling – to tell a non-fiction story.

Craig Strydom was living in Baltimore when *Man on Wire* came out in 2008, and he went to see it at the famous Charles Theatre. By the time the end credits began to roll, he was gobsmacked. How could a non-fiction film be so suspenseful? And then he noticed that it had been edited by Jinx Godfrey, an editor he'd worked with on two commercials for the Maryland State Lottery. Craig was impressed. When, in 2009, Malik mentioned that he was looking for a good editor for the Rodriguez film, Craig immediately recommended Jinx Godfrey. It is not known if Malik ever contacted her.

About a month before his *Man on Wire* musings, Malik had given Sugar another one of his regular updates on the documentary's progress. The date was 14 December 2009:

> The film is going good. It's like a Marathon race. Sometimes I regret I didn't do it in the way I normally do things, fast and flexible. With such an impatient man as Rodriguez it's quite nerve-wracking to do it like this, but when you speak to people who [have] been involved in the documentary world longer than me their advice is always that if you want to do a good film, you need patience and you need time. And our schedule is still on time. It takes time, but it's supposed to. The structuring will be finished in mid-February (after involving a guy who's considered the best editor in Sweden in January and first half of February). After that we'll do three filming trips: to South Africa, to the States and to Israel). The editor quite likes to work on his own, so I might go to South Africa already in a month, mid-January, for location search and some research. Then there will be editing for a couple of months and the film will, if everything goes like it should, be ready in May–June [2010]. The last few weeks has been quite focused on further funding stuff and I'm really dying to start filming!

In the next email Malik wrote:

I'd love to catch up with you already then, but the big question is where will you be in the second half of February? And if you will be in Cape Town – would you have the time to do some filming?? Sorry for always changing the dates and being inconsistent, but it seems it is [what] filmmaking is all about ...

Malik needn't have worried. Sugar was exactly where he'd left him, cocooned in his den.

In February 2010, the filmmaker arrived in Cape Town for his second visit, this time with Daniel Hager, a friend from Denmark. They checked into a guesthouse in Buitengracht Street and immediately began scouting locations with Sugar. It was during one of these expeditions that they drove on Chapman's Peak Drive for the first time. While they scouted, Malik worked with Sugar on a 'dialogue outline'. Something that surprised Sugar, Craig and Matt Sullivan in the final cut of the film was that some of the dialogue originally said by one person would later come out of someone else's mouth. To understand this curious phenomenon, one needs to understand the influence of German director Werner Herzog on Malik's work. The Swede often cited Herzog as a major influence and would frequently bring him up in conversation. In an article on Herzog in the *Financial Times*, journalist Leo Robson explains:

In his own nonfiction films, Herzog wants to tell stories and he doesn't feel beholden to fact. His approach to documentary is an alternative to cinéma vérité, the observational aesthetic that proceeds 'as if presenting facts was everything.' Just because something is factually true, he argues, 'it does not constitute truth per se.' Herzog likes to respond to and collaborate with his subjects; if he bends fact – by inventing dialogue, for instance – it is to the ends of 'truth.' The Manhattan phone directory provides millions of correct entries, he says, 'but it doesn't inspire you'; in the film, he says it doesn't tell you what Manhattanites dream. Instead of fact, which is the 'accountant's truth,' he is after the kind of 'ecstatic truth' available to poetry: 'These moments are rare but I'm trying to find them.'

With some of the dialogue outlines, such as the following example by Sugar, Malik takes a leaf out of Herzog's book:

> I actually got my name from this song! You see when I was in the army Segerman wasn't a common name so everyone used to mispronounce it as 'Sugarman', after the Rodriguez song. So Segerman became 'Sugar Man'. Hence my nickname, 'Sugar'.

In Malik's view, this small distortion of how Stephen became Sugar was 'to the ends of truth'. He would also take certain speeches or chunks of dialogue said by one person and ask someone else to relay the very same story, in order to spread the representation of that particular player in the film. The story about scrutinising the lyrics that Sugar tells in the elevator in Cape Town, for example, actually comes from Craig's original 'Looking for Rodriguez' article that appeared in *Directions* magazine and which Craig himself divulged while shooting with Malik in New York. At the time, the director had crafted the syntactic flow of Craig's speech so as to have palatable sound bites suitable for a documentary. Later, Malik had Brian Currin as well as Sugar relate the same story. In the end, it just made sense to him to have Sugar detail the geographical search for Rodriguez that took place in the late 1990s. Needless to say, this caused resentment among sticklers for the truth. Ultimately, though, Malik was a sculptor of information and understood better than anyone the arcs, rhythm and flow of a story, as well as an audience's craving for a fiction-like progression. As an artist, it was natural to him to use fiction devices to tell a non-fiction story. He would have applied similar logic when he chose to leave out Rodriguez's tours Down Under in 1979 and 1981. The events in Australia just did not suit the narrative.

Malik and Sugar worked on the proposed dialogue until Daniel left and Camilla arrived. All were anxious to start filming again. This time Malik knew exactly what he wanted as he had already started putting the various elements of the film on a workable timeline in Final Cut Pro. With Sugar's help, Malik prioritised which scenes needed to be filmed first. The notoriously volatile Cape Town weather seemed to be holding out, with February being as hot and dry as expected. Of course, the infamous southeaster wind, also known as the Cape Doctor, could blow into town at any time and that would be that. But the weather gods smiled on the production and allowed the small crew to finish filming. Sugar chauffeured the team around in Natalia's Passat, searching for more locations and shooting randomly whenever the opportunity presented itself. Malik wanted a San Francisco-like aerial view of the city, so Sugar took them to the top of Molteno Road in Oranjezicht, a few streets from his own home, where they shot footage of the car driving up the hill to his house.

To recreate the scene in which Craig and Sugar meet for

the first time in 1996 to combine their searches, they found a Mexican restaurant with outdoor seating. The area looked perfect and Malik approached a guy who vaguely resembled Craig having a beer at one of the outside tables. With his customary charm, Malik convinced the guy to be in the scene. As he took his seat opposite the lookalike, Sugar recognised the man as Dutch journalist Aernout Zevenbergen, with whom he had done some DVD business at Mabu Vinyl. Small world. The two had a long conversation, during which Sugar completely forgot that he was being filmed. Once Malik was done shooting, he went over and complimented Sugar on his natural acting skills! Next they filmed Sugar talking to the barman, who also turned out to be a customer of Mabu Vinyl. The film would be truly local. By now Malik had also discovered the value of a $1.99 iPhone app called '8mm', which was giving him the 'Super-8' look he was after on certain scenes for that authentic 'old South Africa' feel.

Malik and Camilla became obsessed with the wide cityscapes of Cape Town and Detroit as stylistic transitions and bookends, and so the team took a room in the Cape Sun Hotel, a high-rise strategically located in downtown Cape Town. The top of the building provided the vista for the now-recognisable external cityscapes, and its exterior glass elevator was perfect for filming the scene in which Sugar explains how analysing the lyrics for geographical locations helped them find Rodriguez. Malik pasted clear plastic decals of the lyrics on the elevator window so that they could use Table Mountain as a backdrop. For the duration of the Cape Town shoot, it was always just the three of them, Malik, Camilla and Sugar. The only time a crew was used was when a jib arm was needed, once for an external shot of Mabu Vinyl as the camera pans from Devil's Peak down to the store's sign, and once for the filming of a mock-celebration of Rodriguez's birthday (complete with hokey *Cold Fact* birthday cake), when the camera pans down and moves through the Mabu Vinyl window and into the store.

Two days were set aside for filming the big opening scene on Chapman's Peak Drive. Malik wanted the film to start with Sugar supposedly driving home from the record store, talking to the camera about the mystery surrounding Rodriguez. He wanted it big and scenic, and so he chose the drive from Hout Bay to Noordhoek via Chapman's Peak. Ultimately, as anyone who has seen the movie can attest, the twisting bends and steep cliffs down to the ocean made for attention-grabbing stuff. But shooting it was not easy, especially for Sugar.

It was already scorching hot by the time the trio set out to film the scene at ten in the morning on the first day, Camilla with her camera and Malik with his iPhone. A bracket on which to mount the camera was attached to the bonnet of the car. They shot all the way along the coast from the city bowl to Hout Bay, with sea on their right and mountains on their left, and from there they drove slowly along the first long sweeping section of Chapman's Peak, climbing with the road as Hout Bay fell away behind them. After about two kilometres, they reached the parking area at the highest point, where tourists usually stop to admire the view back over Hout Bay Harbour and the Sentinel, the mountain peak overlooking the bay. About one kilometre from that first parking area was another smaller car park, but it only had space for a few cars. Malik wanted Sugar to drive that one-kilometre stretch of winding road down towards Noordhoek with the camera mounted on the bonnet and slowly articulate the opening monologue. At the same time, Sugar had to navigate a series of tricky bends, while the sun burnt its way gradually down and across the driver's window. What Malik hadn't told anyone was that he already had the perfect shot in mind: he wanted Sugar's speech to coincide with the sun reaching a height where it was visible through the driver's window. This meant that Sugar – hands sweating and perspiration pouring from his forehead – had to redo the scene about twenty-five times. As he drove back up to the starting point, turned around and slowly drove back down, navigating the bends and reciting his speech for the umpteenth time, Sugar thought that whoever said making a movie was fun should have been on Chapman's Peak that day.

On day two, Malik hired a helicopter to film an aerial shot of the car driving along the perilous cliff pass. But heavy winds put paid to that, and once again, with no real budget to speak of, the filmmaker was forced to improvise. Finally, to solve the helicopter-weather issue, Malik and Camilla set up the camera on a crane and, rogue-style, simply waited for a grey car to come along that they could film to get the overhead shot they were after. They got one pretty close to the Passat, so everyone was happy, especially Sugar, who'd had enough of this acting business for a while. After two weeks of successful shooting, it was time for Malik and Camilla to head home. Over his two visits, Malik had spent about six weeks in South Africa and was becoming quite familiar and comfortable with his new adopted country. Writing from Stockholm, he made it clear that he was satisfied with the footage shot so far.

On 7 March 2010, Sugar watched the Oscars, and afterwards, with a certain amount of prescience, emailed Malik a message of support:

Hi Malik,

I've been awake since two this morning. Yesterday was an unbearable 40 degrees [Celsius]. It was also Ronit and my Silver wedding anniversary, 25 years, how about that! But it was too languidly hot to do anything apart from laze around on the blue couch in the den in front of the overworked fan. But I didn't mind being up, as the Oscars start live on TV at 3 in the morning here, so I watched them live. [...]

I always look to those winners of the smaller categories, not Meryl Streep or Morgan Freeman, or those like James Cameron who will be back there in the front row many more times. No, I like the lesser known winners, those usually unknown creatives who get to experience that once-in-a-lifetime moment, to stand on that stage in front of 3 billion people and get honoured and rewarded for that specific project they have just poured their souls into, and when they do, I think about who they are, their parents, where they grew up, what dreams they had and what complicated road they took to get to that moment, and I'm sure there is always a fascinating story behind each of them, and I feel more for those winners than for the big stars.

And I always feel strangely inspired by them and their success, because it always spells out the same message, and it's that ANYONE can have a dream come true [...] every year I think about what I could possibly do, apart from trying to inspire my kids, to even get a fraction of a glimpse of what that must feel like.

And then, for the first time in my life, while watching the Oscars this morning, which I have done for over 30 years, I realised that there now exists the possibility that something I am involved in could possibly be in next year's Oscar ceremony. What a wonderful thought, and such a positive and powerful and hopeful feeling, and although I am fully aware that it is the same dream that many people making movies right now have as well, there is no harm in having that dream, we have to always completely believe in what we are doing, do the best that we can and do it for that reason and not think of the possible successes or consequences. [...] This year [the Oscars] felt different, and I felt a weird connection to the ceremony.

Malik replied:

Let's bring it home! You're right, it's true that hundreds of films are competing, but it's just as true that every year they need one that is good enough to actually win [...] So without being too megalomaniac, but also without being too unassuming it's quite fair to say WHY NOT?

Malik also told Sugar that he had received an email from Matt Sullivan to say that Clarence Avant had provisionally given them permission to use Rodriguez's music as the film's soundtrack. To have come this far without knowing whether or not the songs could actually be used had been risky, but classic Malik.

The long and lonely editing process continued in Sweden. Financially, Malik was just scraping by. Later in March, he emailed Sugar to let him know that things were on track, and that the editor and animator were hard at work while he spent most of his time searching through old archive footage. It was a satisfying feeling, he wrote, 'that three processes are working simultaneously'. He also told Sugar that he and Camilla were heading back to Detroit in a couple of weeks.

A little later, in May, a quiet and unassuming

fourteen-minute documentary called *Micky Bader* (*Bathing Micky*) was awarded the Jury Prize in the short-film category at the 2010 Cannes International Film Festival. This came as a surprise to many, especially considering the film had been refused by SVT, Danish television and the Swedish Film Institute, and had even been 'criticised quite rudely by the latter', according to Malik. The film, which focuses on a 100-year-old Danish woman who swims in the sea every day regardless of the weather or season, had something in common with Malik's: cinematographer Camilla Skagerström. The short includes tranquil, scenic shots with an emphasis on the terrain, which Camilla treats almost as if it's another character. This is not unlike her treatment of Detroit and Cape Town in *Searching for Sugar Man*, where the cities could be characters themselves. Malik was energised by *Micky Bader*'s success and hoped that a little of the stardust would rub off on him.

Visiting Detroit for the third time, Malik and Camilla finally found Rodriguez in a talkative mood for the cameras and they filmed another full interview with him inside the Brewery. They also filmed some of his friends, including the articulate Rick Emmerson and the animated Jerome Ferretti, and were able to shoot a breathtakingly beautiful sequence of downtown Detroit during a dramatic thunderstorm. It was a quick trip, and on his return to Stockholm Malik settled back into the process of reviewing the footage they had shot to date. He managed to put together a rough cut, which he thought could be final enough to chance his luck with the Sundance Institute. The 2011 film festival was taking entries and he was already thinking ahead. He asked Sugar for his advice:

I'm trying to figure out if the film will be as good as it can get by then ... The festival is in mid-January, and there's quite a lot still to do ... Animations and stuff. We'll see ... The only thing is that Sundance really is the best place to have the premiere (or maybe it's just pure chance that five of the films that won the documentary-Oscar the last six years premiered at the Sundance...?) so if it's not as perfect as it can be by then, maybe it might be a wise decision to wait a whole year. It's a bit of a difficult decision ...

Sugar advised Malik to 'take the extra time. What's the hurry? It's a timeless story and a film for all time.'

In late 2010, Malik sent Sugar a copy of the film as it stood. Sugar's response to the director after watching it was: 'Very powerful and very moving, I cried like a baby!'

Malik decided to send the rough cut to Sundance. Things were falling into place, in spite of the problems he still faced: the money which was increasingly becoming an issue; the music licensing, which was still only provisional and hung over his head; a souring relationship with his producer; and the ever-elusive title. Concerning the title, Sugar made a strong case for *Sugar Man*, because, he said, 'it's very recognisable as a Rodriguez reference for those who already know him. And for those who don't know, they will get the reference soon after. They will also fall under the spell of this amazing artist and his landmark song.' Malik was wavering:

Yes, quite strong and convincing arguments! Maybe it should be called 'Sugar Man.' Maybe it actually is the answer to our dream. How strong is the drug connotation in the English language? Can you hear the words Sugar Man without thinking of drugs? And would that be a problem?

The analytical filmmaker was leaving no stone unturned, but Sugar assured him that it would be fine. Naming issues aside, however, it was money trouble that was proving to be Malik's biggest hurdle. While funding had been coming in in dribs and drabs, it was never quite enough to fully sustain four years without income. In addition, the mounting travel costs, the cinematographer's fees and a film treatment that required expensive animation all meant that Malik's dream film was always just a few kronor away from grinding to a complete halt.

A few weeks after his discussion with Sugar about the title, Malik hit another snag. Writing to Sugar, he said that a woman to whom he showed the film a few days earlier had some problems with the part of the storyline where Rodriguez suddenly wants to become mayor. 'She feels it doesn't really go along with his humble personality. Did you have any problems with that?' Sugar told Malik that, in his opinion, Rodriguez running for mayor showed that the singer was a genuinely caring person. He had wanted to become more involved in his community in order to effect positive change. Sugar therefore didn't see it as a problem.

With the coffers all but dry, Malik sought out freelance video-production work to keep his head above water and managed to secure a shoot through a production company called Protagonist in March 2011. He conveyed the news to Sugar:

I have some good news. A friend of mine asked me last week if I wanted to work in Los Angeles for eight days, earn $1,000 a day and film some fashion models. Why not, I said, and so I did. I just came back yesterday. And it was just one of these weird trips where everything good that could happen happened, and bad as well [...] for example, falling into a Beverly Hills swimming pool with a very nice HD-camera. Anyway, just in case, in the back of my mind I was thinking that if something happens, like the Protagonist girl gets ill or something I just might have a few minutes to spare to add a few shots to the Rodriguez film.

As luck would have it, on the first day he found some time to 'sneak out' and interview Light in the Attic Records owner Matt Sullivan in LA. What he really wanted to get out of the trip to California, however, was to film another scene with Steve Rowland – but Rowland lived in Palm Springs, more than a hundred miles away. Malik realised this would be impossible, as it would cost around $1,000 for a taxi and it would take a full day, during which he would somehow have to give the appearance of still being in LA, because he was supposed to be available for the fashion project at all times. But luck remained on his side:

[B]y pure chance the girls suddenly want to go to – PALM SPRINGS! Why? Beats me! No idea!
But that didn't help much really, in Palm Springs I was still supposed to give my full attention to these girls, there would be no time to do anything else. But – what happens – the girls say they want to go to a fancy hotel and sneak in to the swimming-pool and just do some sun-bathing (models you know) so there was nothing really I could film, it would be better if I did something else for about an hour they said. So immediately I called Steve, who was home and willing to meet, I asked a cab driver how far it was to his house – I was THREE MINUTES away, the girls had driven me to his doorstep. I went over to his house, in one hour

and fifteen minutes I filmed the last missing scene with
Steve, the scene where Steve finds some old photos of
Rodriguez in a drawer. And it turned out really nice.

The girls thought I was out having a coffee ...

With the Steve Rowland shoot now complete, and the
Matt Sullivan interview in the can, one would have expected
Malik to be satisfied with the progress he had made. But
there were still a few bridges to cross. For various reasons
known only to the parties involved, Malik's relationship
with Hysteria Films and Malla Grapengiesser had by now
soured completely. He needed a new producer, but not just
any producer. He had his heart set on the Oscar-winning
London-based producer of *Man on Wire*, Simon Chinn, and
his production company Red Box Films. Now that he had a
relatively complete rough cut, instinct told Malik it was time
to somehow get the film before Chinn's discerning eyes. But
for that to happen he would need a little more luck to come
his way.

And it did. The 'Protagonist girl', as he referred to her in
his email, was in the process of setting up a web-based
fashion network and had scheduled a meeting in London,
which she asked Malik to film on his way back to Sweden. As
his plane took off from LAX and he watched the four-legged
Populuxe-style control tower recede, the filmmaker must
have wondered where his crazy dream would take him next.

18

Butch and Sundance
(2011–2012)

'Even good films are sometimes lost in the wind.'
— MALIK BENDJELLOUL, DIRECTOR, *SEARCHING FOR SUGAR MAN*

The almost 9,000-kilometre trip across the Atlantic was as good a time as any to take stock. Nursing a beer – Malik never quite got through even a single brew – a few things must have been playing on his mind. The footage for the documentary, born out of a *Kobra*-sponsored fact-finding mission, was now largely completed, including a 'bonus' interview with Steve Rowland. But the project, which was supposed to take one year to complete, was now in its fourth year and still had a way to go. Malik hadn't earned a single krona, and by this stage he and his Swedish Film Institute–assigned producer, Malla Grapengiesser, had left a complicated web of contracts and movie deals in their wake. He did, however, have one comforting thought.

Before the late fifties, when promotional films (the

precursors of music videos) came into play, musicians struggled to find illustrative ways to get their music into the public domain. The earliest known form of the music-video genre was the 'illustrated song', a type of performance art used to promote music and songs in the early twentieth century. Tony Bennett claims to have invented the music video in 1956 with his promotional film for the song 'Stranger in Paradise'. In 1959 Elvis made his first promotional film with *Jailhouse Rock*. In 1967, D.A. Pennebaker took the genre one step further with *Dont Look Back*, a documentary film covering Bob Dylan's 1965 concert tour in the UK. By the eighties, with the launch of MTV and music shows on other channels, music videos had become a global phenomenon, and mandatory for any up-and-coming artist. So what Malik was essentially offering Rodriguez was a belated eighty-six-minute promotional music video to introduce his music to the world. If the documentary succeeded, Rodriguez's music would be heard by masses of people. No wonder record companies do cartwheels each time a studio calls asking permission to feature one of their artist's songs in a movie. Film, if done right, has the power to send songs into the stratosphere. This might explain Clarence Avant's willingness to offer up the rights to Rodriguez's songs for the documentary even though it did not portray him in a completely favourable light.

Of course, no matter how good, the film would only succeed in this oversubscribed industry if it had a strong backer, a reputable production company to usher it through the birthing process. It needed an executive producer with connections, someone who knew how to circumnavigate the pitfalls of not just documentary production but also post-production and, most importantly, distribution. It needed an expert who knew how to create publicity for a story in a crowded field of stories all vying for attention in an easily distracted society, because, with no eyeballs on it, even the best film in the world will fail. There is a popular advertising slogan that claims, 'Doing business without advertising is like winking at a girl in the dark.' Malik needed Simon Chinn, the Oscar-winning producer.

By the time the plane touched down in London, Malik's meeting with the aspirant fashion blogger had been cancelled. Finding himself serendipitously with a free day in London, he headed straight for Chinn's office. Of course, anyone other than Malik would have realised that he couldn't just waltz in and expect to see Chinn without an appointment. But the Swedish filmmaker, improvising and summoning his trademark charm, asked the receptionist to please tell Mr Chinn that he, Malik Bendjelloul, had a film better than *Man on Wire*. It was a ballsy thing to say, considering that the film in question had won an Academy Award. The producer could have reacted in a number of ways, particularly with annoyance, as he probably had a lot of wannabes knocking on his door in search of Oscar glory. But Chinn, as cool as ever and to his eternal credit, agreed to see the eager young director. And so it came about that Malik met Simon Chinn, son of British businessman and philanthropist Sir Trevor Chinn, and the filmmaker's infectious charm soon won over the producer, who consented at least to watch the rough cut.

It was a coup, but the joy would be short-lived, as Malik returned to Stockholm to find an email in his inbox from Rodriguez's youngest daughter, Regan, bearing bad tidings. It was the kind of email that came with the territory. As a documentary filmmaker with no real budget, Malik often found himself having to placate his films' subjects. He wrote to Sugar about the new fire he had to stomp out:

> Just got an email from Regan, saying, 'please take most of my parts out', hmmm … I've heard before that she's a bit worried about looking too stiff … Well, that's the danger in showing stuff too early to people, they start [to] worry … I'll tell her that I'll do my best, and kindly ask her to wait with her final decision until she sees the final product … I was anyway thinking to film all the family interviews again, and then I could really try to customize her lines in a way that she's completely happy with … And if there's still a problem like in September – three daughters might not be needed, two might also do alright maybe … There's always ways of working around things, I guess …

Sugar disagreed with this last assertion. Featuring only two daughters would have impacted negatively on Malik's already fragile understanding with the publicity-shy singer. Not only did the film need the exclusive look into Rodriguez's life that only the three daughters could provide, but as long as they were happy and on board, their over-protective father would be happy too. Sugar responded to Malik:

> Regan is a bit stiff on camera, but what she is saying is serious and important to the movie. So I think it works. Nobody likes what he or she looks like on camera (me included) but that's no reason to start changing scenes to keep the 'actors' happy. If the opportunity arises I would also like to re-record sections of some of my speeches ('Love' is not a San Francisco band, for example) but I

would never insist, and I have to point out to you that this is your movie.

He might have been correct about it being Malik's film, but ultimately a documentary filmmaker relies on the goodwill of others, who give up their time to participate in a film that has financial gain as one of its primary goals but for which they themselves earn little to nothing in return. Malik's only real leverage with his subjects in this film was that it had the potential to ignite interest in Rodriguez's music.

In the midst of all this, Sugar watched *Man on Wire* and was inspired to do a curious thing. After watching the documentary, he looked up in his den and noticed that two of the bookcases resembled the World Trade Center towers. Inspired by the 'art crime of the century', he strung a piece of wire between the two bookracks and balanced a miniature Manchester United soccer-player figurine (he is a committed fan), holding a tightrope walker's pole, on the wire to replicate Philippe Petit's endeavour. He took some photographs, which he then emailed to Malik. He called the installation *Sugar Man United on Wire*:

I took these pics to show you. Not sure why. But if it does turn out that [Simon Chinn] is interested in getting involved then this would turn out to be quite a prophetic sculpture, don't you think? 'Sugar Man,' 'Man On Wire,' and 'Man United,' phew!

After reading what was perhaps the zaniest email he had ever received, Malik wrote back, adding his own crazy banter to the mix:

290

> HAHAHA! I love it! It's like that rock star called 'Boy George
> Michael Jackson Browne.'

Malik was actually making a reference to the 2002 epi-
sodic web film by Memo Salazar called *Boy George Michael
Jackson Browne* (most reviewers agreed that the title was the
best thing it had going for it). Malik also told Sugar that he
had had a long chat on Skype with Steve Rowland who had
just watched the latest cut of the film:

> He said he thought the film was fantastic and his girlfriend
> came to the Skype-cam and said that she was crying for
> the whole last part of the film … and also thought it was
> incredibly good.

The next day, 1 May 2011, Malik emailed Sugar with
amazing news. Simon Chinn had called to say he was keen
and would like to be involved, although he needed the
go-ahead of his US co-funders, the Independent Television
Service (ITVS). The producer thought the film was 'really,
really good, and that he didn't have much to add, maybe just
a little bit more on why Rodriguez never became famous in
the US, despite the quality of the music'. In a follow-up
email, Malik reported that 'all is good with the film, this
week the animations and the original music are the top priority'. He planned to visit Detroit in July to do some extra
filming, and was 'still trying hard to get Simon Chinn on
board' officially. Although Chinn was interested, he was still
waiting for a reply from ITVS to see what deals Malla
Grapengiesser had made and to assess if the film was still
financially viable for him. Malik wrote:

> And then the next step is to convince Malla – or maybe, since no contract between Malla and myself is written – to just leave her, which might be quite an interesting option. We have no contract, I can actually do whatever I want to do with the film.

Malik was not that kind of person, however. Although he was unhappy about what his relationship with Malla had become, he would never imagine that an agreement between them did not exist.

In late June 2011, Malik returned to Detroit to fill in the blanks. He could no longer afford a cinematographer, so decided to operate the camera and record sound himself. He said he found Rodriguez to be 'another man':

> We were together just he and I and sometimes his new girl-friend for eight or ten hours a day, just talking, talking, and talking [...] He is one of the most intelligent, humorous, thoughtful, creative, generous and interesting persons I have ever met. I'd rather sit and have coffee with Rodriguez than fifteen of my closest friends in Stockholm, for no other reason than that the dialogue would be more interesting. And COFFEE – it was all about coffee now, we went to a new coffee house just close to his house instead of the usual bars. Last time he couldn't walk because his eyesight was so bad, now his eyes work again, we walked all over town. Every night he took me to different events, concerts, exhibitions, and cultural stuff. What a wonderful thing. Most of the time we spoke about the film. I think he really is hoping for this film to happen.

Rodriguez had separated from Konny and was now dating

a woman named Bonnie Stempeck Bulyk, whom he had met at the shop where he often had his boots mended. Malik thought she was good for the singer, even though she was much younger than him. He found her calm, kind and helpful.

While he was in the US, Malik called Craig Strydom. At one point he said to Craig, 'I have someone here who would like to talk to you.' And then Rodriguez came on the line. It was the first time Craig had spoken to him since the first South African tour in 1998. He enjoyed catching up with the singer on the phone. Rodriguez was warm and gracious, enquiring about Craig's family and Baltimore, and expressing his happiness with how the documentary was proceeding. Craig was excited to tell his house guests who it had been on the other end of the line, but it didn't mean anything to them at the time.

Malik arrived in Baltimore a week later to see Craig. After dinner they watched the latest cut of the film. It was the first time Craig was seeing any of it and he voiced his shock at hearing his own story coming from other people's mouths. Malik told him about his technique of reassigning parts of the story to peripheral players so as to make the film more interesting. In spite of this, Craig was impressed. The person he had thought of as a film student when he first called back in 2008 had turned out to be a consummate filmmaker. The next day Malik shot several scenes in Craig's house, which went a long way towards alleviating some of Craig's concerns. On the Sunday of Malik's departure, he and the Strydom family went to the historic Charles Theatre to see Woody Allen's *Midnight in Paris*. It was Craig's daughter Isabella's first grown-up film. Before he left, Malik told Craig about the difficulties he was experiencing making the Rodriguez documentary. How he had been forced to learn the techniques of animation in order to complete those portions of the film. How he had started scoring parts of the feature because there was no money and he had no choice. And other than a festival licence, he also had not yet – and this was crucial – obtained definitive permission to use Rodriguez's music. This was serious. The whole thing was obviously taking its toll on the filmmaker. Craig noticed how thin he'd become. After leaving Baltimore, Malik went on to shoot a few additional scenes with Mike Theodore in New Jersey. The air miles certainly were racking up.

A short while later Malik wrote to Sugar saying that he and Simon Chinn 'now speak a couple of times a week' and that Malla had agreed to let Malik buy her out. But this posed a new problem, as she wanted what seemed to Malik to be a considerable amount of money. 'But now it's negotiation time,' wrote Malik, 'and that's at least something [. . .] Simon seems quite convinced that everything will be sorted out. It's really quite inspiring that he is so interested.' Malik had supreme confidence in Chinn, explaining to Sugar:

Rotten Tomatoes is a 'review aggregator,' it collects and summarizes all major American film critics' reviews into 'good' and 'bad' reviews. In the left hand column you can see that the best-reviewed film right now in the US, all genres, is the James Marsh/Simon Chinn film 'Project Nim' (about a chimp, have you heard about it?) In the right hand column you can see that the second best-reviewed film EVER in America is 'Man On Wire.'

Around this time, Malik received an email from John Battsek, who Chinn was putting forward as executive producer on the film. Battsek had just seen the latest cut and wrote that he was 'not sure if I ever found it so easy to watch a cut of a film, it just drifts by'. After such positive feedback, Malik had obviously begun to think about the documentary's critical reception, writing in an email to Sugar that 'it might be important that Rodriguez is preparing and gets himself into shape for next year. Maybe we all should.' The director was probably hoping Bonnie would help Rodriguez 'get into shape'. Malik also mentioned that he had spent some time with Dennis Coffey, who he found to be an all-round 'cool guy'. In addition, he had spoken with Bob Babbitt on the phone. Babbitt, the session bassist on *Cold Fact*, had played on many landmark Motown recordings, and when Malik asked him about Rodriguez, 'he replied with a whiskey voice "I don't re-mem-ber any-theeeeng"'.

John Battsek, who by now had confirmed his interest in being the new executive producer on the film, and Malik both wanted to enter the film for the 2012 Sundance Film Festival (nothing had come of Malik's 2011 entry), but Chinn was hesitant. He requested an editor by the name of Joe Walker to have a look at the film. Walker had edited Steve McQueen's *Hunger* and the Ridley Scott-produced *Life in a Day*. Malik, however, was ambivalent. He wrote to Sugar:

> so I guess I can't be too against it, but then we need to find time in [Joe Walker's] calendar and then things might be delayed ... I want to finish this! Gah!

Later, he went on to say:

> The film looks pretty good, I can send you a copy of the
> new cut, it would be interesting to hear what you think ... I
> don't particularly think it needs another editor. It's just
> about [being] a bit humble to these British guys – I'm a first
> time director and they are both Oscar-winning producers.
> They should know how to do this better than I do ... or ...
> who knows?

But then, on 4 October 2011, Chinn called. He had just
watched the latest cut of the film and had changed his mind
about Sundance: he now thought they should enter it immediately. He had shown it to Andrew Hulme, who had edited
Dutch director Anton Corbijn's previous two movies, and
thought it would be a good idea to have Hulme get involved,
even if just for a couple of weeks. Walker, it seemed, was too
busy. Malik apprised Sugar of the situation:

> So it might still be Sundance [...] If we are going to go for
> Sundance we will probably not have time anymore to raise
> any more funding, people, including both the British guys
> and myself won't get our salaries until the film starts to sell
> [...] If it sells ...

The only problem, however, was that the submission
deadline for Sundance had come and gone. The very next
day, Chinn asked the institute if they would permit a late
submission. Their reply was positive.

They needed to act quickly, but things were not yet cast in
stone. Malik was still in negotiations with Malla to buy her
out of her contract, and only once that was done would he be
able to confirm Chinn and Battsek's participation. On top of
that, it seemed at first that the cash-strapped Malik would

have to pay for the editor out of his own pocket. On 10 October, Sugar advised him:

> [B]e cautious ... although I know you always are! Once you buy Malla out it becomes your film completely ... right? If so, then, although the film has put you in an uneasy temporary financial situation, you have to gamble on it being a massive success and paying back in spades all you have put in. In that case you can't allow anyone else to hijack the movie and get you to do stuff you may not want to do, at your own cost. Just to remind you ... This film features the most wonderful story in rock history, about the most amazing musician/person, who wrote some of the greatest songs, told and made absolutely brilliantly by one of the most dedicated, passionate and talented new filmmakers. Wherever you are on your journey with this film, don't EVER forget that ... Clear Eyes, Full Hearts, Can't Lose.

Sugar had obviously been watching *Friday Night Lights*. Malik responded:

> Hey Sugar! Thanks for your support and help! It's really crucial to be surrounded by believers [...] My impression is that the more power someone has in the film industry the less he believes his own personal thoughts and tastes. Everyone who sees the film just loves it, and cries and applauds, but the ones who are in charge of the money are always suspicious. Now for example the BBC didn't just say, 'we'll take it' when Simon screened [it] to them, but said it was interesting but a bit 'niche.' Which is kind of crazy, I mean it's less 'niche' than 'Man on Wire' at least.
>
> I had a long conversation with Simon last Friday and told

him I won't pay for an editor myself unless I would be really convinced I can't live without one. He completely understood [...] I certainly still have the possibility to skip the British guys and just produce it myself, when I buy Malla out the film is mine, there are no real financial commitments to anybody. I just pay 20,000 euros and then another 10,000 every third month to Malla, costs that I actually could cope with myself more or less. But I'm not sure it's smart. The British guys have been nominated for Oscars every time the last three years. They just contacted Sundance and I saw the reply saying 'of course the dead-line has expired, of course we can't take any more film, of course we will make an exception because it's you'. I wouldn't be able to get it into Sundance this year without them. I think with them the film is guaranteed the attention it deserves. Without them, who knows ... remember 'Deep Water' – a brilliant doc that didn't have any success anywhere ... Even good films are sometimes lost in the wind.

By November 2011, Malik had finalised the film and sorted out his financial situation. Malla Grapengiesser had signed a contract releasing Malik from her debt for the amount of €50,000. A second agreement made Simon Chinn the official producer of the film and John Battsek the executive producer. 'Oh yeah!' wrote Malik to Sugar and Craig. 'We're submitting the film to some festivals right now, so far it has been sent to Sundance, Berlin, SXSW, Gothenburg and Ann Arbor.' The two fans were elated by the news that there were now some heavy hitters on board. As mentioned before, Battsek's oeuvre included documentaries such as *Restrepo*, *Fire in Babylon* and *One Day in September*, which had won the Academy Award for best documentary feature in 2000. He and Chinn had an impressive record between them and it wasn't long before the new alliance started bearing fruit. Malik reported that Chinn had informally received a very positive response from one of the members of the Sundance jury, who said their film was one of his favourites. It was great news, considering around 10,000 films are entered annually and only sixteen are selected in the World Cinema Documentary category. A few days later, Sugar received the following email from Malik:

> Just got an email. Bring out the champagne.
> WE'RE IN SUUUUUUNDAAAAAANCE!!!!!!!!
> It's not official until next Wednesday so please don't tell anyone.
> But. 16 films selected from 10,000 submissions. And:
> WEEEEE'RE IN SUUUUUUNDAAAAAANCE!!!!!!!!
> Sugar, it's all because of YOU!!! Without you – no film. THANK YOU SO MUCH for EVERYTHING Sugar! You made it all happen with your energy, kindness and spirit! I really mean it!

Sugar emailed his congratulations, ending with the question: 'P.S. What's it called?' The film had made it to Sundance, but Malik still did not have a title. By now a few more suggestions were being kicked around, including:

Thanks for Your Time
After the Fact
My Songs Will Set You Free
A Blue Coin
Climb Up On My Music
Rodriguez

I Wonder
Rodriguez: Coming from Reality
Coming from Reality
Sugar Man
The Motor City Messiah

It was in an email to Sugar about something unrelated that Malik first mentioned 'Searching for Sugar Man'. He said that Chinn had been in contact with a sales agent in the US who had voiced his concern that Hispanic names might still be a problem in America. After all, it was the reason why, in 1967, Rodriguez had recorded under the name Rod Riguez. But in 2011? Malik was annoyed, but added: 'Right now, the first contender is something like *Searching for Sugar Man*.'

Although Rodriguez and his family were mostly happy with the film, they requested some cuts for the sake of privacy. Firstly, Konny, who had been interviewed earlier in the process and who in fact had made it into an earlier cut, asked to be left out of the film. (For some reason, Malik decided not to approach first wife Rayma for an interview – the wives' absence in the film would come up later in the press.) The second request involved Juan Introna and Ethan. Over the years, Eva's marriage to Juan had fallen apart and by the time Malik was doing his final edits in 2011, they had split up, with Eva retaining custody of their only child Ethan. The family wanted to excise both Juan and Ethan from the film. Malik wasn't too pleased about this. 'I'm really against it,' he wrote to Sugar. 'Music is one thing but LIFE is another. That this story created life, in ten generations one thousand new persons will inhabit this earth because of this story.'

Malik also felt that by expunging Juan, he would be robbing Ethan of a film about the 'beautiful saga of how his parents met'.

With the Sundance announcement approaching, Sugar advised Malik on how to handle the situation:

> I really don't think they should have ANY say at this stage with regards to the final edit. I'm sorry to hear that Eva and Juan split up, but that's just too bad in context of the movie, same with Ethan. Let me understand this, we are about to give Rodriguez the biggest publicity push he's ever had, but they don't want anything personal in the movie?

The incident brought up an unpleasant memory for Sugar. In 1997, when he first made contact with Eva, she sent him some photographs of Rodriguez and his family but she was unhappy when Sugar put them up on the Great Rodriguez Hunt website. 'It seems nothing has changed,' he told Malik. 'They want their privacy protected while at the same time collaborating on a movie.' Can one have it both ways? But not wanting to upset Rodriguez, Malik found a way to exclude Juan. Sugar had filmed footage during one of the singer's trips to South Africa in which Alec McCrindle, the co-creator of the Great Rodriguez Hunt website, can be seen putting his arm around Eva. Malik put this shot into the movie, with a voiceover referencing Eva's marriage to a South African. The idea was that when audiences saw that scene, they would assume Alec was Juan, the man she married.

With the problem now solved, there came the first of two major breakthroughs. The matter of the title was finally settled. The honour went to Simon Chinn's wife Lara, who, after watching her husband agonise over the title (if only to get the Sundance people off his back), with exasperation brought up an earlier suggestion that had been floating around, saying, 'Just call it *Searching for Sugar Man.*' They did, and now it's hard to imagine that it could ever have been called anything else. The second breakthrough took both Sugar and Craig by surprise. On 30 November 2011, two months before the festival, they each received the following note from Malik:

There will be a press conference in LA in one hour. Big news. Searching for Sugar Man is the OPENING FILM!

Craig immediately got up from his desk, barged into his boss Chris Denney's office and asked for leave. *Searching for Sugar Man* would be opening the 2012 Sundance Film Festival! He could hardly say the words. And all because of an effusive Swede who had walked into Mabu Vinyl nearly five years earlier with his trademark greeting, saying, 'I have this idea.' Sugar was mindful, too, of Simon Chinn and John Battsek's role. He would say later:

So when Butch Cassidy and the Sundance Kid, as I had nicknamed them, our two hot-shot producers, galloped into Sundance with two films, not only ours but one of theirs called 'The Imposter', the Sundance gang sat up and took notice. And they really liked both films, but we heard that they loved ours, so the signs were good and we started making plans to get to the festival.

Malik was ecstatic:

This is FANTASTIC!!!! What started when you introduced me to your pet turtles in your garden has ended up as the OPENING FILM!!!!!

Sugar replied:

So how are YOU doing there, after such a momentous day? I've been walking around on cloud nine, as they say, just breaking out into giggles all day (doing it now!). Had an empty house so watched 'Searching For Sugar Man' for the nth time! Still love it.

(The main thing that had Sugar giggling was the thought that the opening documentary at Sundance would start with him singing along to 'Sugar Man'.) Malik replied, saying that he was not laughing as much, since there were now far too many things to take care of that demanded maximum concentration:

Right now we're trying to arrange for Rodriguez to perform in Park City. I checked the Internet; the title already has almost 2,000 hits on Google … WE'RE IN SUNDANCE!!! RODRIGUEZ IS GOING TO MEET ROBERT REDFORD!!!

It was panic stations all round as the different parties involved scurried to figure out how to get to Sundance, where to find accommodation and how to obtain tickets. For starters, accommodation gets booked up long before the list of successful films is announced. And buying tickets at Sundance is not so simple. Robert Redford, who founded the Sundance Institute, has a lottery system in place, plus a locals-first ticket policy. And while Craig just had to catch a flight west from Baltimore, Sugar had to cross the ocean, at great cost. The solution came from a very unlikely source: Prince Roger Nelson, best known by his mononym Prince. Malik had recently filmed and edited one of Prince's live concerts and had even hung out privately with the star in his editing suite where they worked together on the cut. With the money from that job, Malik was able to pay for Sugar's trip to Sundance. Within a few days, the generous director had booked a return flight from Cape Town to Sundance, and organised for Sugar to be accommodated in a large house rented by Chinn and Battsek for the duration of the festival. Only one issue remained. In all the excitement, Sugar had forgotten to check if his US visa was still valid. It wasn't. How to renew a visa in record time? As luck would have it, when Sugar eventually reached the front of the queue at the US consulate, the woman behind the counter who called his number turned out to hail from Park City, Utah, the skiing village that has played host to the Sundance Film Festival since 1981. The US official was as excited as he was and spent the entire interview giving him tips about the weather (freezing) and the many Los Angeles and New York film types that overrun her town during the festival (locals have their own acronym for these interlopers: PIBs, for 'people in black'). Needless to say, Sugar got his visa and it was all systems go.

Before flying out, Malik emailed Sugar a press release from the newly installed production team. Aside from some very complimentary stuff, it read:

> We love working with accomplished directors, but there is also a tremendous amount we can bring to a young film-maker like Malik. He didn't know what he had.

Sugar was quick to point out to Malik:

Wow, but ahem, I have to say, and feel fully qualified to say this, I think you ALWAYS knew what you had!

With that, Sugar packed his bags and headed for Cape Town International Airport. As the team from the UK made the trek across the Atlantic, Craig and his wife Philippa checked in at Baltimore–Washington International, hoping that the customary inclement weather that occurred at that time of the year would not ground their plane. Matt Sullivan got on a plane at LAX, while the Rodriguez clan bundled into the Detroit Metropolitan Wayne County Airport. Last but not least, Malik Bendjelloul, his girlfriend Ann-Sofie Rase and director of photography Camilla Skagerström boarded a flight in Sweden. They flew to Paris, where they met up with Sugar. Together the four flew to Salt Lake City, Utah. It is not known what Malik was thinking as the lights dimmed for take-off from Charles de Gaulle, but one thing was certain: now there was no turning back.

19

The path to glory
(2012–2013)

'I don't mean to be a sore loser, but when it's done,
if I'm dead, kill him.'
— PAUL NEWMAN AS BUTCH CASSIDY IN BUTCH CASSIDY
AND THE SUNDANCE KID

It used to be that train stations defined one's first impression
of an American city. Today it's airports. At Denver
International, it's the peaked 'tepees' that attract one's gaze,
while at Washington Dulles the distinctive suspended curve
of the terminal building's roof whispers for attention. In the
case of Salt Lake City International, as the plane circles to
land, it's not the buildings that one first notices; it's the eerily
flat expanse of Salt Lake Valley and the dramatic snow-
capped mountains surrounding it on two sides, the Wasatch
Range to the east and the Oquirrh Mountains to the west,
that define Utah's 'Crossroads of the West'.

On 18 January 2012, after arriving on a plane filled with
film and media people, Malik, Ann-Sofie, Camilla and Sugar

made the forty-five-minute drive to Park City in light snowy conditions. It is on this road, the road to Sundance, that the journey to the Oscars really begins for many filmmakers. As the first major film festival of the year, Sundance is the early litmus test. If there is even a hint of success at Sundance, the filmmaker and production company have exactly one year to create a groundswell until the Academy Award nominations are announced in the following January. Everyone who comes here knows the drill.

Making that first pilgrimage to Sundance, Malik would have been all too aware of the previous rainmakers. Independent, low-budget directorial debuts like Quentin Tarantino's *Reservoir Dogs* (1992), Kevin Smith's *Clerks* (1994) and Daniel Myrick and Eduardo Sánchez's *The Blair Witch Project* (1999) had all premiered at Sundance and gone on to earn both exponential profits and critical acclaim. The ultra-violent *Reservoir Dogs*, for one, had caused such a sensation that *New York Daily News* film critic Jami Bernard had compared its impact to that of the Lumière brothers' infamous 1895 silent film, *The Arrival of a Train at La Ciotat Station*, which instilled panic among early movie-goers. According to legend, when *The Arrival of a Train* was first shown, the audience was so overwhelmed by the moving image of a life-sized train coming directly at them that people screamed and ran to the back of the room. Likening the reaction of contemporary audiences to *Reservoir Dogs* with that of nineteenth-century viewers, Bernard wrote, 'People were not ready for it.' Now, twenty years after Tarantino, it was Malik Bendjelloul's turn to premiere his own masterpiece.

The co-production teams from Red Box Films (founded and headed by Simon Chinn) and Passion Pictures (headed by John Battsek) settled into the oversized log cabin–style house they had rented for the duration of the festival. It was well stocked and conveniently situated a short walk from the town's steep main road. While Sugar was put up in one of its many rooms, Rodriguez and his family stayed in a condo on the other side of town, and Craig and Philippa booked into a hotel in Heber City, a short drive away. It was promising to be a grand reunion. The festival would officially open the following day, 19 January.

That year there were four competition categories: US Dramatic (featuring sixteen world premieres), US Documentary (sixteen world premieres), World Cinema Dramatic (fourteen world/international premieres) and World Cinema Documentary (twelve world/international/North American premieres). On day one, the festival would screen one narrative film and one documentary from both the US and World Cinema competitions. *Hello I Must Be Going* directed by Todd Louiso, *The Queen of Versailles* directed by Lauren Greenfield and *Wish You Were Here* directed by Kieran Darcy-Smith would open the American narrative film, American documentary and world narrative film categories respectively. Rounding off the opening night from the world documentary category would be *Searching for Sugar Man*.

On the morning of the premiere, Malik was whisked off to a number of interviews. By the afternoon there was a buzz around the house that the two main guys from Sony Pictures Classics, Tom Bernard and Michael Barker, were about to put in an offer to buy *Searching for Sugar Man*, sight unseen. Chinn and Battsek advised that they wait until after the screening that evening. Still, it was a positive indicator of things to come.

The producers hosted a dinner on the second floor of Café

Terigo on Main Street before the premiere later that night. Here, for one memorable moment, the trajectories of all the players in the search for and the subsequent story of Rodriguez converged. What was supposed to be a ceremonial get-together turned out to be a comedy of errors, however, with Rodriguez and family breezing in long after the agreed-upon time, Malik too nervous to eat or to remain seated, the endless phone calls interrupting conversations (Chinn and Battsek had a film to sell), and a desperate waiter trying to get the attention of the crowded table to announce the evening's specials.

After a rushed dinner, everyone headed off to the auditorium where *Searching for Sugar Man* was to make its debut. It was a Winter Wonderland moment, made all the more exquisite by the knowledge that they were about to see a film in which they had all played some or other role. Aside from Malik and Chinn, no one had seen the final edit, and even they had not seen the film on the big screen. Nothing can prepare one for the intimacy of such a moment.

The 448-seater Library Center Theatre was chosen as the venue for the first screening of the film. The team was led to a seating area reserved for filmmakers and others attached to the documentary. Rodriguez was seated at the back and out of sight. The screen, with that year's official pre-screening slide projected onto it, had the appearance of a fine bead curtain. Strings of letters forming the words 'Sundance Film Festival' ran vertically in a step-and-repeat fashion. Large areas of these letters were punched out to form the official tagline of the 2012 festival: 'LOOK AGAIN'.

A festival representative stepped up onto the low stage and announced the film with a carefully prepared introduction. His words heightened the anticipation without giving away the story. The slide behind him faded to black and the theatre lights dimmed, leaving only the comforting glow of the emergency lighting. It would take five seconds for the film to begin; five seconds that felt like an eternity. Four years of hard work had led to this moment; would it be like the arrival of the train at La Ciotat Station?

The auditorium filled with the familiar strumming of 'Sugar Man'. A beat later the room lit up with a wide-angle shot of Chapman's Peak Drive as seen from the driver's perspective. *'Sugar man, won't you hurry / Cause I'm tired of these scenes.'* The driver is singing along to the song on the radio. Cut to the interior of the car and it's none other than Stephen 'Sugar' Segerman. 'I got my nickname from the song,' he says, as he navigates the bends.

In the theatre, Sugar viscerally recoiled, sliding deeper into his seat at the sight of his face magnified on the screen. Craig felt like he was dying a slow death as he saw the progression of time on his own face, from late youth to near middle age, in three passing shots: at the Rodriguez concert in 1998, talking to the camera in New York in 2008, and then again in 2011. But seeing Camilla's breathtaking wide-angle cityscapes of Cape Town and Detroit on the big screen for the first time made both men forget their embarrassment.

The film held together remarkably well, thanks in large part to Malik's musical score and his inspired choice of which songs to use where. The final version was as perfect as Malik had promised. The 'silkworm' speech by one of the unexpected stars and the unofficial sage of the film, construction worker Rick Emmerson, had been put back in at the end. It was a clip for which Sugar had fought long and hard after it had been cut from an earlier version of the film.

Plumber Jerome Ferretti, too, had done a sterling job. Filmed at one o'clock in the morning on the sidewalk in front of a Detroit bar in sub-zero temperatures, he had scored two vodka tonics for his efforts. And Rodriguez's daughters all came across extremely well. After eighty-six minutes, the last of the credits scrolled up and the theatre was plunged into darkness once more. For three or four excruciating seconds, there was nothing but silence. And then it began – a wave of applause that built and swept around the theatre, pulling people to their feet in a standing ovation that seemed as if it would never end. Nervously, Sugar and Craig rose too. Are you allowed to applaud a film that you appear in?

Surprisingly, no one left the theatre after the applause died down. Sundance is no place for banality. As anyone who has been there can tell you, the cineaste quotient at Sundance is significantly higher than at most other film festivals. Malik was called up onto the stage and, after another enthusiastic round of applause, began answering a barrage of questions. It was at this point that everyone involved realised just how much *Searching for Sugar Man* had resonated with the audience, most of whom had never even heard of Rodriguez before. Malik, instantly likeable as always, announced that he had a surprise and called up Craig and Sugar, the two so-called fans. A second round of questions ensued, the crowd getting pretty worked up. The film had clearly touched a nerve. Then, just as there was a lull, the film director said that he had one more surprise. It was almost as if this thing – this surprise – had slipped his mind. 'Ladies and gentlemen,' he said, 'Rodriguez!' And with that, Sixto Rodriguez, who no one knew was present, took to the stage. A tidal wave of emotion spread through the audience as they jostled to ask him questions and express their admiration. Were it not for the late hour, the Q&A would have gone on longer. All in all it was a crazy evening. The response to the film couldn't have been better, but, naturally, everyone feared that it might have been a once-off because it was an opening crowd. The true test would be the first public screening at nine the following morning at the Yarrow Theatre, on a freezing Park City Friday.

After only a few hours of sleep, bleary-eyed and nursing slight hangovers, the team gathered once more to pose for photographs in front of the pale-orange Sundance publicity backdrop. It was freezing outside, and thankfully the cinema had arranged a green room for them to hang out in during the screening. It was a new experience for most. With Rodriguez now an emerging hero, and the success of the film depending initially on no one knowing that he was alive and knocking about in Park City, it made sense to keep him under wraps for as long as possible. A few minutes before the end, the team was ushered into the theatre through a side entrance and took their seats in the front row. When the credits rolled, the entire audience rose as one and gave the film a robust standing ovation. Sugar and Craig cowered in the front row, desperate to look back but not wanting to blow the surprise. The Q&A session unfolded in pretty much the same manner as it had the night before, with Rodriguez's entrance bringing the crowd to their feet. The drama of it all was fantastic. Here was a mostly American audience, who until that morning had never even heard of Rodriguez, being told that he was dead, no . . . he's *alive!*. . . and he's *here*, playing his guitar on stage. Magnificent in black, with his back to the audience, Rodriguez performed an impromptu version of Paolo Nutini's 'Last Request'. When the show was over, everyone in the audience was given a piece of paper on which to grade the film for the much sought-after Audience Award.

Two showings in and the positive responses had strengthened Sony Pictures Classics' desire to buy the movie with immediate effect, before their usual competitors came riding in. Later that morning, Mike Barker and Tom Bernard arrived at the production team's house and went straight into a meeting with Chinn, Battsek, Malik and Matt Sullivan (who had helped facilitate the music licensing agreement), where a deal was struck that saw *Searching for Sugar Man* become the first film to be sold at the 2012 Sundance Film Festival. As is usually the case, the deal made headline news: there is a certain cachet attached to the distinction of being the first film sold. With such a powerful film company now behind the documentary, everything seemed possible. Over the next ten days, the *Sugar Man* squad travelled in convoy and followed the same, tried-and-tested, post-screening Q&A procedure. And each time they would enjoy the look of astonishment on the faces in the audience. It was as if they had just witnessed a miracle. *Searching for Sugar Man* soon became the talk of the festival, along with *Beasts of the Southern Wild*, a mind-blowing film in the US Dramatic category about a young girl in the swamps of Louisiana, by yet another first-time director, Benh Zeitlin.

One could say that Sundance officially launched Rodriguez 2.0. Notwithstanding the fact that his music had been re-released in the US in 2007, he now had a promotional vehicle, essentially a music video, to take his music to American audiences, directly and by word of mouth, more than ever before. Not a screening went by where someone didn't ask where he or she could buy a copy of the soundtrack. And wherever the film played, there were full cinemas, ecstatic responses, standing ovations and fuelled Q&A sessions. All the attention allowed Rodriguez to pontificate a little, too. For example, later in the week the team drove to a nearby town called Ogden for a screening at a mock Egyptian-style cinema. During the Q&A, someone asked Rodriguez a straightforward question about his songs and, typically, he avoided answering, this time by launching into a rambling commentary about an incident that had occurred in Ogden a few weeks earlier in which six policemen had been shot and one died. He spoke at length on the subject, leaving both the team and the audience bewildered as to how he even knew about the shooting. As usual, Rodriguez was up to date with political and current affairs. Very soon, incredible reviews began to pour in.

In one instance, Davy Rothbart for *Grantland* described the story as a 'dark and dismal tale' that becomes 'stirring and triumphant'. He also described how Malik Bendjelloul 'emerges along with a couple of the subjects of his documentary, the packed house rises to its feet for a series of four standing ovations'. He concludes the first part of his review with, 'but I have no doubt that *Searching for Sugar Man* is one of the best documentaries I'll watch this year.'

The awards ceremony and after-party took place on the final evening of the festival. Sugar recalls it being 'a fun-filled, but mostly irreverent awards ceremony with [comedian] Tim Heidecker being his usual funny dickhead self'. *Searching for Sugar Man* picked up two awards: the not-unexpected Audience Award and a Special Jury Prize. The Grand Jury Prize for World Documentary went to *The House I Live In*, directed by Eugene Jarecki. Again according to Sugar, who was told in confidence from a reliable source, it was 'a close and controversial decision, with the jury apparently keen to spread the awards around'. Malik went up to collect the Audience Award, and then he and Rodriguez together received the second, to thunderous applause. Coincidentally, both awards were presented by American actor Edward James Olmos, who was later touted as one of the possibilities to play Rodriguez in a proposed biopic.

When it was all over, Sugar flew home. At a stopover in Atlanta, someone at the airport called out, 'Hey, Sugar!' It was a film industry person from Toronto who he'd met at Sundance. One thing was becoming clear; after only a few showings, and now with a theatrical release pending, he could no longer take his anonymity for granted. Commenting on the response to the film, his new friend predicted that in the near future Sugar would become either very rich or very famous, or both, but not neither. And he was right.

With Sundance over, Malik and Red Box Films busied themselves with the upcoming festivals, hoping to build on the initial success of the film and gain momentum towards the grand prize – the 2013 Oscars. Malik and Sugar spoke about getting *Searching for Sugar Man* onto the South African circuit (the possibility of it not showing there was absurd). The first stop for the newly acclaimed documentary was to be the European Film Market in Berlin, where some South Africans would be in attendance. This would be followed by the True/False Film Fest in Columbia, Missouri, and then South by Southwest (SXSW) in Austin, Texas, where Malik would be accompanied by Rodriguez. Amid all the festival chaos, the filmmaker still had to find time to do all the paperwork. He complained to Sugar about this chore:

The last month has, strange enough, been the most stressful AND boring in years! To create some balance in my life

[...] I don't know. Tons of 25-page contracts in extremely complicated English, release forms, archive clearances, from early morning to late night. For a month! I want to have a holiday. Go on a whale safari in [South Africa].

True/False went well – the reviews were great and all tipped *Searching for Sugar Man* as the best film at the festival. Not everything was smooth-sailing, though. Clarence Avant had not signed the document licensing the songs for the film. Malik had erroneously thought this had already been taken care of, but now Avant would not sign until he had seen the film. In a state of panic, Malik, who was in New York at the time, wrote to Sugar that he was planning to fly to Los Angeles and back that very day in order to facilitate an emergency screening for Avant. Sugar, in his by-now-familiar role as sounding board and adviser, suggested that Avant would sign in the end, as it would reflect badly on him if he refused to.

Malik responded:

I didn't sleep for a second this night ... You're right, the film is a bit difficult to stop now, I hope, without making a bit of a fool of yourself. But it's a pretty nerve-wrecking situation ... How come it's been like this from day one on this project. You go from glorious triumph to nightmares every second day. A bumpy ride.

Malik put off the emergency trip to LA and headed to Austin instead. After SXSW, he wrote to Sugar:

The screening went great with two standing ovations and Rodriguez's performance was fabulous. Everyone says we would have won the audience award but the head of SXSW

Film told me they accidentally forgot to give out ballots for our screening, so now that Paul Simon film won instead.

Also a music documentary, *Under African Skies* chronicles Paul Simon's return to South Africa twenty-five years after his groundbreaking and controversial album *Graceland*.

The licensing saga continued after SXSW. By now Malik had managed to organise a special screening in LA, but no one was playing ball. Unable to hide his desperation and annoyance, he emailed Sugar once again:

We thought bringing [Matt Sullivan] to the screening with Clarence would be a good idea [but] Matt wasn't available until tomorrow. But we just got an email from Interior music that Clarence is not going to come to the screening anyway, only his assistant, so now Matt isn't going to come. And probably I wouldn't need to go [either], but the tickets are bought and I'm going. Oh, filmmaking ...

Malik caught the next plane to LA only to have the screening cancelled at the last minute.

Clarence didn't want to attend but wanted his colleague Courtney to be there, which we said was fine. But then two hours before the screening he said that he wanted the head of Netflix to be there as well. Sony told Clarence's people that we want to screen the film to Clarence out of courtesy, if he doesn't want to see it, fine, but we have no reason to screen it to someone else. So the whole thing was called off and I returned to Sweden without the screening. Now I'm just extremely tired. Next steps will be Tribeca, Sheffield and Los Angeles!

Malik could not understand why Avant would nominate the head of Netflix, an organisation with no link to *Searching for Sugar Man* whatsoever, to view the film on his behalf. What no one realised at the time was that the so-called 'head of Netflix' was actually Ted Sarandos, the head of content acquisition for Netflix and the husband of Nicole Avant, a former US ambassador to the Bahamas and Clarence Avant's daughter. Eventually Sony Pictures Classics arranged for a special screening for Nicole, and a few days later her father signed the last of the papers needed for a Light in the Attic soundtrack release. The news was huge. That Avant agreed to sign a licensing deal for a film in which he is not portrayed in the most favourable light is remarkable to say the least.

It was around this time that Malik heard that *Searching for Sugar Man* would open Doc/Fest, the Sheffield International Documentary Festival held annually in June. But before then, it was off to the 2012 Tribeca Film Festival in New York City. Craig attended the April festival, where he met Mike Theodore in person for the first time. After their phone call in 1997, Mike had featured heavily in Craig's first article, 'Looking for Rodriguez'. He was accompanied by his wife Neica, the very same Neica Lee Rompollo who had been both the 'glue and unofficial psychiatrist' to the numerous musicians who had passed through the doors of Tera Shirma Studios in the late sixties. Rodriguez attended the festival too, and both he and the film received several standing ovations. Putting a slight damper on the event, for some unknown reason the singer refused to talk to Mike. Thankfully the audience, filled to bursting with goodwill, did not notice. The infectious enthusiasm displayed by the New Yorkers boded well for the film and its trajectory in the months to come. Among those who saw *Searching for Sugar*

Man at Tribeca were actors Mark Ruffalo and Sam Rockwell, and director Michael Moore, whose *Fahrenheit 9/11* is the highest grossing documentary of all time. After the screening, Moore found Malik and told him it was the best documentary he had seen all year and asked for it to be the opening film at his own festival, the Traverse City Film Festival. Malik was thrilled. Rumour had it that Moore was going to head the 2013 Oscar jury, so there was buoyancy all round.

Seated with Craig and Philippa at Republic on Union Square the next day, Malik went into detail over a bowl of pad thai about his money troubles. As the film's director and roving ambassador, he had to attend back-to-back film festivals (he would end up participating in over forty) and was therefore not able to earn a living. He was living a strange double life: having to sleep on a friend's sofa in New York but driving around in a limo provided by the production company. As in publishing, the money only comes later.

Among the many filmmakers present at Tribeca was Brittany Huckabee. Her new documentary *Sexy Baby* premiered at the festival, and in between Q&A sessions she found time to watch *Searching for Sugar Man*. She ran into Malik a few days later at a party, where they chatted about their films. A little while after that, a friend stumbled on a photograph on a social website of the two of them together and called Brittany to teasingly ask who the young man was. Brittany, so engrossed in the publicity of her own film, had forgotten about the young Swede, but now a seed had been planted.

From Tribeca, social media took up the mantle of film promoter. Musician Pharrell Williams was the first major influencer to tweet about Malik's movie:

@Pharrell: Just saw 'Searching for Sugar Man,' new music doc coming out in July. Highly recommend it, crazy story!

Actress Susan Sarandon did not hold back either, tweeting:

@SusanSarandon: I only saw one [film] and loved it. Searching for Sugar Man.

With the documentary now gaining massive momentum, Malik's next goal was to screen it at the Cannes International Film Festival in France. Interestingly, one of the many fall-outs between Malik and his Swedish producer Malla had been over which festival the film should premiere at. Malik had wanted Sundance, while Malla, he said, had insisted on Cannes. For European directors, Cannes holds the most gravitas. Unfortunately, for a film to play at the festival, it has to premiere there as well. (The same rule applies at Sundance.) Malik told Craig at the time that there was talk of including *Searching for Sugar Man* as part of the Cinéma de la Plage, the festival's outdoors theatre for films that are out of the running. It would, Malik said, be 'as a favour, because *normalement* it is not done'. The director was happy to take what he could get. But showing the film at Tribeca was the last straw for the French. With Gallic candour, the selection representative stated, 'Over our dead bodies are we going to screen a film that has been in both Sundance and Tribeca.' *Tant pis.* Turns out the human condition is never far from proceedings, as the hierarchy at Cannes made clear by their decision. Their dismissal mirrored the situation in South Africa. In spite of the Rodriguez story emanating from that country, and notwithstanding its two South African protagonists, for the longest time it seemed as if the film would not be released in South Africa. It took several interventions, including ones by Sugar and Eva, to finally get the cinema operator Ster-Kinekor to release *Searching for Sugar Man* on the local circuit. It is not known why the company dragged its heels; nevertheless, an official theatrical release and roll-out eventually kicked off with a press preview on 15 August 2012.

Towards the end of Tribeca, Bob Dylan watched the film in his tour bus and loved it. This is interesting considering Dylan's name comes up several times in the movie. At around the same time, Malik wrote to Sugar:

> I'm staying in New York after Tribeca for a couple of more days; I'm staying with a friend here. Right now I'm at the Public Library reading stuff to find stories. Just received a tentative release plan from Sony, it looks like the film will be screened in over 80 cities in America! It will spread slowly with premieres in new cities every Friday for about six weeks starting July 27. Pretty cool. And Alec Baldwin liked the film so much that he wants to be involved in some way, he was even talking to go to the Detroit premiere.

The next day, director Phillip Noyce popped into Mabu Vinyl to say hello. Mabu was fast becoming the *Searching for Sugar Man* 'ground zero'. Noyce was back in Cape Town to film a Hilary Swank movie and was once again talking about a potential feature film, this time starring Johnny Depp as Rodriguez.

As the year progressed, the film became a runaway train and opened in many countries around the world. Malik was along for the ride, trying to attend as many festivals as the budget would allow. The list of countries where *Searching for*

Sugar Man was screened included Russia, Bosnia and Herzegovina, Australia, South Africa, Switzerland, the Czech Republic, South Korea, Sweden, France, Greece, Finland, Japan, Brazil, Mexico, Bulgaria, the Netherlands, Qatar, Argentina, Chile, Serbia, Israel and Colombia. Along the way, Malik and his film picked up a long list of accolades.

In July 2012, Malik and Ann-Sofie attended the Moscow International Film Festival to accept the Golden George, a statue of Saint George slaying the dragon, for Best Documentary. This would be their last outing together as a couple, as they broke up shortly afterwards. One of the world's oldest film festivals – founded in 1935 – Moscow put on a show of Hollywood proportions. To help lighten the director's load, Sugar made the trek to the Durban International Film Festival to accept the Audience Award, and Craig took an overnight flight to Berlin to accept the Most Valuable Documentary of the Year Award from the Cinema for Peace Foundation, where, at a lively post-awards charity auction, actress Charlize Theron invited bidders to 'bid the dress right off my body'. She worked the room like a champion and raised an incredible amount of money for her charity, Africa Outreach Project. Also in attendance were Ukrainian heavyweight boxing champions the Klitschko brothers, although they were not nearly as adroit as the South African-born beauty when it came to getting the Berlin *Oberklasse* to part with their euros. Craig met Mexican actor Gael García Bernal, who was present at the awards for his performance in the Sony Pictures Classics film *No*, the story of an advertising executive who comes up with a campaign to defeat Augusto Pinochet in Chile's 1988 referendum. *No* won the Cinema for Peace Justice Award. Another notable winner on the night was *Call Me Kuchu*, a documentary about murdered Ugandan LGBT rights activist David Kato. The film was awarded the Cinema for Peace Human Rights Award.

In November, Malik attended the IDFA in Amsterdam, where he had met Dutch filmmaker Willemiek Kluijfhout a few years earlier. It was business as usual for Malik, until he unexpectedly ran into Brittany Huckabee, whose documentary had also been selected to play at the festival. This time she did not forget meeting him. Within days, she was with him in Sweden, and he in turn followed her to Florida where she had a shoot. They vowed never to be apart for longer than two weeks.

After the festivals came the cinema releases. *Searching for Sugar Man* was released in numerous countries across the globe. And as the film gained momentum, so Sugar and Craig began to find it increasingly difficult to appear in public without being recognised, questioned and/or hugged!

The year between Sundance and the 2013 Academy Awards was a busy one for the newly discovered Rodriguez. Wherever possible, Malik roped the singer in to attend film festivals. Again and again, the Q&A sessions were energised as he entered the auditorium, the man whom the audience assumed to be dead when they started watching the film. And as the success built on itself, the phone began to ring.

On 14 August Rodriguez appeared as a musical guest on *Late Night With David Letterman*. 'First of all,' David Letterman declared to the audience, 'if you are near this movie, *Searching for Sugar Man*, go and see it. It's jaw-droppingly fascinating.' Rodriguez then sang 'Crucify Your Mind', backed by a twenty-five-piece orchestral interpretation of Theodore and Coffey's transcendent arrangement. Also in mid-August, the singer appeared on a heavily rotated CNN feature story, in which he discussed his life and belated fame.

On 7 October, Rodriguez appeared on the most successful show in US history, CBS's *60 Minutes*, hosted that night by Bob Simon, who would sadly die in a car accident on 11 February 2015. On 16 November 2012, Rodriguez crossed the Atlantic to appear on *Later . . . with Jools Holland* on BBC2, and on 11 January 2013, back on American soil, he performed 'Can't Get Away' on *The Tonight Show with Jay Leno*.

Not one member of the Rodriguez family was spared the media onslaught. Konny and all three daughters were interviewed on several occasions. Only Rayma declined to speak to the press.

It was during this time that the film began to crystallise in the annals of popular culture. British soap opera *Coronation Street* featured a scene in which a character walks into a room carrying a *Searching for Sugar Man* DVD and asks something like, 'Have you seen this yet?' It also made background appearances in films and advertisements, usually on a marquee or a poster. But it is a Japanese television show called *Kiseki Taiken! Anbiribabō* (meaning 'Miracle Experience! Unbelievable!') that took things to a whole new level. *Anbiribabō* focuses on stories that have a miraculous conclusion. Hosted by Beat Takeshi Kitano, one of Japan's most famous film directors, the show has some serious money behind it. The set itself is a dynamic, neon-filled, high-budget blend of pinball machine meets Broadway musical. A guest panel oversees the show alongside the host. The segment featuring *Searching for Sugar Man* begins with a recap of the Rodriguez story. Loud, echoing Japanese voices, like something out of an Akira Kurosawa film, narrate over those of Sugar and Craig, and are dramatically punctuated by orchestrated music. In the background, the panel reacts vocally and occasionally a tight inset of one of the panellists is shown. This is followed by a seemingly well-shot re-enactment of several of the film's scenes, specifically those relating to the two South Africans' search. The actor playing Sugar is a complete caricature, made even more incredible by a level of overacting not even seen in Bollywood. The man playing Craig sports a thin neck-beard and a head full of hair, badly cast on several counts. But it's the dramatic par-celling of the story that takes the cake, especially in the scene where Craig and Sugar receive that first call from Rodriguez. Their response is so throaty and guttural that if you close your eyes you can't be sure if you're watching porn or kung fu. Even the scene in which the pair imagines Rodriguez shooting himself is hammed up – an actor in a Rodriguez-style wig circa 1979 puts a revolver to his head, and as he pulls the trigger the camera cuts away to a long cylinder of cigarette ash falling off a cigarette in slow motion.

Finally, the day came for Seth MacFarlane and Emma Stone to announce the 85th Academy Awards nominations. It was Thursday 10 January 2013 and the *Sugar Man* camp was tense. The Oscars are notoriously unpredictable, and often favourites are left out of the running. In spite of the over-whelming success of *Searching for Sugar Man* at practically every awards show it was entered into, and its widespread proposed release (unusual for a documentary) in cinemas around the world, no one wanted to get their hopes up. Unfortunately, Rodriguez's songs were not eligible for the Academy Award for Best Original Song, as the rules for that award state that a song released prior to a film's production and which had nothing to do with the film cannot qualify for nomination. Still, the film itself was in with a chance.

Sugar couldn't bring himself to watch. It was only when his brother Michael called from Australia to say 'Mazel tov' that he was able to breathe once more. That year, the nominations for best documentary feature were not announced by the presenters. Instead, a band running across the bottom of the screen read: 'Also announcing nominations for ... BEST DOCUMENTARY FEATURE'. And then scrolling across were the names of the five nominees, which included *Searching for Sugar Man* as the last title to scroll by. Such is the category hierarchy. Not that anyone from *Searching for Sugar Man* cared how the news was delivered. It was enough to be nominated. Malik, who heard the news with Brittany by his side while on a trip to Los Angeles, was finally able to exhale. It was as if he had been holding his breath for five years. He was now only one step away from moviemaking's greatest accolade. Craig went for a long walk after the announcement, remembering his statement to his army friends in 1984: 'I am going to find out what happened to Rodriguez.' His words may have dissipated into the ether, but they had been the genesis of an idea. An idea that was later energised by the liner notes of a CD and eventually realised. Now, thanks to an indefatigable Swede and a young record dealer who literally begged for the rights to re-release the music of the rock star who never was, that idea, that story, was world-famous. And so, at long last, was the withdrawn poet-sage-musician-activist who started it all.

20

All aboard Amy's train
(2013)

'Nobody cares about the bronze or silver medals.'
— Buzz Aldrin, second man on the moon

You haven't made it in the entertainment industry unless your star is on the Hollywood Walk of Fame, that eighteen-block concrete monument to celebrity. It's the pinnacle, towards which everything is geared. Filmmaking has its own Walk of Fame: a short hop across the stage at the Academy Awards to accept that much-coveted golden statuette, the Oscar. It's the goal, desired not only for the recognition of genius it bestows, but also because it guarantees bums on seats for one's masterpiece.

Contrary to popular belief, Hollywood is not as old as the hills. Before it became a municipality, the Cahuenga Valley was a fertile farming area planted with vineyards, barley fields and citrus groves. By 1900, the original small settlement of Hollywood had grown big enough to have its own post office, hotel, newspaper and two markets. But it was only around 1910, when Hollywood merged with the city of Los Angeles, that motion-picture studios began to be established in the area. Out east, Thomas Edison's film company, which held many of the patents associated with filmmaking, was prosecuting filmmakers, often forcing them to shut down production. Out west, in California, Edison's patents were harder to enforce. It was D.W. Griffith who made the first motion picture in Hollywood, a seventeen-minute short called *In Old California*. Today, 'Hollywood' is a metonym for the entire motion-picture industry in the United States.

The first Academy Awards presentation took place in 1929 at a private dinner at the Hollywood Roosevelt Hotel. The ceremony was seen by an audience of around 270 people and lasted just fifteen minutes. It wasn't until 1944 – less than two years after Rodriguez was born – that the Academy created a category for the 'documentary feature'. In that year there were five nominees: *Desert Victory*, *Baptism of Fire*, *The Battle of Russia*, *Report from the Aleutians* and *War Department Report*. *Desert Victory* took home the Oscar, which, in support of the American war effort, was made of plaster. (The statuette, along with all the others, was traded in for the real thing after the war.)

Now, seventy years later, *Searching for Sugar Man* was a contender in what had been officially rebranded 'the Oscars'. It was up against four other films: *How to Survive a Plague*, a film about the early years of the AIDS epidemic and two groups who helped turn the disease from a death sentence into a manageable condition; *The Invisible War*, an exploratory documentary about sexual assault in the US military; *The Gatekeepers*, a film about the secretive Israeli security agency, Shin Bet, as told by six former agency chiefs; and *Five Broken Cameras*, a first-hand account of the tension between the Israeli army and Palestinians in the West Bank village of Bil'in.

Malik would have immediately gone into research mode, studying, analysing and making every attempt to ascertain his film's chances. One thing he was not was fatalistic. The first thing he would have noticed was that the four films he was up against were issue-based: AIDS, rape and the Israel–Palestine conflict. He would also have discovered that *Searching for Sugar Man* was not the first music-based contender in history. In fact, several music-themed documentaries had already taken home the sought-after statuette. In 1969, *Arthur Rubinstein: The Love of Life*, a film about the Polish-American piano virtuoso, won the Oscar; in 1970, *Woodstock*, a film about the 1969 Woodstock Festival and edited by (among others) Martin Scorsese, took home the award; and in 1980 the prize went to *From Mao to Mozart: Isaac Stern in China*, a documentary about the Ukrainian-American violinist who toured China in 1979.

The mad scramble for tickets to the 2013 Oscars began almost as soon as the nominations were announced. Apparently being the subjects of a nominated documentary and the original writers of the story didn't necessarily guarantee entry to the prestigious event, as Craig and Sugar soon found out. Typically, the director gets first dibs, followed closely by the companies who invested their money in the film, then their affiliated companies, their associates and so on. If they are lucky, documentary subjects *might* crack the nod and get to attend. Money, it seems, outmanoeuvres artistic input even in creative industries. Rodriguez was a special case in that he had 'promotional value'. Ratings rule, and having Rodriguez there to bring up on stage should they win would have been hugely beneficial for both the film's and the Oscars' ratings.

The only problem was that Rodriguez didn't *want* to attend the awards show. He was ending off a tour of South Africa at the time, and so logistically it would be difficult, although not impossible, to get him there. The boys from Sony Pictures Classics seemed to be holding out on giving Craig and Sugar tickets to the Oscars in an attempt to get them to coerce the singer, but it didn't work. According to his family, the reason for Rodriguez's refusal was apparently fatigue – it would be too draining on him to travel the long distances. Sony countered by offering to fly him first class from Cape Town to Los Angeles, but it was still a 'no go'. Sony then decided to pull out all the stops, sweetening the deal by offering to fly his daughters out too, also first class. But Rodriguez dug in his heels, much to his daughters' chagrin. When Craig tried to find out later why Rodriguez had not wanted to attend the ceremony, a source close to the family said, 'Think Brando.' When Marlon Brando won the Oscar in 1973 for *The Godfather*, he boycotted the ceremony, sending Native American civil rights activist Sacheen Littlefeather in his place to read out a refusal speech on his behalf. Brando was protesting America's handling of the Native American situation, as well as the depiction of Native Americans by Hollywood. Rodriguez, who had arranged pow-wows to highlight the plight of Native Americans, obviously identified with the actor.

Two weeks before the Oscars, on 10 February, *Searching for Sugar Man* won the British Academy of Film and Television Arts (BAFTA) Award for Best Documentary. While not quite the same calibre as the Academy Awards, the BAFTAs come damn close. Simon Chinn and Malik were present to accept the award, which would have opened up a new line of analysis for Malik: how many BAFTA-winning films had gone on to win at the Oscars?

With Rodriguez out of the running, Craig and Sugar finally got word that they would be attending the awards in Hollywood. The Western Cape Department of Economic Development and Tourism kindly paid for their airfares and accommodation so that they could attend the ceremony along with Rafiq Samsodien, the South African producer of the Oscar-nominated short film *Asad*, and two of the young Somali actors who starred in it. Directed by Bryan Buckley and filmed in Paternoster on the West Coast of South Africa, this brilliant coming-of-age short is about a young Somali boy struggling to survive in his war-torn country.

A double-header screening of the two local Oscar-nominated films was held in Cape Town with Rodriguez in attendance. At the crack of dawn the following day, Sugar and Craig boarded an Emirates flight for Los Angeles. Somewhere over California, as the plane was coming in to land, the clouds took on the surreal, dream-like quality of a Hollywood movie backdrop. The two fans would remain in a haze for the rest of their stay in Tinsel Town. Like gate-crashers, Craig and Sugar, who had begun this journey with no other goal than to track down a presumably dead singer, now found themselves breathing the same exclusive air as the stars of the silver screen.

Malik, Battsek and their partners were staying in the historic Beverly Wilshire Hotel, while Sugar and Craig checked in at the Hollywood Roosevelt Hotel, where the very first Academy Awards had been presented eighty-four years earlier. Walking down Hollywood Boulevard to find a bowtie, Craig saw the preparation crew laying the red carpet (more maroon than red) and setting up the grandstands for the spectators, whose tickets were nearly as difficult to come by as the real ones. He stopped for a moment and watched with other hopefuls, who no doubt daydreamed about the day when they would cross the divide from anonymous minimum-wage earner to famous celebrated actor too busy to answer Kevin Spacey's call.

The next evening, Sony Pictures Classics hosted a function for the films in its Oscar stable: *Searching for Sugar Man*, *Amour* and *No*. Gael García Bernal was there, as was Michael Haneke, the Austrian director of *Amour*, which won the 2012 Palme d'Or at Cannes. The function was at the London West Hollywood and featured its own red carpet and a menu by famed British chef Gordon Ramsay. The evening was made particularly memorable by Tom Bernard's vein-popping rant about how Rodriguez had let him down by refusing to attend the Oscars. Here was a man unaccustomed to not getting his way. With three Oscar nominations, however, Sony had nothing to complain about.

The next morning was taken up with chores. Steaming tuxes, ensuring shirts were starched and ironed, and visiting Light in the Attic Records, a major contributor to the late blooming of Rodriguez's career. Matt Sullivan, Malik, Sugar and Craig all paid a visit to the Amoeba Music store as well. It was one of the highlights of the trip, especially for Mabu Vinyl owner Sugar. The whole day, however, was made remarkably stress-free by virtue of a large canister of pot that Sugar had somehow acquired. Still without a bowtie, Craig had to borrow one from a friend of Matt's at the last minute. As relaxed as everyone was, no one could conceal the excitement and trepidation of what awaited them that night. How had the Academy voted? Had the process been fair? Craig recalled a list he had read of all the brilliant documentaries that had *not* won, let alone been nominated. Examples included *The Thin Blue Line*, *Touching the Void*, *Hoop Dreams*, *Paris is Burning* and *Fahrenheit 9/11*, which was ruled ineligible because director Michael Moore had allowed it to be screened on television before it opened in cinemas. But it was the debacle surrounding *Hoop Dreams* that led the Academy to change the voting system. This American documentary about two African-American teenagers who dream of becoming professional basketball players was listed by the *Guardian* as the most successful documentary in British cinema history, and film critic Roger Ebert declared it the 'best film of any kind' for 1994. Writing about its failure to receive even an Oscar nomination, he said:

> We learned, through very reliable sources, that members of the committee had a system. They carried little flashlights. When one gave up on a film, he waved a light on the screen. When a majority of flashlights had voted, the film was switched off. 'Hoop Dreams' was stopped after 15 minutes.

According to Steve Pond in his book *The Big Show: High Times and Dirty Dealings Backstage at the Academy Awards*, after the *Hoop Dreams* fiasco the Academy's executive director, Bruce Davis, took an unprecedented step:

> He called Price Waterhouse and asked to see the complete results of the voting. The accounting firm prepared a rundown for Davis that left out the names of the voters, but showed how each voter had scored every movie in contention. In voting, members of the committee were asked to rate each documentary on a scale of zero to ten – a

departure from other Oscar categories scored by committee, which used a scale of six to ten. 'What I found,' said Davis, 'is that a small group of members gave zeros to every single movie except the five they wanted to see nominated. And they gave tens to those five, which completely skewed the voting.' Choosing his words carefully, Davis summed up the results. 'There was one film that received more scores of ten than any other, but it wasn't nominated,' he said. 'It also got zeros from those few voters, and that was enough to push it to sixth place.'

Fears such as these sat with the *Searching for Sugar Man* hopefuls. Perhaps it was better not to think about it.

When it came time to leave the hotel for the Oscars ceremony at LA's Dolby Theatre, Craig and Sugar, whose hotel was only a three-minute walk away from the venue, caught a taxi to the Beverly Wilshire. This is because it is not encouraged to walk to the Oscars if you are attending, as a tight security cordon is set up at most entry points around the theatre, making it almost impossible to arrive on foot. In any case, it was decided that everyone should arrive together. On the way, the taxi stopped to pick up a heavily pregnant Camilla Skagerström, who had just flown in with her husband. Forty minutes later, they arrived at the Beverly Wilshire, where they found Malik loitering in the hotel entrance (with Michael Douglas) waiting for the wives and girlfriends to get ready.

The ride to the Oscars was an eventful one. Dressed to the nines, the *Searching for Sugar Man* entourage cracked jokes and Chinn and Battsek told war stories of previous Academy Awards shows. At one point Chinn's phone rang – it was

Philippe Petit, the star of *Man on Wire*, calling to wish them good luck. Panic set in when Craig realised he might have forgotten his ID in the hotel room, without which one could not enter the area, let alone the auditorium. He eventually found it in his top pocket. Among the crowd gathered at the police checkpoint was a demonstration by the members of the Westboro Baptist Church. Although most in the *Sugar Man* car didn't know it at the time, Westboro Baptist is known for its hate speech, especially against homosexuals, and often organises anti-gay pickets. On their website they state that 'the entertainment industry is chock full of filthy perverts'. When the entourage eventually arrived at the Dolby Theatre, they were met by a publicity person whose job it was to show the newbies the ropes of how to negotiate the red carpet. The group was ushered into a holding tent, where they waited until the assigned publicist indicated that it was the optimal time to walk past the press in the hopes of being interviewed. Interviews are not guaranteed, and this drip-method of only releasing a film's entourage onto the red carpet when the time is ripe is designed to optimise the film's publicity. It's also customary to let the lesser-known filmmakers pass by the press area earlier in the afternoon, before the likes of Charlize Theron and Hugh Jackman arrive and suck up all the red-carpet airtime later in the day. When the team finally got the go-ahead to walk down the carpet, Ryan Seacrest, standing in the long shadow of Casey Kasem, showed no interest in interviewing either Malik or Chinn, but Piers Morgan, perhaps because he was British and perhaps recognising Chinn or Battsek, was a little more accommodating. *Searching for Sugar Man* had not yet been screened extensively in the US, so it was understandable that most of the press had not heard of it. Malik seemed more relaxed than he had been for some time. Perhaps he realised that it was no longer up to him. Brittany Huckabee looked resplendent in an off-the-shoulder gown. They made the perfect pair. Sugar wore a Rodriguez badge below his bowtie, while Craig was just thankful that his borrowed bowtie – which had required science (or magic) to tie – was still around his neck and had made it this far. He had spent a considerable amount of time watching YouTube videos in his room on the mechanics of tying a bowtie, only to give up and have a hotel receptionist do it for him. The red carpet is actually split into two channels. The left is for stars and those who are to be interviewed, while the right is for partners and those not directly involved in a particular film. One high-light of Craig's slow amble down the red carpet was when someone tapped him on his shoulder and said assertively, 'You're standing on Amy's train.' Looking down, Craig dis-covered that his shoe was indeed positioned squarely on the train of Amy Adams's silver-grey Oscar de la Renta gown.

In the reception area of the Dolby Theatre, Craig, Malik, Sugar and Camilla milled about with Battsek and Chinn. A rare tray of canapés created a small flutter among the stars, most of whom probably hadn't eaten all day. Robert De Niro shook his head as he missed the last morsel of whatever it was. Looking around the room, it became clear to the Hollywood novices that almost all the male actors present were shorter in real life than they appeared on screen, with the exception of Larry David and Conan O'Brien. It also quickly became apparent that the Oscars is, in actual fact, not an awards ceremony, but a television show. Perhaps many years ago it was an awards ceremony that just hap-pened to be televised. Today it is a television show that just so happens to have a live audience. Everything that occurs when the doors to the auditorium close is in service of the broadcast to the rest of the planet. A typical television count-down precedes the show's commencement (and all subsequent segments): 'Ladies and gentlemen, the show will commence in ten, nine, eight, seven . . .' And, as in the Super Bowl, the show stops for commercial breaks – a complete interruption in which the house lights come on and people mill about making small talk. Old hands like Jack Nicholson know exactly how long they have to shoot the breeze before returning to their seats. Newbies like Sugar and Craig often find themselves locked out for an entire segment until the next commercial break. And while the television audience sees only what the cameras are focused on, those in the audi-torium see everything, the full ultra-wide shot. For example, at one point an electrician on a ladder was changing a light bulb stage left with Adele in the foreground waiting to per-form, while on stage right host Seth MacFarlane, lit by a spotlight, was in full throes with one or other comedic inter-lude. The auditorium was able to take in both experiences, while the viewer at home only saw MacFarlane.

As the time for the feature documentary category approached, Craig and Sugar, sitting in the nether reaches of the theatre, became antsy. Then, Ben Affleck took to the stage:

The documentary filmmaker uses the camera to show real life and real people in a way that is insightful, often aston-ishing, but above all, truthful. This year's films illuminate the tension and resentment of those living in the West Bank, behind-the-scenes operatives working in secret in that same land, the life-and-death battle waged thirty years ago by activists trying to stop the spread of Aids, the war being waged against our nation's female warriors, and a journey to find a long-lost musical legend.

He then announced the nominated documentaries: *Five Broken Cameras*, *The Gatekeepers*, *How to Survive a Plague*, *The Invisible War* and *Searching for Sugar Man*. And then it came, the moment that was almost too much to bear:

'And the Oscar goes to . . .'

A pause that felt like an eternity.

'. . . *Searching for Sugar Man*, Malik Bendjelloul and Simon Chinn!'

Like Philippe Petit, Malik had pulled off a heist of astronomic proportions. Sugar, with tears running down his cheeks, recalled the first time the Swede had walked into Mabu Vinyl with his trademark effusive greeting.

The filmmaker and his producer made their way up to the stage, and a statue was handed to each of them. Malik's speech was confident and generous:

Oh boy, thank you so much. Thanks to the Academy ... very, very kind. Thanks to one of the greatest singers ever, Rodriguez. Stephen 'Sugar' Segerman, Craig Bartholomew, Camilla Skagerström, SVT, SFI, all my friends and family, and Sony Classics, the best distributor on this planet. Thank you!

Chinn was up next. In his speech he offered an explanation for Rodriguez's absence:

Rodriguez isn't here tonight, because he didn't want to take any of the credit himself and that just about says everything about that man and his story that you want to know.

At the next ad break, the two fans – a former Quiz Kid and a so-called musicologist detective – stepped outside to drink a toast and call home. Both forgot that it was practically impossible to get back into the auditorium before the next break.

Back in Ängelholm, mum Veronica Schildt Bendjelloul and dad Hacène Bendjelloul leant in closer to the radio. It was a quarter to four in the morning in Sweden when Ben Affleck announced the Oscar for best documentary. 'We did not watch the Oscars on TV because we do not have that channel,' Veronica told journalist Lasse Mauritzson. 'But we were tipped off by Malik's brother Johar. He told me what time it would be on so we set the alarm clock for 3:30 and listened to the live broadcast. We cheered.'

The couple went to bed after the announcement. But by 5:30 a.m., the phone was already ringing off the hook. The Swedish press was not going to let this story go unnoticed. 'It feels a bit odd, it is the son who made the film, but it is us who gets the attention,' says Veronica. When asked how she planned to celebrate, Malik's mother said, 'I do not know, it's not us who won. But I'll buy a big houseplant.'

Before the show, the publicist had briefed the team: 'If you win an Oscar, then we will be going to the *Vanity Fair* after-party. If you don't, then it is off to another party.' Surprisingly, even at the pinnacle of the accolade totem pole, there was still a clear demarcation between the winners and the losers. Chinn had booked two limousines for the night, and there were now two statuettes in the team's possession. This meant one statuette per limo. It was very important, they were told, to walk in as a group holding the Oscar. Failure to do so would make it extremely difficult to gain entrance to the hottest event of the night. So the entourage split into two groups and made the slow journey to the *Vanity Fair* party. Crowds had lined the streets, and someone in the first limo, the one with Camilla, Craig and Sugar, conducted them by sticking the Oscar out of the window and then pulling it back in again. With each thrust into the air the crowds went wild, and each time the statuette was withdrawn the cheering died down.

The *Searching for Sugar Man* posse spent most of the evening at the after-party at the same table as astronaut Buzz Aldrin. Below his gold bowtie, the second man to walk on the moon sported his congressional gold medal. The golden statuette, placed in the centre of the table, seemed to exert a planetary effect as people orbited around it. Seth Rogan invited Sugar for a smoke, while Craig hit the head alongside Quincy Jones. Bono, Sarah Silverman, Elton John, John Travolta and Quentin Tarantino were among the long list of celebrities to make their way through the *Sugar Man* team's temporary solar system.

Malik had to step outside from time to time to field calls coming in from Sweden. 'It was fantastic, as if the whole world went into slow motion,' he told Swedish news agency TT Spektra, referring to the Oscar stage, 'but the steps were actually quite slippery.' To SVT's *Good Morning Sweden* he said, 'It feels like the final leg of a long journey. Tomorrow is Monday, then it is time to start working.' When asked about the statue, he added, 'It feels good, it is heavy and shines a lot.'

Sugar, whose first brush with fame was as the longest-running Quiz Kid in South Africa, was relishing this next, more auspicious encounter. Craig, denied a trip to the moon in 1969, was spending the evening in the company of the second man to set foot there. And the musician who started it all? Well, Sixto Rodriguez chose not to watch the show, opting for bed instead.

While there is no star for a documentary filmmaker named Malik Bendjelloul on the Hollywood Walk of Fame, there is one for Apollo 11 and its three astronauts, Neil Armstrong, Michael Collins and Edwin 'Buzz' Aldrin.

21

Working-class hero
(2013–2015)

'But thanks for your time, then you can thank me
for mine, and after that's said, forget it.'
— Sixto Rodriguez, 'Forget It'

It is the evening of 25 February 2013. Seated at a fashionable
sushi restaurant in Santa Monica, California, Craig, Sugar,
Camilla, Simon Chinn and Josh Braun rub their tired eyes
and share their stories from the night before – the night
Searching for Sugar Man won the coveted Oscar. Chinn orders
off the menu for the table, while Craig regales the group with
a tale of how, directly after using the urinal next to Quincy
Jones, a song from *Thriller* began to play. What are the odds?
Chinn has already placed the Oscar at the centre of the table
for all to see. A group of passers-by ask if they can hold it and
take a few photographs. Sure, says Sugar. Be careful, it might
be cursed, shouts someone else, referring to the so-called
'Oscar jinx', the idea that winning an Oscar can put an end
to one's film career. Think F. Murray Abraham, Linda Hunt

and Roberto Benigni. After taking a few snaps that are uploaded directly into the social stratosphere, the group moves on, leaving the revellers in peace.

Malik and Brittany bounce in. They are late but radiant. To celebrate, the couple spent much of the day in Malibu, walking on the beach and hiking, a far remove from the madness of earlier when they had to sneak out the back door of their hotel to avoid the Swedish paparazzi who had been camped out in the lobby since the night before.

Malik has the other Oscar with him. That too gets pride of place on the table. What if it gets stolen? Impossible to sell it if it does, says Malik. As it happens, Oscar winners are required to sign a contract giving the Academy the right to buy back the statuette for one dollar if the recipient ever wants to sell it.

Such is the nature of the dinner on the evening after the ceremony: light, funny and poignant. The stress is gone. What are your plans? That's the question on everyone's lips. Good question. It's mission accomplished for most parties at the table and now it's time to reset and recharge. What a year it's been. Craig and Sugar pilfer what's left of the Oscar swag and it's goodbyes all round. Hope to see you soon.

For all those involved in *Searching for Sugar Man*, the rest of the year went by in a flash. Each had to deal with the price of success, which was intense for some, less so for others. The mercurial nature of fame and too much praise is more of a challenge than many realise. 'Applause is the beginning of abuse,' said English poet Ted Hughes.

Sugar went home to Cape Town and had to deal with the highs and lows of co-owning a now iconic record store. Brian Currin, keeper of Rodriguez facts and trivia and the administrator of Sugarman.org, finally succumbed to an offer to work for Mabu. Part of his daily routine is to shield Sugar from curious tourists who have made Mabu Vinyl a port of call.

Craig returned to his advertising job in Cape Town, and a week later he found himself walking the crowded aisles of the outdoor markets in Lagos, on a site visit for a Dutch milk company. A four-man military escort guarded him and his colleagues. A week earlier he had walked the red carpet; now he looked down at his feet and almost stumbled over a basket of rats for sale. 'For voodoo,' said the soldier in charge. On arrival back in Cape Town he was happy to see the February issue of *Rolling Stone* on the racks featuring his latest Rodriguez article, 'This is not a song, it's an outburst'. He had also been commissioned by *China Newsweek* to write a Rodriguez article, which was slated for March 2013.

In Detroit, Rodriguez was back at the building site. But this time it was *his* building site. After forty-something years of living in the house in Woodbridge for which he had allegedly paid $50, he had finally decided to renovate. Also – if the rumours are to be believed – he surprised his first wife with a new car. Financially speaking, his troubles were over.

For the first time, the music of Rodriguez seemed to resonate around the globe. The new *Searching for Sugar Man* soundtrack, consisting only of Rodriguez compositions, began to chart around the world, reaching number one in Sweden, nine in New Zealand, two in Denmark, twenty-two in Switzerland, seventeen in Australia – and the list goes on. More importantly, this time Rodriguez was receiving his royalties. Both *Cold Fact* and *Coming from Reality* were re-released in a number of countries, often charting in the top 100. According to the Nielsen SoundScan figures quoted by the

Detroit Free Press in May 2013, *Cold Fact* sold 140,000 copies in the US, *Coming from Reality* 69,000 and the *Searching for Sugar Man* soundtrack 108,000.

As a result of all the attention that the movie and record sales were getting, the singer had to drop his reluctance to be interviewed. He simply had no choice but to be more accommodating with the press. He did several interviews in which he skilfully avoided the questions, but in a March 2013 interview with the *Hollywood Reporter* he said more than usual. When asked about the guitar and what he liked about it, he cleverly answered, 'I like that it is lightweight.' When asked what he liked about his role in music, he said, 'I only had to come up with a three-minute song' – which is a bit like a scientist who cures a disease saying, 'I only had to put liquid into a test tube.' Rodriguez went on to talk about the importance of a vocal signature, and it soon became clear that the man who had given up on music in 1974 never stopped thinking about music. When the journalist asked Rodriguez what it felt like when 'his music career went away' – referring to the period post-1974 – the singer answered, 'I was too disappointed to be disappointed.' He added, 'Nothing beats reality.'

Later in the interview, with great insight, he goes on to explain how 'music is a moveable art, others can take it and make it their own' – a sentiment that echoes Mario Ruoppolo in the film *Il Postino* (*The Postman*). Ruoppolo tells the exiled Pablo Neruda that 'Poetry doesn't belong to those who write it; it belongs to those who need it.'

A month or so later, quite unexpectedly, Rodriguez got a call from Wayne State University, which wanted to confer on him an honorary doctorate for his 'musical genius and commitment to social justice'. This, perhaps, was the Oscars ceremony that the singer had been holding out for. The commencement ceremony took place at Ford Field on 9 May 2013 before 3,500 new graduates. Rodriguez, dressed in the billowing Wayne State University emerald-green, white and black graduation gown with gold piping, looking more Shakespearean than rock star, was immensely proud to be honoured by his alma mater.

'Over the years, you have remained politically involved and connected to the Detroit community, living humbly in the city, working to improve conditions for the inner-city working class,' said Wayne State University president Allan Gilmour as he named Rodriguez a Doctor of Humane Letters. But anyone hoping for pearls of wisdom from the singer-songwriter was sadly let down. In a short speech Rodriguez said:

> I wouldn't pass up the opportunity to congratulate the graduates at Wayne State University. Good luck to you. Congratulations on your hard work and to your family and to your friends who helped you get through. The best of luck. Well done, or as it's said in Spanish, *bien hecho*.

Later, when a journalist asked how he wanted to be treated now that he had an honorary doctorate, he answered: 'I want to be treated like an ordinary legend.'

These were strange times indeed for Dr Rodriguez, who was about to turn seventy-one. He was finally able to sell out a venue in his own neighbourhood, at a concert that had been announced a day after *Searching for Sugar Man* won the Oscar. On 18 May 2013, Rodriguez filled the 4,400-seater Masonic Temple Theater just down the road from his Woodbridge house. The artist with the guitar slung over his back, walking the streets of Detroit in *Searching for Sugar Man*, finally had a large gig to go to.

A formal review of the show appeared in the *Detroit Free Press*. Journalist Brian McCollum wrote:

> You could only marvel looking on at Rodriguez: this dignified spirit, clad in black, coolly crouching toward his microphone, making his way into Detroit's musical canon four decades after he should have ... But alongside his low-key vibe was a light and approachable demeanor. Chatty between songs, Rodriguez came armed with an arsenal of goofy jokes and punny maxims, with a ribald crack about Minnie Mouse and a deadpanned moment early on: 'I just want to be treated like an ordinary legend.'

The post-doctoral quip seemed to be gaining traction.

In a less formal review in the news blog *DetroitYES!*, a fan wrote:

> Everyone had their focus on the soft-spoken man in black who kept reminding us he was a 'solid seventy' and although he knew it was the drinking, he loved us, too. I cannot remember another show in all my years of concert-going with as plentiful the quantity and quality of crowd heckling, nor the gentle humorous retorts from the man of the hour.

The spotlight was clearly on the singer from Detroit. Just the day before, on 17 May 2013, the *Detroit Free Press* reported that, 'After decades of murkiness about his record sales and royalties, a legal and accounting team has begun an inquiry for the enigmatic singer-songwriter.' The article quotes New York attorney Mark Levinsohn, who had been retained by the singer: 'An attorney and a royalty auditing firm have been engaged by Rodriguez to try and find out what's going on with respect to his royalties – or lack of royalties.' According to the article, a veteran New York record-label auditor, Gary Cohen, had been enlisted to help sort out the mess. Clarence Avant was reported as stating: 'I wish him the best. The fame will be over in a year.' This, from the man who in the movie said, 'You think somebody's going to worry about a 1970 contract? If you do, you're out of your goddamned mind.' Perhaps to soften the insult, Avant defends himself in the article by saying that he had been unaware of Rodriguez's South African album sales at the time, and that they were bootlegged copies not licensed by him. But in keeping with the tone he set earlier in the conversation, he concludes, 'Even when I tried to give his [recording] masters away, nobody wanted to take them.' The 4,400-strong audience may not have been fully aware of all this, but it must have been on Rodriguez's mind as he played that night.

The singer continued to get booked in 2013, playing a host of summer shows including the Coachella Festival in California in April, the famous Le Zénith in Paris in the first week of June, and Glastonbury later in the month.

On 2 May the following year, the *Hollywood Reporter* dropped a bombshell. In an article headlined '"Searching for Sugar Man" star's amazing journey erupts into fraud lawsuit', the magazine revealed that a complaint had been filed in a Michigan federal court by Harry Balk, the owner of Gomba Music and the person who gave Rodriguez his first break, against Clarence Avant. According to a follow-up story in the

Hollywood Reporter dated 28 May 2014, Interior Music is defending itself and has made a third party complaint against Rodriguez, adding the musician to the confusion. The *Hollywood Reporter* goes on to say that Rodriguez is also defending himself.

The complaint, rewritten in plain English, reads:

July 25 1966, Rodriguez entered into a contract with Harry Balk and his publishing company, Gomba Music, which stipulated that Rodriguez was to write music compositions exclusively for Gomba for the period of five years until July 25, 1971.

As a reminder, *Cold Fact* was recorded in 1969 and *Coming from Reality* in 1970, although the latter was only released outside the five-year window (and perhaps for this very reason), in November 1971. The complaint goes on to say that:

In 1969, Avant entered into a series of agreements with Rodriguez for the album Cold Fact, but because Rodriguez was still legally contracted to Harry Balk and Gomba, a fraudulent scheme to conceal the writing of the compositions was concocted, whereby the compositions written by Rodriguez would falsely be credited to other individuals or entities with whom Gomba has or had no agreements.

As a result, in 1970, Avant and Interior music entered into a series of agreements with among others, Jesus Rodriguez (allegedly Rodriguez's brother, and the reason for the confusion of his name in South Africa) and one other entity, namely 'Sixth Prince.'

The complaint goes on to 'demand a trial by Jury'.

In the song 'Cause', Rodriguez once sang the words, *'Cause they told me everybody's gotta pay their dues, and I explained that I had overpaid them.'* Now, in his 'solid seventies' (to use his own phrase), Rodriguez is making up for lost time with a string of global shows that suggest the dues he overpaid are finally paying off. He played at the posh Royal Albert Hall in London on 7 May 2015, which was also British election day, a fact he commented on before breaking into a rendition of 'This Is Not A Song, It's An Outburst: Or, The Establishment Blues': *'The mayor hides the crime rate, council woman hesitates, public gets irate but forget the vote date . . .'* Successful ticket sales resulted in a second performance on 27 May. In July he opened for Brian Wilson of Beach Boys fame, playing a fifteen-city tour – two legends, two septuagenarians, one a survivor of showbiz, the other a survivor of obscurity. And the tours aren't expected to stop just yet. He is returning to South Africa for a multi-city concert series in early 2016 – and these days it is safe to say that the carriage no longer turns into a pumpkin on the flight back home.

There is no doubt that even with the unsolved royalty issue in the wings, and the pending court case hanging over his head, Rodriguez is having more fun than he ever could have expected. This, from his interview with the *Hollywood Reporter*:

HOLLYWOOD REPORTER: But basically, you're a happy man, a content man?
RODRIGUEZ: I am a fortunate man . . . quite fortunate.

Epilogue

It started out so nice
(2014)

> 'As a child I never really was an actor, but just a
> child who adults told where to stand, what to do,
> what to say, and when not to say it.'
> — MALIK BENDJELLOUL, IN CONVERSATION
> WITH CRAIG STRYDOM

"SUGARMAN" DIRECTOR WAS "TRUE CAPE-
TONIAN"'. So reads the headline on the *Cape Times*
billboard. The date is 14 May 2014. It is a Tuesday. For anyone
driving by, there seems to be a typo, something wrong with
the tense. What do they mean 'was'? Do they not have proof-
readers at Cape Town's leading English newspaper?

Rewind to April 2013, Malik and Brittany, now living in New
York, took a well-earned break, embarking on an extended
trip to South Africa, the country that gave Malik 'the best
story you will ever hear in your life' (one can almost hear the
enthusiasm of his voice effervescing through his trademark

lilt). It was during this trip that he started seriously thinking about his next project, first as a documentary and then as a dramatic feature: the story of South African conservationist Lawrence Anthony, who during the invasion of Iraq by US forces made an emergency trip to save the last surviving animals in the Baghdad Zoo. His noble endeavour took six months and was recounted in the book *Babylon's Ark*, which he wrote with author Graham Spence. Malik was so taken by the story that he began writing a script for a full feature film. His choice of subject was not surprising: Malik had told Sugar that he wanted to make a film where 'something incredible happens that would go on to change the world'. For him it was the day man discovered how to communicate with animals. Malik's childlike naivety and 'belief in magic', in Brittany's words, made him extraordinary.

In the year after the Oscars, he was also toying around with a few other documentary ideas. At the end of July 2013, on the radio show *Sommar i P1* produced by his brother Johar, Malik spoke candidly about his hopes and dreams and the ideas he had not yet realised. He recalled how he had once interviewed the eccentric South African-born pop musician Bill Drummond from the band KLF (later K Foundation), who burnt one million pounds sterling in cash in a disused boathouse. The reason, according to Malik, was to reignite the group's hunger to be creative; to once again feel what it felt like when they had no money and survived only on creativity; to feel what it felt like before disillusionment set in. Drummond, however, talking to Andrew Smith from the *Guardian*, posited a different and irreverent reason: 'It wasn't to destroy the money. It was to watch it burn.'

One can easily understand why Malik was fascinated with the burning of one million pounds as a subject for a documentary. He seemed absorbed by the figurative line that separates 'making it' and 'not making it', or between 'making it' and not knowing that one had 'made it'. This is what the Rodriguez story was all about. What Malik seemed to be struggling with within himself was how to reignite the raw desire to create again. The way he had felt when he had nothing. 'Money meant nothing to him,' Johar Bendjelloul told Craig in 2015. 'He had no use for it.' A little like the way Konny described Rodriguez's attitude to money in *Dead Men Don't Tour*: 'He has absolutely no use for money. He will give it away.' And in an echo of the Rodriguez story, a forgotten KLF tune – a track that they had recorded in a day, never released as a single, thought was crap, and had forgotten about – later came to be used as an anti-Milošević rallying cry in Serbia. This was the kind of thing Malik was interested in, given his love for miraculous stories, stories tinged with fantastical outcomes and overtones, stories where fact was stranger than fiction.

One other subject Malik spoke passionately about on *Sommar i P1* was the 'moon illusion', the phenomenon by which the moon appears larger near the horizon than it does high up in the sky. This – and one could hear it in Malik's voice – appealed to his sense of wonder, and he seriously considered making a documentary about it, although he also spoke about the inherent difficulties of shooting such a film.

In February 2014, a year after that magical night, Craig flew back to the US to deliver a speech at his former employer IMRE's 'vision meeting'. Next, he took a train to New York to interview South African songwriter Dan Heymann on his influential anti-apartheid protest song 'Weeping', which he had recorded with the band Bright Blue in the eighties and which had been covered by many others, including Josh Groban. Over the years the song had become one of the official anthems on the South African struggle playlist, a subject that has long fascinated Craig. After several hours of talking, Dan and Craig made their way through thick snow to SoHo, where Craig was to meet up with Malik. Before saying goodbye, Dan pointed out his first New York apartment, where 'free jazz' musician Ornette Coleman had once lived. This simple fact meant a lot to the highly musical keyboard player and songwriter. Malik, too, loved the Ornette Coleman story when Craig told it to him later that evening.

They met at a Cuban restaurant on the corner of Prince and Elizabeth streets. Over a beer, which naturally Malik didn't finish, the Oscar-winning director spoke enthusiastically about his plans for the future, mentioning the script that he had written, which at that point was only loosely based on the Lawrence Anthony story. Philip Seymour Hoffman had died of acute mixed drug intoxication just a few weeks earlier and they briefly discussed the topic. Malik also mentioned that he'd had problems with insomnia, but did not elaborate. He was planning a visit to Sweden in the upcoming months for his mother's seventieth birthday. Later over coffee at McNally Jackson Books, however, Craig noticed that the filmmaker began to fidget and seemed increasingly concerned about the time. They said their goodbyes and Malik took the subway while Craig slipped and slid his way back to his hotel. It was the last time he saw Malik in person.

On 14 May 2014, the world woke up to the news that Malik Bendjelloul had taken his own life. The idea that he would commit suicide struck everyone who knew him as completely absurd, and still does. To his friends, there was not a single incident that they could refer back to as a pointer – a clue – of what was to take place that day. The press, especially the *Hollywood Reporter*, highly dramatised the coverage of his death, causing a lot of pain to those whom Malik had loved and who loved him in return. Brittany told the *Guardian* on 13 July 2014 that she and Malik were together almost constantly for the year before he died. She had plans to follow him to Sweden in the spring. After his death she could find no evidence whatsoever that he was planning or had ever planned suicide.

Simon Chinn was just as perplexed by what had happened. He'd had two meetings with Malik in the last few weeks of the director's life, and in the first, on 17 April in New York, he noticed for the first time that Malik was going through some kind of professional crisis. As a way to help him, Chinn disclosed that after *Man on Wire*, he too had developed what he termed 'second album syndrome'. During their lunch, Malik spoke about wanting to go back to documentary-making for his next project. He had written his feature over the previous year or more and at that point had shelved it because it had seen some rejection, and this was, Simon believed, the source of his artistic dilemma. It was also at that meeting that Chinn introduced Malik to Sacha Gervasi, the director of the rockumentary *Anvil! The Story of Anvil*, about the woes of a Canadian metal band. But ultimately, according to the producer, 'Malik wanted to free himself from the noise. He needed to fall in love with something.' Rumour had it that Malik had already turned down several director-for-hire jobs, including a series of twenty-plus vignette-type commercials that he had told Craig about over dinner in New York.

Chinn's second meeting with Malik was over breakfast in London on 25 April 2014. (Malik would also meet with John Battsek later in the day.) Malik had come to the UK when asked to consider directing a feature about Portuguese football star Cristiano Ronaldo, which was being produced by the same team that had made *Senna*, the 2010 biopic about Formula One driver Ayrton Senna da Silva. Simon told Malik about the television projects he was working on and Malik got quite excited by some of them. But as for the Ronaldo documentary, both Chinn and Malik had their doubts about whether it would be a suitable project for him. While it was fast becoming clear that Malik was keen to start working again, it was important that the subject be something close to his heart. He also wanted to make it on his own terms. Call it naive or purist, but Malik felt that he had earned the right to do so.

Ultimately, the cause of Malik's suicide will remain a mystery. Talking to Andrew Anthony from the *Guardian*, Brittany confirmed what his friends, colleagues and family already knew, and have always known: 'His creativity came from a place of light, never darkness, and he truly sought to uplift and inspire the world with his work.'

On 15 May 2014, the *Chicago Tribune* reported that at a near-capacity Chicago theatre, Sixto Rodriguez addressed the crowd about the filmmaker's apparent suicide. 'He will be sorely missed,' he said solemnly. 'Sweden has lost a favourite son there. So have the States.'

In writing this manuscript, not a day has passed during which the authors have not inadvertently thought about giving Malik a quick call to resolve this or that question, only to realise that he is no longer with us. But his spirit lives

on in this book and the work he did on what will undoubt-
edly go down in history as one of the greatest documentaries
ever made, a film about a search for the Sugar Man.

Were you tortured by your own thirst
In those pleasures that you seek
That made you Tom the curious
That makes you James the weak?
– SIXTO RODRIGUEZ, 'CRUCIFY YOUR MIND'

Authors' Note

Rodriguez's small but mysterious oeuvre has long been a subject of fascination to South African and Australian audiences alike. Today, thanks to the intervention of his fans and the popular documentary *Searching for Sugar Man*, the interest in Rodriguez's music has at last become global.

The intersecting stories that make up this book are an attempt to chart the singer's long journey from obscurity to fame. Writing it, however, presented certain challenges. The first was how to solve the problem of collaborative non-fiction – in this case a story told by two authors who are also protagonists of the story. In the end we drew inspiration from the book *All the President's Men*, in which journalists Carl Bernstein and Bob Woodward solved a similar problem by writing about themselves in the third person when telling the story of Watergate and their role in uncovering it.

The second challenge was how to structure the book, with its three main overlapping stories set on different continents and spanning several decades. With the help of our managing editor Robert Plummer, the problem was soon solved, resulting in the tetralogy of stories that you now hold in your hand: the Mystery, the Man, the Music and the Movie.

We are grateful for Robert's insight and intellect, as well as the sharp eye and narrative skills of our editor Bronwen Maynier, the courage and foresight of our publisher Marlene Fryer, and the support of all at Penguin Random House South Africa. It was serendipitous that at the exact moment you were looking for someone to write the Rodriguez story, we came calling. Thanks also to Transworld publisher Doug Young and rights manager Ann-Katrin Ziser for believing in this book and taking it to a wider audience.

Pinning down the facts of Rodriguez's life has been as difficult as tracking him down in the first place. We would like to acknowledge the many people who were forthcoming and generous in their responses to our numerous requests for information: Mike Theodore, Dennis Coffey, Steve Rowland, Camilla Skagerström, Johar Bendjelloul, Simon Chinn, Janice Prezzato, Matt Sullivan and Josh Wright from Light in the Attic, Kevin 'Sipreano' Howes, Ralph Terrana, Roger Armstrong, Tonia Selley, Graeme Currie, Willem Möller, Kelly Moore, Willemiek Kluijfhout, Maurice Greenia, Brian Currin, Brittany Huckabee, Terry Fairweather and Gerardo Ramos. Thanks also to everyone who has researched Rodriguez and contributed to our knowledge of him, such as Glenn A. Baker, Jerry Schollenberger, Harry Young and the many people who have posted on the websites The Great Rodriguez Hunt/Site, Climb Up On My Music and Sugarman.org.

Sugar would like to extend special love and thanks to Ronit, Natalia, Raphael, Daniell, Joyce, Sheila, and all the Segerman and Benjamin families, for your continued love and support and for sharing this wonderful journey. Thanks also to Brian Currin for your loyal and continual commitment to the Sugarman.org website, which has proved to be an invaluable part of this whole story, and to Andre Bakkes, Andy Harrod, Alec McCrindle, Josh Georgiou, Alan Freedman, Henri Talerman, Jacques Vosloo, Alan Levin, Justin Cohen, Tyrone Rubin, John Samson and Buddy.

Craig would like to thank Henry and Pat, Bert and Gladys, Michelle, Adrian, Gina, Bernice and Isabella, for your constant love and encouragement, and Philippa, whose love and affection permeates each and every page of this book.

Our eternal gratitude goes out to the late Malik Bendjelloul, whose wonderful film finally achieved what we had been trying to do for so long: getting Rodriguez's music the global recognition it deserves. Thank you to Hacène Bendjelloul and Veronica Schildt Bendjelloul for giving us permission to reprint Malik's correspondence.

Last but not least, we wish to acknowledge the legend himself – Rodriguez – and his daughters Eva, Sandra and Regan, for their friendship and participation over the years.

Craig Bartholomew Strydom
Stephen 'Sugar' Segerman
Cape Town, July 2015

References

Twenty years ago we didn't know what Rodriguez's first name was, which city he came from, or even that he was alive. Through a long process of investigation, we now know a fair amount – but not everything – about the singer and his life. In writing this book we have drawn from interviews, newspaper articles, books, reviews, liner notes, websites, films, and TV and radio shows. We have not used academic-style footnotes in this book, but we do acknowledge that we have relied on a wide range of sources.

Interviews
Mike Theodore
Johar Bendjelloul
Simon Chinn
Dennis Coffey
Graeme Currie
Brian Currin
Terry Fairweather
Kevin 'Sipreano' Howes
Brittany Huckabee

Willemiek Kluijfhout
Kelly Moore
Janice Prezzato
Steve Rowland
Tonia Selley
Ralph Terrana

Books, articles and web pages

Andrew Anthony, 'Searching for Malik Bendjelloul – a tragedy revisited', *Guardian*, 13 July 2014

Glenn A. Baker, *Rodriguez 'Alive'*, sleeve notes

Jami Bernard, '*Reservoir Dogs* film review', *New York Daily News*, 1992

Big Fat Magazine: The Midwest's Magazine of Rock, 1970

Classic UK Recording Studios Resource, philsbook.com

Roger Crosthwaite, 'New Look, New Sound Rodriguez', *Telegraph*, 26 March 1979

DETROIT: A Young Guide to the City, edited by Sheldon Annis. Detroit: Speedball Publications, 1970

DetroitYES! blog, detroityes.com

Tim Forster, 'Cold Fact – Sixto Rodriguez', *Fuzz, Acid and Flowers*, January 2001, reposted on http://sugarman.org/rod_timforster.html

———, 'Buried Treasure', *Mojo*, July 2002

Eriq Gardner, '"Searching for Sugar Man" star's amazing journey erupts into fraud lawsuit', *Hollywood Reporter*, 2 May 2014

Bob Gendron, 'Review: Sixto Rodriguez pays tribute to Director Bendjelloul', *Chicago Tribune*, 15 May 2014

Emelie Henricson, 'Malik – från barnens favorit till världsstjärna', *Expressen*, 26 February 2013

R. Hernandez, 'Many Movements, One Struggle', online article, *Oakland North*, UC Berkeley Graduate School of Journalism, www.oaklandnorth.net/many-movements-one-struggle/

'John Watson, the South End and the Elite Ruling Class', *The Last Columnist*, 28 September 2012

Kevin 'Sipreano' Howes, *Cold Fact* liner notes, Light in the Attic Records

———, *Coming from Reality* liner notes, Light in the Attic Records

Rian Malan, 'Bizarre is a word for it', *Telegraph*, 6 October 2005

Lasse Mauritzson, 'Oscarsyra i Ängelholm', *Helsingsborgs Dagblad*, 25 February 2013

Brian McCollum, 'Sixto Rodriguez pursues review of contracts, sales in search of royalties', *Detroit Free Press*, 17 May 2013

———, 'Sixto Rodriguez takes Detroit stage to enchant hometown crowd', *Detroit Free Press*, 19 May 2013

Willem Möller, 'Jamming with Sugar Man', *YOU*, 1 November 2012

Tom Panzenhagen, 'U. Council Committee to Recommend Monteith College Closing', *South End*, 23 October 1975

Alexis Petridis, 'The singer who came back from the dead', *Guardian*, 6 October 2005

Jean Petra Phillipson, 'My Voice', www.petrajeanphillipson.com/my-voice/

Steve Pond, *The Big Show: High Times and Dirty Dealings Backstage at the Academy Awards*. New York: Faber & Faber, 2005

Lee Robson, 'Cave Man, Werner Herzog discusses his new 3-D movie about cave paintings and his approach to documentary', *Financial Times*, 26 March 2011

Eva Rodriguez, 'Eva's Memories', http://sugarman.org/rodmemories2.html

Davy Rothbart, 'Sundance Journal No. 1: Cold Facts', *Grantland*, 27 January 2012

Jan B. Sands, 'Student Claims Police Brutality', *South End*, 22 October 1975

Sugar Segerman, 'Sugar and the Sugarman', online article, http://sugarman.org/rodriguez/sugar.html

Jerry Starr, 'Academic Values and Mass Education', monteith-college.org

Craig Bartholomew Strydom, 'Looking for Rodriguez', *Directions*, October 1997

——— (writing as Craig Bartholomew), 'Fact: Rodriguez lives', *Mail & Guardian*, 20 February 1998

———, 'In search of Rodriguez: from hooker bars to opera houses', *Sunday Independent*, 8 March 1998

———, 'This Is Not a Song, It's an Outburst', *Rolling Stone*, January 2013

———, 'Working Class Hero', *China Newsweek*, March 2013

Joe Tangari, *Cold Fact* review, *Pitchfork*, 17 September 2008

'The Family Dogg: "The View From Rowland's Head"', *Melody Maker*, 2 December 1972

'Thoroughly Unconventional Eva Rodriguez', *George Herald*, 2012

Brian Wawznek, '46 Years Ago: Beatles Pose for 'Sgt. Pepper' Cover Photo', *Ultimate Classic Rock*, 30 March 2013, http://ultimate-classicrock.com/beatles-pose-for-sgt-pepper

Josh Young, 'About Light in the Attic', http://lightintheattic.net/about

Films
Dead Men Don't Tour, directed by Tonia Selley (1998)

Looking for Jesus, directed by Justin Cohen (2000)

Searching for Sugar Man, directed by Malik Bendjelloul (2012)

A Singer with Mexican Blood, directed by Hector Hugo Jimenez, Hora Cero Films (2014)

Television
60 Minutes, David Simon, CBS (7 October 2012)

The Breakfast Club, SABC 2 (1998)

Ebba och Didrik, directed by Peter Schildt, SVT (1990)

Hollywood Reporter interview, March 2013

Kiseki Taiken! Anbiribabo, Fuji TV (2012)

The Late show with David Letterman, CBS (14 August 2012)

Later . . . with Jools Holland, BBC 2 (16 November 2012)

The Tonight Show with Jay Leno, NBC (11 January 2013)

Radio
Sommar i P1, produced by Johar Bendjelloul , 30 July 2013

Acknowledgements

A Most Disgusting Song
Words & Music by Sixto Diaz Rodriguez
© Copyright 1971 Interior Music Corporation, USA.
Universal/MCA Music Limited.
All Rights Reserved. International Copyright Secured.
Used by permission of Music Sales Limited.

Can't Get Away
Words & Music by Sixto Diaz Rodriguez
© Copyright 1979 Interior Music Corporation, USA.
Universal/MCA Music Limited.
All Rights Reserved. International Copyright Secured.
Used by permission of Music Sales Limited.

Cause
Words & Music by Sixto Diaz Rodriguez
© Copyright 1971 Interior Music Corporation, USA.
Universal/MCA Music Limited.
All Rights Reserved. International Copyright Secured.
Used by permission of Music Sales Limited.

Climb Up On My Music
Words & Music by Sixto Diaz Rodriguez
© Copyright 1971 Interior Music Corporation, USA.

Universal/MCA Music Limited.
All Rights Reserved. International Copyright Secured.
Used by permission of Music Sales Limited.

Silver Words
Words & Music by Sixto Diaz Rodriguez
© Copyright 1971 Interior Music Corporation, USA.
Universal/MCA Music Limited.
All Rights Reserved. International Copyright Secured.
Used by permission of Music Sales Limited.

Sugar Man
Words & Music by Sixto Diaz Rodriguez
© Copyright 1970 Interior Music Corp.
Universal/MCA Music Limited.
All Rights Reserved. International Copyright Secured.
Used by permission of Music Sales Limited.

The Establishment Blues
Words & Music by Sixto Diaz Rodriguez
© Copyright 1970 Interior Music Incorporated, USA.
Universal/MCA Music Limited.
All Rights Reserved. International Copyright Secured.
Used by permission of Music Sales Limited.

Index

371